Roger Penney.

FIRST CENTURY
CLOSE-UPS

Printed and bound by Antony Rowe Ltd, Eastbourne, England

Published by Crossbridge Books
345 Old Birmingham Road
Bromsgrove B60 1NX
Tel: 0121 447 7897
www.crossbridgebooks.com

First published 2005

ISBN 0 9543573 9 6

British Library Cataloguing in Publication Data. A catalogue
record for this book is available from the British Library.

Other books published by **CROSSBRIDGE BOOKS**:

It's True! Trevor Dearing (Imprint *Mohr Books*)
Total Healing Trevor Dearing (Imprint *Mohr Books*)
Called to be a Wife Anne Dearing
Schizophrenia Defeated James Stacey

For children:
The Kentle-Shaddy Eileen Mohr
The Kentle-Shaddy Knows Something E.M. Mohr
The Kentle-Shaddy in Felmunia E.M. Mohr

FIRST CENTURY CLOSE-UPS

Roger Penney

CROSSBRIDGE
BOOKS

Acknowledgements

It has been my great pleasure and providential blessing to come into contact with Mrs Eileen Mohr of Crossbridge Books. I want to thank her for her patience and for her always helpful criticism and advice.

I am also grateful to those people who have read some or all of the manuscripts, including John Wilson and John Locke from Scotland, Professor Howard Marshall, and my granddaughter Miss Charlotte Penney (aged 14). These have all encouraged me and do encourage me. Thank you, all of you!

Roger Penney

BIBLICAL QUOTATIONS

Where quotations are taken from the Torah, the King James (Authorised) version of the Bible is used, to reflect the archaic feel of the language.

In other instances, quotations are from the New King James Version of the Bible.

Contents

FOREWORD

The problem, whether one is writing a history of an historical novel or stories, as I have done, is twofold. First there is the matter of historical accuracy; of time, of place and of the smaller details of dress, modes of speech or everyday matters in different situations and conditions. The second is somehow easier in part, though often having towering difficulties. It involves the skill of empathy needed by the journalist, by the historian and, for that matter, by the artist and the actor and even by the detective.

All the people I have dealt with are, in a real sense 'everyman' and 'everywoman'. God is showing us our need and His solutions to our need. The process may be painful, sometimes very painful.

Though writing about these people who met Jesus or encountered Him in some other way, the writer also creates, out of his own imagination, fictional characters which may or may not be like the real historical ones. This is the problem for any writer including the historian, that finally his character, even of a well-known personage, is the product of his imagination. So, my stories, written for your consideration, for your enjoyment and to challenge you, are after all, just that: they are stories. If you want the reality you must read the Gospels for yourself and then let the reality of your own self dawn on your own soul.

1

A STRANGER ON THE SHORE

The scrawny, thorny bushes hardly moved in the breeze from off the lake. It was incredible that only a short time before there had been winds of storm force sweeping down from the hills to beat the surface of the water into a frenzy of waves and wind-driven spray. Storms like this happened from time to time. The wild wind howling with anger and frustration through the mountain gorges to whip up the surface of the sea into fury was one of these.

But it had been more than one of these. That late afternoon destructive, demonic forces were walking the earth and the atmosphere. The Prince of the Power of the Air himself had roused himself to do battle. Without warning, out of a clear sky the winds drove down with a malignant intensity never before experienced. A monster ravening after its prey, a black cloud of hatred, vicious hatred intent upon destruction; that is what it had been. Prey there was; an object of hatred there was. A man, calm yet purposeful, dignified in humility, weary and hungry yet with all the power of the universe and more, infinite power to command. A fishing boat of the larger sort, crammed not with gear and catch but with upwards of a dozen men.

From his hideout among the rocks, looking down to where the cliffs which surrounded the lake gave way to a flattened stony beach, he watched. The boat, its sail in

1 A Stranger on the Shore

לְהַלְבֵּשׁ לְנִשְׁבְּרֵי־לֵב ׀ רָא לִשְׁבֵוּיִם֙ דְּרוֹר וְלַאֲסוּרִים־ פְּקַח־קָוֹחַ ׃

tatters, but pulled strongly by four men at the oars, made slowly, as if the boat itself was weary with the effort, for the small beach.

Part of him, that part which could, from time to time think and reason, told him that no boat could have lived in such a storm. Something strange and fearful was going on. The beings stirred; they were readying themselves; he cried, a weird pitiful cry. It was a cry without hope, a cry of dread for the torment that he knew was to come. Like a man dying in an agony that comes and goes, his cry was of pain, of fear and of deep despair knowing that he had to face the inevitable and that he could not face the inevitable.

The agony forced itself from his lips again and again. The torture went on and on and there was no respite. The hurt, instead of getting less only got worse. Sometimes it would die away but he knew it would return with greater power, deeper intensity and with destructive force to body and to soul.

The storm had caught him out in the open. He usually hid from the light of day but towards evening he would go out to find food. Not that these days he needed much food. He seemed to stay alive on nervous energy alone, the things inside him driving and driving, giving him superhuman strength so that, at times, he could lift and throw great boulders. Then, leaving him aching with exhaustion to collapse onto the stony ground or to seek shelter in the limestone caves which abounded and which were the burying places for the dead of the area, they would slink and seemingly creep away. They did not go away but stayed, as if asleep and resting themselves, deep inside him, deep down in his body and yet in his mind in ways he could not understand.

He watched. He always watched. He was still wet

לַחֲבֹשׁ לְנִשְׁבְּרֵי־לֵב ׀ זָרָא לִשְׁבֻיִם֙ דְּרֹ֔ור וְלַאֲסוּרִים־ פְּקַח־קֹֽוחַ ׃

and cold; so very cold. Now they were coming, people were coming. But these were not the ordinary people. Them he hated, for had they not driven him out into this desert place to live out his tortured existence among the tombs? He hated them for their fear of him when he suddenly appeared, shrieking his hatred and his bitter mental pain. He hated them for their smug, satisfied little lives which could not, or would not, understand his bitterness and his hurt.

These were not ordinary, for there was one among them. One special, yet an enemy; the enemy. And yet he knew, part of him knew, that he could not be the enemy. They were stirring; it was their hatred, their bitterness and their pain he felt now. His own too, as if someone were sawing away at his raw nerves, giving him a double intensity of pain and of horror which made the mental pain and the physical pain and sickness an ever multiplying screaming agony of horror. It was as if hell, the gehenna of fire, the eternal pain of the abyss were opening up before him. Boiling hatred and horror surged about in his mind and he wanted to hurt, to kill, to destroy, to smash and to crush. He saw Him. Oh, yes! He saw Him.

He stepped out of the boat, the others hanging back either in dread or to attend to the boat and to make it fast, near the shore, but held by anchors fore and aft, safe from the stones and the rocks.

The rain had knifed down, drenching him but seeming to wash clean his sores and his wounds where he had cut and bruised himself with sharp stones. Now, watching that small figure stepping out onto the stones of the beach, he felt fear churning his stomach. As the rain had washed the dirt and dust from his skin, so the fear turned to anger and hatred and washed away all human

לַחֲבֹשׁ לְנִשְׁבְּרֵי־לֵב ۚ זְרָא לִשְׁבֻּיִם דְּרֹיר וַלַאֲסֹוּרִים־ פְּקַח־קָוֹחֵ ۚ

feelings. Indignation that his privacy should be invaded by this visitor from the other side changed to bitter hatred. The anger he felt at his fellows who had driven him out turned to fiery rage at this one who suddenly seemed to be the representative of all humanity.

He began walking up the slope to where he crouched in his cave watching and grinding his teeth, growling now, like a beast while saliva drooled from the corners of his mouth. He was to be driven out, he knew. Driven even further away, driven into the abyss where there was no forgetfulness, where there was only weeping and crying, where there was only pain and anger and frustration. He and they knew all this.

His heart was pounding, his breath coming in great gasps, while the curses stumbled and jumbled and tumbled from his lips. He no longer felt the pain of his broken teeth as he began to swear and curse, spraying the spittle which had flooded his mouth down himself and over the ground where he still crouched. He tried to drag himself down, to curl up protectively into a foetal posture, but he could not. They were in control. He lost all consciousness of himself as a separate being. He was one of them. He *was* them.

"Kill! Kill! Kill!" they screamed. His bowels twisted and writhed within him, but it was not his bowels that twisted and writhed and emptied themselves, it was theirs; he was theirs; his was their hatred and their murderous obsession. He burst out of the cave and plunged headlong towards the shore to where the lone figure came on gently and remorselessly.

He showed no fear; why did he show no fear? But he, they, knew why. They knew but they called on their, his, implacable hatred and malignity, to drive away the fear and to drive him, them, down the slope to destroy, to

4

לְהַבֵּשׁ לְנִשְׁבְּרֵי־לֵב ֹ קְרָא לִשְׁבוּיִם ֹ דְּרוֹר וְלַאֲסוּרִים־ פְּקַח־קוֹחַ׃

smash and to kill. The blood in his arteries throbbed with the strength of emotion, and thought began to intrude through the frenzy which filled his being. something wanted him to rush back up to the high ground and from there, to the cliffs which overhung the lake, to throw himself down.

They were confused. Suddenly they did not know what to do. They wanted to destroy him. They wanted to destroy the being on the shore, but the despair showed that they could not. Fear and fury, cunning and malevolence skipped through the turmoils that wracked him and he knew that they wracked them as well.

He was close now. He felt fresh emotions. As the rain had tried to wash him clean so these, compassion, kindness, love, pity, held out the hope of freedom, of cleansing and of life. Just the possibilities, no more. They had tried to blank them off, but they could not. These were far stronger than the malevolent hatred they projected, and he knew, as in a flash of blinding white light of insight, that they were defeated.

With the realisation came another burst of pain. It seared into his brain. They could not hurt the Stranger on the shore but they could turn on him. Even as this fresh realisation flitted across his consciousness, another wave of pain tried to stop it. But he knew they were losing; their hold on him was weaker.

No longer did he think their thoughts as his thoughts. The little thoughts; the thoughts that angered them, were his own. And yet they were not his own, for they came in response to the calm of the Stranger and the mental completeness that was his. It was this also which angered and terrified, yes! and terrified, them. They were afraid.

He looked at the Stranger, no longer strange, but with

לְהַלְבֵּשׁ לְנִשְׁבְּרֵי־לֵב ֫זְרֹא לִשְׁבֻיִם דְּרֹור וְלַאֲסוּרִים־ פְּקַח־קֹוחֽ׃

all the knowing love of mother, of father, of wife and of children; knowing yet forgiving, loving and knowing but still loving, still wanting, longing. A great longing reached out to him but he could not yet, not quite accept it. They still tried to force him away, but the pain no longer mattered; they no longer mattered; a surge of hope began to make itself felt in the depths of his being.

They felt a surge of despair, of dread but with no remorse. There was a dread of the inevitable yet their hatred and loathing of the Stranger only intensified with their helplessness in His presence.

The superhuman strength which had broken chains and fetters with which people had bound him, fell from him. He was weak. And yet the weakness which had led him to succumb to the demons, now began to set him free from them. They had, at first at least, given him the things he craved for. And then everything had turned to dross and to ordure. He began to loathe himself, for what he had been and for what he had become. He wanted to go to the Stranger, yet he dared not do so. The Stranger was clean, He was holy, good and pure. And what was he? He was dirt. No, not quite, but yet so filthy as to be almost as worthless as dirt.

He fell down onto the ground. He was almost at the Stranger's feet and he wanted to crawl that last yard but he could not. Fresh fears filled his heart. Fear that the Stranger who was no stranger, would reject him. Did he not deserve to be rejected? There was fear too that the Stranger, who was no stranger, might yet be a stranger and judge him. And did he not deserve to be judged? He knew Him. It came to him in another blinding flash of insight. He had heard the Name. Imploringly he lfted himself to look at Him.

"Jesus, Son of God Most High," he said, "what do you

לְהַבְּשׁ לְנִשְׁבְּרֵי־לֵב ;רָא לִשְׁבּוּיִם וְדֻרֹור וְלַאֲסוּרֵים־ פְּקַח־קֹוֹחַ:

want with me?"

Hope, faint and miniscule, stirred within him. The voices and the emotions that had stirred and roiled within him were now stilled. No longer could they shout and swear, no longer shriek abuse at passing strangers. No longer would he try to hurt people or terrify the herdsmen who brought their flocks of goats or their herds of swine to these desolate places. No longer would he be afraid of his fellow men because they had been afraid of him. The destructive, self-destroying impulses were all gone.

Then a fear manifested itself. Would they come back? Would the powers and the voices come back again? Would they again invade his soul? Would they suck out his personality so that his soul became their soul, leaving him a shell which the demons controlled and used for their own fell purposes?

No sooner had he had the thought than he knew he could be set free. He knew that he could be taken and enfolded in those arms of love. He could be safe for ever and for ever. Ever to be with the Stranger who was now no stranger.

They were held now. The power of light kept them fast. They had no power. Theirs was the power of bitterness, of hatred and of all the lusts and of all the greeds. Powerless now confronted by the power of love. The hatred was there but it could not speak and it could not move. They were bound and could only respond if He bade them respond, or move if He gave them leave.

A whine escaped his lips. They were still there, still using him, but their power was diminishing and he knew that this was the end game. There was fear there now, much fear but a little bluster too.

"Don't torment us! Not yet, it isn't time!" Like a child

לַחֲבֹשׁ לְנִשְׁבְּרֵי־לֵב ׃רָא לִשְׁבוּיִם דְּרֹ֑ור וְלַאֲסוּרִים־ פְּקַח־קֽ֥וֹחַ ׃

defying an adult there was a half-scared protest there too. But He knew. Of course He knew. He who had designed all things from the beginning knew it all.

"Come out of him!" It was a command which it was impossible to resist. They knew, they knew they had to leave their victim. They knew that there was nowhere else for them, not unless there were other victims for them to destroy as they had almost destroyed him. They knew.

He felt their defiance. Not that there was nothing he could do about it; it simply did not matter. Indeed it was his opportunity. They had chosen a dialogue and He would now expose them, an object lesson to all eternity for those who should come after.

"What is your name?" They had not expected that. Now He could almost read their thoughts, the roles were being reversed, the situation changed. The whine changed, now despair and timidity entered and it quietened, seeming to hang in the air and to come out of the ground rather than from his lips. They were losing their grip and losing their defiance. Now they were beseeching. He sensed it and he knew it, he could almost smell their terror and their despair.

"Legion." At the sound spoken softly in awe, he realised what he had called up. He had wanted to be like the Romans, strong, feared and hard. He had wanted men to cringe in terror as they now cringed in terror. And he saw what he had never seen before – that it was not others that one should control. That was not the real victory; the real victory was to have control over oneself.

The words of the Hebrew proverb began to come back to him. Painfully and slowly they formed themselves in his mind. At the same time he remembered when he had sat at the feet of the rabbi in

לְהָבֵשׁ לְנִשְׁבָּרֵי־לֵב זָרָא לִשְׁבֻיִּם דְּרוֹר וְלַאֲסוּרִים־ פְּקַח־קוֹחַ:

the synagogue school and learned the sacred words. He had been a scholar in those far-off happy days: "He that is slow to anger is better than the mighty. And he that ruleth his spirit than he that taketh a city." He had hardly been slow to anger; contempt for his fellows and impatient ambition had burned within him. Certainly he had wanted to take and control cities and armies. And look where it had got him.

"Legion," the voices repeated, humble now, before their creator and their judge. As if owing an explanation to Him who knew all things they went on: "Legion! For we are many."

The voices, instead of driving, were now being driven. It was not they who had brought about the near total disintegration of his personality but he himself. He was filled with self-loathing again and his head drooped onto the ground in bitter, tearful, remorse.

"We are many." The words crawled out as if ashamed. They crawled out of the hidden cracks and fissures in his broken, soon to be mended personality. They crawled out from the hidden mines and springs of his soul and prostrated themselves before the Lord who stood there on that lonely shore, now no longer lonely, no longer desolate.

They cringed and the words cringed. It was not if but when. "The pigs," they implored, "send us into the pigs."

He did not speak. He made no gesture but it was as if He had simply inclined His head giving gracious permission, all the while watching them as, powerless, they crept away in the shame and ignominy of utter defeat. They did not go out cohort by cohort. They did not go with their weapons and their standards. They did not leave him shrieking and howling their defiance, as the winds had, but a little while before, howled their

9

לַחֲבֹשׁ לְנִשְׁבְּרֵי־לֵב זְרָא לִשְׁבוּיִם דְּרֹוֹר וְדִיוֹר וְלַאֲסוּרִים־פְּקַח־קֹוֹחַ׃

defiance. They left stooping and cringing. They left crawling and crying. They left in terror but with some relief which was no relief, for they knew what was to follow. They went eventually in headlong flight as a vanquished army quits the battlefield which has become a field of shame. Indeed they were truly vanquished. Vanquished and defeated utterly. And, as if to salve the pain of defeat, they threw themselves into the herd of pigs feeding nearby on the slopes.

The boys and the men who had been watching the pigs had crept closer to observe what was happening. Many a time they had been disturbed by the demoniac and they wanted to see the fun when he turned on these intruders. They came from the cities of the Decapolis which were Greek settlements with some Syrian foundations among them. The Greeks sacrificed pigs to Zeus, and the Syrians, whose own culture was mixed with that of their Greek conquerors in the time of Alexander, practised similar sacrifices and saw nothing unclean in the use of pork. The Romans too enjoyed pork and so leaving Jewish wisdom and business acumen for mere opportunism, these people grew rich on the proceeds of the pigs that fed in the region.

It was with horror that they saw the source of their livelihood suddenly cease their grubbing for roots and nuts and race madly down an ever-steepening slope leading to the cliff edge. Indeed the Greeks there would have reflected, though they may not have appreciated the loss of their revenue, how the god Pan fills men and animals with the blind terror which we call panic.

First the pigs milled about. The movement became more aggressive and the boars slashed with their tusks while others squealed as bloody gashes were opened in their sides. Quickly the aimless milling about turned to

לְהַבְּשׁ לְנִשְׁבָּרֵי־לֵב זְּרָא לִשְׁבֻּיִם דְּרֹור וְלַאֲסוּרִים־פְּקַח־קֹוחַ׃

the panic that led to the flight down from the hill and which ended with them all drowned in the sea. Some tried to swim but others tried to save themselves by climbing onto their backs while others made futile swimming motions with their trotters.

The owners of the pigs and, of course the curious, as with any unusual phenomenon, came out in their droves to see what had been going on, for it is certain that the tale lost nothing in the telling.

There, to their astonished eyes, a sight met them which was the last they had expected to see. A Stranger was seated on a rock and round Him were a group of Galilean fishermen. In the middle of them, seated on the ground, as if in a place of honour, at the very feet of the Stranger, was one whom they did not at first recognise. Closer inspection brought a shock to their senses. He was changed! It was not that he was sitting still. It was not even that he was clothed. But most remarkable of all was that he was talking to and listening to the Stranger who smiled gently at him and seemed to address most of His remarks to him.

"What about our pigs?" some were going to ask. But they did not. The words seemed to die on their lips. "What about our living?" they wanted to say. But they could not.

However, there was a sense of alienation. A madman they could understand; but how a madman could be cured and how a herd of pigs suddenly took off down a suicidal slope they could not understand. They were deeply respectful but they did not want the Stranger. Some said, later, that they could see He meant trouble for them.

So He did. So He has. He has been a trouble and will go on being a trouble to all those who care more about

לִתְבָשׁ לְנִשְׁבְּרֵי־לֵב ;רָא לִשְׁבַיִם וְדִרֹוֹר וְלַאֲסוּרִים־פְּקַחַ־קֽוֹחַ׃

their worldly goods and their money than for goodness, justice and freedom. But to the poor, the afflicted, the confused and the hurt; that is a different matter.

"Come to Me, all you who are weary and burdened," He calls, "and I will give you rest." But He does not just call, He actually comes to where we are before He calls us. Even if it is to come through a storm, to the ends of the earth, to the deserts and the dark places.

"But what about the man who was tormented by demons?" you ask. "Surely he wanted to stay with the Lord Jesus?" Of course he did and that is what he asked for. But it is not exactly what he got. The Lord told him to, "Go home to your friends, and tell them what great things the Lord has done for you, and how He has had compassion on you."

This is what he did. But do you think that the Lord was not with Him there?

(The quotations from the Bible are from Luke's Gospel chapter eight. You can also read about this in Mark chapter fiv.)

2

Sabbath Rest

Passover had come and gone. The homer of the first fruits of the barley harvest had been reaped and presented before God in the Temple at Jerusalem. Two weeks had gone by and soon it would be the time of the wheat harvest.

The Lord and His disciples had not travelled far, little over a quarter of a mile from where they had spent the night. The short journey, much less than the two thousand yards allowed on the Sabbath, had, however, taken a long time. People wanted to see and to talk to the prophet from Nazareth. Others brought relatives who were sick or crippled, seeking healing for them. No one was sent away disappointed, no one but did not have his questions answered. That short journey seemed interminable; it was certainly tiring. They had started early, as if the Lord knew of the crowds who waited for Him. It was as if He had determined beforehand to satisfy all their needs and to clear their minds of their doubts and their worries.

People usually hurried to the Beth HaKnesset, the house of meeting, the Synagogue. It showed how eager they were to hear the Law read and commented on. On that particular Sabbath day they had other priorities and other things on their minds, though had they but known it the man they sought was Himself the Word of God.

They were still eagerly discussing the events of the

לְהַבֵּשׁ לְנִשְׁבְּרֵי־לֵב זְרָא לִשְׁבוּיִם דְּרוֹר וְלַאֲסוּרִים־ פְּקַח־קוֹחַ:

morning and of the doings in the synagogue, as they
walked slowly away though the fields along a road that
was barely more than a field path. Wheat grew to the
very edge of the road where the rich soil of the field
turned to stones and the stones to trodden earth which in
winter was often slippery with mud and potholes.

Why had the Lord taken them to that particular
synagogue? He had not said anything, nor had He done
anything apart from talk to many of the local people. It
was a question nagging at all of their minds.

Behind them, the Lord, still surrounded by eager
questioners, answered questions and argued with His
enquirers. Further back still they could see, just emerging
from the synagogue, a group of Pharisees, the Pharisees
who had occupied the chief seats that morning. More
questions to disturb their walk; what was going on; why
were Pharisees following them instead of going back to
the town?

Some of the people had hailed the Teacher as "Lord,"
others as "Son of David," and yet others as "Rabbi" or
"Teacher", though He had never graduated from the
schools.

Hours had gone by and the disciples were hungry.
Moses allowed travellers to pluck ears of corn and to eat
them. It had been a long day and it was little more than
half over. They wondered where they would be bound
for next and where they would rest that night. There
were plenty of villages in the area. Some of them were
within the distance still allowed by the Law for them to
walk. They slowed down to let the Lord catch up with
them and chewed on the ears of wheat as they did so.
Had not Moses written, "When thou comest into the
standing corn of thy neighbour thou mayest pluck the
ears with thine hand; but thou shalt not move a sickle

לְהָבֵשׁ לְנִשְׁבָּרֵי־לֵב זְרָא לִשְׁבּוּים דְּרוֹר וְלַאֲסוּרֵים־ פְּקַח־קוֹחַ׃

unto thy neighbour's standing corn." As they chewed they thought about the morning and the presence of prominent Pharisees, some of them all the way from Jerusalem. They were not aware that those same Pharisees were watching them, some with horror, some with malicious glee and some with contempt.

Had the Lord known about them, those Rabbis from Jerusalem, one of them even a senior member of the Sanhedrin? Had He purposely come to this synagogue? Had they known of His intention and so had they purposely made it the object of their visit? It was all very puzzling, especially since the opposition of the Pharisees to the Lord, to His teaching and to His miracles seemed to be hardening and getting more vehement.

Was He seeking a confrontation, they wondered. He could easily have avoided it and He had the uncanny ability to be in control of every situation. It was more than having a ready answer, it was as if, as they believed, He knew all about things in advance. His was not just a ready wit, or a facility with words. No! It was something more, something deeper and more powerful. So if He knew, why seek out a confrontation? His teachings were about peace and about love for one's enemies. Did He love them, those Pharisees, who, if looks could kill, would have struck Him dead on more than one recent occasion?

People had been packing into the building that morning. The disciples had not noticed anything unusual until they entered the vestibule and saw in front of them, already seated on the raised bema before the ark holding the sacred scrolls, a group of senior Rabbis. Who were they and what were they doing? These were the questions which immediately sprang to their minds. As for the Lord Himself, He seemed completely unperturbed. As other men squashed up to let them sit

15

לְחָבֵשׁ לְנִשְׁבְּרֵי־לֵב ־ זְרָא לִשְׁבֻּיִם֙ דְּרֹ֗ור וְלַאֲסוּרִ֖ים ־ פְּקַח־קֹֽוחַ ׃

He took his place with smiles of thanks and of greeting to those round about.

The senior Rabbi, an important Pharisee, and an honoured guest in the synagogue looked about him with a patronising and benign expression on his face. As he caught sight of the Lord his eyes narrowed. It was only momentary and not noticed by the throng, yet the Lord had seen it and had answered it with a sad and gentle smile.

Several aspiring Pharisees, youngish but studious sons of the richer families, who approved of one son, at least, giving himself to the full-time study of the Law, the Prophets and the Writings, sat in the front rows. These, hoping later to be called upon to read, or to perform some other service during the proceedings, had satisfied smug expressions on their faces, or they carefully wore the features of mock humility. They had all hoped to be noticed by the eminent guests from the capital and their names noticed when they too went up there to study in the schools.

In accordance with custom they wore phylacteries on their foreheads and on their wrists, tied with seven knots. The fringes on the corners of their upper garments were enlarged so as also to be noticed. Everything was as orthodox as they could possibly make it. A Jew always ought to dress his best on Sabbath; if possible he should dress above his station in life, though it was also recommended that he eat below his station in life.

These, already showing the religious pride of their chosen brotherhood, had arrived very early. Not only did that show their eagerness but it enabled them to avoid contact with the common people who, by their touch, might defile them. You could never be sure whether the ignorant might well be ritually unclean and so would

16

לְהַבֵּשׁ לְנִשְׁבְּרֵי־לֵב זְרָא לַשְּׁבֻּיִם דְּרֹור וְלַאֲסוּרִים־ פְּקַח־קֹוחַ ׃

transmit their contagion even with a passing touch from their garments. They dreamed of graduation and the coveted title Rabbi. Oh to be addressed as Rabbi and to be accorded the respect it gave! Maybe even, after marriage, entrance to the outer court of the Sanhedrin, and then, to the Sanhedrin itself, the governing council. It was dominated by Pharisees and even the priests had to conform to their strictures on the teachings of the Torah regarding the Temple and its service.

There had been a slight stir as the Lord Jesus entered followed by His disciples. They sat near the back. Not for Him the chief places, not for Him to take the places of honour unless they were freely accorded Him. Craftsmen and labourers surrounded them. These were the common people who heard Him gladly, but who were despised by the learned and the strictly religious. Some of the disciples stood towards the back near where the women's gallery extended round from the sides.

The building was a mass of humanity. The disciples felt, or imagined they felt, a deepening hostility underlying the tensions that crackled in the air. It was fraught with emotion; all were clearly expecting something, but what, they did not know. Some crisis was at hand; they felt it, but could not say what form it would take, or even if it concerned Jesus from Nazareth and His disciples and the Pharisees. The tension hovered there on the fringes of their understanding, just out of their grasp.

Having settled on His seat between two workmen all dressed up in their best robes, He had sat patiently with that gentle but enigmatic smile on His face. He was clearly where He loved to be and He was, with equal clarity, among those people whom He loved most. "Blessed are the poor in spirit, for theirs is the Kingdom

לַחֲבֹשׁ לְנִשְׁבְּרֵי־לֵב זְרָא לִשְׁבֹּיִם דְּרֹוֹר וְלַאֲסוּרִים־פְּקַח־קֹוֹחַ׃

of Heaven." And here among them, in their very midst was the King Himself; what joy and what blessing they had derived from His own presence! He had sat, calm and relaxed, among friends, oblivious, it seemed, to the tension in the air. Yet He who knew all things could not have been unaware of that tension. He knew of it with a certainty, for He was the cause of it.

In the women's seats in the gallery round the sides and the back of the room, they had cast meaningful glances at their neighbours and exchanged remarks behind their hands. The remarks grew louder and the disciples could hear what the women were saying. They came in snatches at first then whole sentences. "The Prophet of Nazareth ... ", " ... carpenter's son!" "Thinks he's the Messiah!" That one spoken with contempt, disparagingly. " ... Elijah?" And, "did not Moses promise ... ?" Then, in worried tones, "Whatever will the Rabbis from Jerusalem be thinking?" The question was asked querulously but the answer came back with a chuckle from one of her neighbours: "I imagine we'll soon be finding out."

The women fell silent at a severe glance from one of the senior Rabbis, though a little whispering still continued in tones that did not quite reach the important seats at the front. Even that was soon subdued and a respectful hush had fallen over the concourse as the Ruler of the Synagogue got up to begin the proceedings.

First there were the two set prayers said at the opening of every synagogue service. The first prayer began: "Blessed be Thou, O Lord, King of the world, Who formest the light and createst the darkness, Who makest peace, and created everything ... " The second prayer left the theme of God's creative acts and gave thanks for His love and His mercy to His people. "With great love hast

18

לְהָבֵשׁ לְנִשְׁפְּרֵי־לֵב זְרֵא לִשְׁבֻּים דִּרֹור וְלַאֲסֹורִים־ פְּקַח־קֹוחַ־:

Thou loved us, O Lord our God, and with much overflowing pity hast Thou pitied us, our Father and our King ... " It went on to beseech His grace upon His people: "Enlighten our eyes in Thy Law; cause our hearts to cleave to Thy commandments; unite our hearts to love and fear Thy Name and we shall not be put to shame, world without end ... "

After that came the "Shema", so called from the word with which it began, "hear". It began, "Hear O Israel, the Lord our God is one Lord ... " and continued as the recitation of three passages from the Torah, almost a Jewish 'creed'. This assertion of the unity of the Godhead also implied the unity of God and His people and the unity of all Jews wherever they were to be found. More prayers followed and readings from the Law and the Prophets.

So the proceedings went forward according to the ancient prescribed pattern which had hardly changed since the time of the Maccabees. Even before that it had changed only in some features since the time of Ezra, "the ready scribe in the Law of the Lord." It went on to readings from the Law. One of the readers was the younger rabbi who had received the honour of starting off with the first two prayers and the Shema, having already been warned by the Ruler of the Synagogue or the Minister who was in overall control of the service.

Other men had been also called and took their place before the Ark to read from the sacred books, while the 'methurgeman' repeated what he said in the common tongue, giving a translation and sometimes words of explanation, called a 'targum'. Everything was conducted in the Hebrew language, but there were always those who were ignorant of the ancient language.

Many of the stricter rabbis frowned on this practice of

לְחַבֵּשׁ לְנִשְׁבְּרֵי־לֵב ־קְרָא לִשְׁבוּיִם דְּרוֹר וְלַאֲסוּרִים־ פְּקַח־קוֹחַ׃

giving a targum, considering that everyone should only speak in Hebrew. Hebrew was, after all, the sacred language in which God had called Abraham out of Ur of the Chaldees, in which He had conversed with Isaac, with Jacob and with Moses. It was Hebrew in which the God of Israel had written the tablets of the Law given to Moses and in which Moses had written the five books of the Law. For all they knew, and they thought it most likely, it was the Hebrew tongue in which God and Adam had talked during those happy days before the fall when, "God walked with Adam in the cool of the day".

However, since many wealthy Jews came regularly to keep the specified festivals in Jerusalem, who had no knowledge of Hebrew and who spoke in gentile languages, they could not be too insistent and make this a rule. Jews from Rome, from Alexandria and from Babylon as well as from many more far-flung parts of the empire and beyond the empire, came to the Feasts of Passover, of Pentecost and of Tabernacles. With them they brought their wealth, rich offerings for the Temple treasury and, as special religious good deeds they would pay for the sacrifices to be offered by their poorer brethren who could not afford anything more than two pigeons.

Jerusalem's hungry coffers rang with the silver and gold of these pious but ignorant bankers, merchants and, sometimes, administrators. It was not only rich Jews who thronged the city at festival times but visitors from all over the world. They were the proselytes, that is gentiles who were in the process of learning about Judaism and who were eventually to take on the yoke of the Law.

All the time while people had been settling down, the rabbis from Jerusalem had been casting covert glances in the direction of the Lord Jesus. They clearly did not think

לְחַבֵּשׁ לְנִשְׁבְּרֵי־לֵב זְרָא לִשְׁבֻים דְּרֹור וְלַאֲסֹורִים־ פְּקַח־קָֽוֹחַ־:

of Him as anything but a nuisance and a danger. Some looked with suspicious hostility, others with puzzled dislike. The chief of them sat in the place of honour with a confidence that it was his by right. How could he have understood that before him, in the body of the building, among the common folk, sat One greater than the synagogue, greater even than the Temple and certainly greater then the High Priest and the chief Rabbis. He was greater than the Law, for He had given the Law since it was an expression of Himself. How could they have known? Yet they should have known.

Was not that Pharisee who presided there with such a regal air, a member of one of the branches of the lesser Sanhedrin when the magi came to King Herod and asked where Messiah was to be born? He had since been promoted to the Great Sanhedrin but his father, who had been one of the supreme governing Council at that time had told him about the incident. The prophet Micah had said: "And thou, Bethlehem Ephrathah, though thou art little among the thousands of Judah, yet out of thee shall He come forth unto Me who shall rule My people." The spies of the High Priest had since confirmed that Jesus of Nazareth had indeed been born at that time in Bethlehem and had escaped the massacre by a dangerous flight into Egypt until after Herod had died. Apparently, because Archelaus, Herod's son, had been confirmed as ruler in Judea in his father's place, the family had moved to Galilee. This, thought the rabbi, was a wise move considering the character of Archelaus.

This was not widely known, for the saying went, "Can any good thing come out of Nazareth?" Nor did the Pharisees and the priests wish it to be known, for surrounding the Man from Nazareth, there were already enough possibilities for trouble. They knew all about the

לַחֲבֹשׁ לְנִשְׁבְּרֵי־לֵב ؛רָא לַשְׁבִּם וְדִּרֹּור וְלַאֲסֹוּרִים־ פְּקַח־קֹוחַ׃

miracles and the signs. They knew of the healings he had performed and how the blind had been made to see. The lepers were cleansed and the paralysed and the deaf had been restored and made well.

These of themselves would not have worried them; everywhere there were stories of healings in answer to the prayers of this or that rabbi. This man's were too well attested by reliable witnesses for them to be denied. On the other hand, their very credibility and their numbers made him even more dangerous and most of those in authority were nervous about what he might do or say next, especially since any Messianic claims might upset the Romans and the notoriously inconsistent Roman governor.

Relations with Pilate had always been precarious and the least thing, the least threat to his authority or to that of Rome, which amounted to the same thing, might cause him to react with bloody violence against the Jews.

If the man from Nazareth had simply claimed to be a prophet, or even some unlettered rabbi, it would not have mattered. They had always had their share of these and they did no real harm. If anything they helped to increase the religious devotion of the masses. However, they found him threatening to their system when he taught things contrary to their ideas and to their teachings. They saw themselves as the only accredited teachers in Israel, yet this man taught with an authority which even they would not dare to claim. He appealed to no rabbinic texts nor to the authority of the ancients, but spoke as if he were equal to the Law. He became even more obnoxious in their eyes when they found that they could not contradict him nor vanquish him in argument, but that he met all their criticisms with such wisdom that it became dangerous and self-defeating for them to

לְהָבֵשׁ לְנִשְׁבָּרֵי־לֵב זָרָא לִשְׁבוּיִם דְּרוֹר וְלַאֲסוּרִים־פְּקַח־קוֹחַ׃

challenge him.

The senior Rabbi was lost in his own thoughts for some time while waiting for the Synagogue service to begin. His outward show of confidence was not reflected completely by his inner state of mind. The man called John the Baptist worried him too. The common folk were fickle and some had stopped following him and had gone on to follow this Yeshua ben Yosef. However, many of the common folk thought of John as the Elijah who was to announce the Messiah. He had not in so many words pointed him out as such. There were tales of miraculous signs when Yeshua had been baptised.

Then there was the enigmatic announcement concerning him by John: "Look, the Lamb of God, who takes away the sin of the world!" What could that mean? It worried him but he could not explain to himself why it should do so. Only God could forgive sin and yet this Yeshua had told people he had released from their afflictions, "your sins are forgiven you." This too had been confirmed by reliable witnesses and this had gone on from one end of the country to the other. He was infecting more and more people with these teachings and he bypassed or ignored the proper teachers of the Law. That was surely not right?

Countless times had he gone over the arguments and the counter-arguments in his mind, assessing every point both for and against. The man was clearly an impostor, yet every time he expressed that conclusion to himself he was torn by doubts. They were doubts he did not wish to recognise, doubts which everything he knew and believed said were ridiculous. Yet the doubts lingered and caused him grave difficulties and unease. He even lost sleep over the matter.

He found himself going over again in his mind the

לְהַבֵּשׁ לְנִשְׁבְּרֵי־לֵב ִ זְרָא לִשְׁבוּיִם֙ דְּרֹור וְלַאֲסוּרֵים־ פְּקַח־קֹֽוחַ־ ׃

chain of reasoning he had tested, link by link, times without number. The man must be an impostor. Were he not, then, since the Pharisees were the true heirs of the Hassidim, the Holy Ones, or Godly Ones, then if he were a prophet he would have allied himself with them. How could he not if he were from God?

Then there was the Messianic claim. It was madness, but even allowing, which he did not, that he were Messiah, then there again, he must have allied himself with the Godly party in Israel. How could he not? Who represented the true teachers of the Law? Clearly the Pharisees. Who represented the true nationalists? Not for sure the demented Zealots, clearly only the Pharisees could claim to be the true descendants of the Maccabees. With the priests concerned with their own positions and placating the hated Romans. With some of them, even those in the highest positions in the state and the religion of Israel, concerned with nothing but profit, the feathering of their own nests. Again, how could a prophet not ally himself with the party that kept the priests in the Temple up to their duties regarding the observances of the rituals and the laws?

The true Messiah must have shown himself to the Pharisaic party and then set about the cleansing of the nation. He would have then brought the whole of the twelve tribes together and overthrown the Roman power before, like the true Son of David, extending Israel's borders as far as the Euphrates River, where the prophet had indicated them to be. No! He concluded for yet another time: this Yeshua could not be Messiah. He might be so to the common people who knew not the Law, but he was nothing more than a Messiah look-alike, an impostor, a pretend Messiah.

Perhaps he was sincerely deluded; he thought about

לְהַבֵּשׁ לְנִשְׁבְּרֵי־לֵב זְרָא לִשְׁבֻיִם דְּרֹור וְלַאֲסוּרִים־פְּקַח־קֹוחַ ׃

the possibility. No! That could not be. The man was too clever to be a deluded fool. He was someone who, without deluding himself, made a success of misleading the people. Messiah he most certainly was not. Trouble he most certainly was, and trouble that had, somehow, to be quickly and effectively nipped in the bud. He must not be allowed to subvert the Jewish people any more. He certainly must not rob the people of their natural leaders, the Pharisees. His teachings must not be allowed to stir up trouble with the Romans. No! He concluded, the sooner the man was dealt with the better. The sooner things were back to normal the better it would be for the religion and the people of Israel.

His reason for coming had been in answer to all the reasons that churned round in his mind. They needed a public confrontation and an arrest that would discredit Yeshua of Nazareth in the eyes of all the people. They had lost arguments; his teachings undermined their own, and their pride had been seriously dented. Worse still, their standing in the eyes of the people had been seriously diminished and it had to be restored. He had to confront the teacher from Nazareth himself and to catch him out in some obvious fault concerning the Law. Only thus might the status and standing of the Pharisees be restored; only thus would things return to normal, and only in that direction lay safety.

He mused on; an arrest for blasphemy would be the best thing for them, but any arrest for any serious breach of the Law would help and then they could deal with matters at their leisure. He looked forward to interrogating, himself, the carpenter from Galilee, but that would be for the full Council presided over by the High Priest to decide. His lip curled in dislike at the thought of Annas and his son-in-law the odious Caiaphas. However,

לְחַבֵּשׁ לְנִשְׁבְּרֵי־לֵב ;רָא לִשְׁבֻוּיִם דְּרוֹר וְלַאֲסוּרִים- פְּקַח־קוֹחַ:

it had to be admitted that Caiaphas had his uses; no one else had his skill in dealing with the Romans and in keeping the Governor Pilate sweet and from interfering in matters where he was not welcome. No! Caiaphas did have his uses but he was too clever by half. On the other hand, though, for Caiaphas to be the man who trapped Yeshua into an indiscretion, would be loss of face for the Pharisees. But then, in the end it did not matter, since the end justified the means, and the end was to be the downfall of Yeshua ben Yosef from Nazareth.

It was not a regular custom for the rabbis from Jerusalem to visit provincial synagogues. However, in this case they could disguise the true reason by implying that they were there to commend the piety of the rulers and the people. Having a group of Jerusalem rabbis visiting for a Sabbath service gave the local leadership greater status in the eyes of the locals and it also encouraged the local up and coming younger would-be rabbis in their studies and in their religious exercises.

They had known that Yeshua was in the area and would attend, he reflected, so other senior men from Jerusalem would have been in other synagogues in the locality. The local ruler of the synagogue and the senior men would be a little nervous during the visitation but afterwards, with a few words of commendation, they would be suitably gratified. Meanwhile they would watch the man they had come to trap and would follow his words and his actions with extreme care. They had even debated whether they should follow him if he travelled further than the specified Sabbath day's journey of about two thousand yards. They would follow him as far as they dared but could find no precedent for exceeding the amount allowed on the Sabbath.

As the people filed out after the conclusion of the

לְהָבֵשׁ לְנִשְׁבָּרֵי־לֵב זְרָא לְשְׁבוּיִם דְּרוֹר וְלַאֲסוּרִים־ פְּקַח־קוֹחַ׃

service, the Pharisees watched. Yeshua was in conversation with His disciples and with some of the common people who were gathering round Him in a respectful circle. At last He got up, having listened with genuine interest to the comments and questions of the people. There was not a question that He had not answered to the full satisfaction of the questioners. There was not a comment which He had not listened to, and had responded to with deeper teaching of His own. He was all kindness and courtesy, treating everyone with the interested encouragement which a gifted teacher would give to his most promising students. To their annoyance the rabbis from Jerusalem were being ignored.

As the prophet from Nazareth led His disciples out through the imposing main entrance, they were followed by two of the younger Pharisees. The more senior ones remained behind to exchange pleasantries with the Ruler of the Synagogue and with the other senior officials there. They explained that they must visit another synagogue at the other end of the town so must reluctantly tear themselves away.

"We know your hospitality Rabbi," they said to the Ruler of the Synagogue, "and we need to keep our wits about us, so we really must be on our way." With this and like pleasantries they made their departure and moved on slowly after their more junior colleagues who, in turn, were following the prophet from Nazareth and His disciples. They did not hurry, for one hurried to the Synagogue but not away from it.

He, for His part, had turned aside as if to strike out along the roadway that led between the fields of corn. He walked very slowly, still in conversation with some of the earnest older men who had been in the synagogue that morning and followed as well by some of the womenfolk.

27

לְחָבֹשׁ לְנִשְׁבְּרֵי־לֵב ָרָא לִשְׁבוּיִם דְּרֹור וְלַאֲסוּרִים־ פְּקַח־קֹוַח׃

His disciples were by now a little ahead but lingered when He seemed to hold back, slowing His pace to bid a courteous goodbye to the folk who had been questioning Him.

The party consisting of the Lord and His disciples was strung out along the road between the rich and ripe fields of corn not two hundred yards ahead of the two groups of Pharisees, now scenting success to the real reason for their visit. They watched with sharp, eager and critical eyes, hoping, expecting him to make some slip, to transgress in some way or another so they would have an excuse to show him up before the people. Anything at all would do to raise sufficient doubts in the minds of the common folk. He had to be shown up as having no possibility of being Moses' promised prophet, nor Elijah, and certainly not Messiah.

There were so many regulations concerning the Sabbath that it took a Pharisee with the mind of both a lawyer and an accountant to be sure that he observed every little matter with scrupulous care. You must not carry anything weighing more than a fig weighed. If you did you were working. You took care to wear only the necessary clothing or you might be carrying a load on the Sabbath day.

The Pharisees themselves, of course, were convinced that he was none of the things people were saying he was. That is, with the exception of men like Nicodemus who seemed to be somewhat under his spell. But he was only one and did not count when it really came to it. After all, did not Yeshua of Nazareth consort with tax gatherers? He could not possibly be the Messiah. Nor could he indeed be any sort of prophet with such a man among his closest associates. Matthew Levi was well known for his previous despised and hated occupation.

לְהַבֵּשׁ לְנִשְׁבְּרֵי־לֵב זְרָא לִשְׁבֻּיִם דְּרוֹר וְלַאֲסוּרִים־פְּקַח־קוֹחַ:

There were others too; he talked to harlots. Not that anyone could find anything improper – but even to be in the company of one was a seriously defiling matter. As for the rest of his disciples, they were fishermen, workmen, a zealot even. He could not be Messiah, for if he were he would have chosen the qualified teachers of the Law to be his friends. It was an open and shut case and his popularity among the ignorant folk was dangerous, for he was misleading them. Giving them ideas above their station in life and making them question the constituted authorities.

The visiting rabbis had spoken of the sacredness of the Sabbath. They had explained how the guidance given by the rabbis was designed to prevent transgressions of the Law itself. God had given the Torah containing the Law but Israel had to obey and carry out every precept and every prescription of the Law – that was the responsibility of every Israelite. To this end they stressed the need for all Jews to study the rabbinic texts or to ask for guidance from their leaders and teachers.

Most of those who had been present felt they had been privileged to be lectured to by the famous teachers from the capital. They felt that the presence of such prominent men in their synagogue conferred some special favour upon them and they glowed with pride that theirs was the one chosen for the privilege. Some thought that the presence too of the prophet from Nazareth conferred an additional blessing upon their congregation. Generally they left, that morning, bathed in the warm glow of pride and of honour. Some of the more sensitive souls had felt something of the tension in the air, but most of these simply put it down to nervousness due to the presence of distinguished guests. Maybe one or two as well as a few of the disciples sensed

לְהָבֵשׁ לְנִשְׁבְּרֵי־לֵב זְרָא לִשְׁבֻּיִם דְּרֹור וְלַאֲסוּרִים־ פְּקַח־קֹוחַ׃

the impending clash between the Pharisees and Yeshua ben Yosef.

As they were setting out in the heat of the day the disciples too wondered about the antagonism of the Pharisees. Certainly the Lord, on more than one occasion, had rebuked these sticklers for every part of the Law. They found it hard to understand why men did not love Him as they did. No one who had seen His miracles could doubt that He was sent by God. They found it hard to see how anyone could doubt Him, or think that He would knowingly cause trouble for the authorities. Yet the authorities did not like Him and they seemed to want to catch Him out. They had been unsuccessful so far but there was an ominous feeling that there might yet be trouble.

That He was actually God the Son they could not yet understand. It was, perhaps, too difficult a concept for them to take in. As for the Pharisees, the very idea could not enter their rigidly closed minds. The thinking of the disciples was as yet unformed, inchoate and rudimentary; they had much yet to learn and much to put together in their minds as they meditated on all the things He had taught them, and would teach them. He was their teacher and their Lord. That He was the Lord Himself, God, could not yet enter their thinking; it was too big, too enormous to take in. And yet, in time, that too would come, as miracle, parable and teaching came together pointing to only one incontrovertible conclusion.

It was a long time since they had eaten. They were hungry and so began to pluck the ears of corn, to rub them in their hands to remove the husks and to pick out the kernels to eat. It helped somewhat to allay the pangs of hunger and it filled in the time while the Lord caught up with them. This practice was sanctioned by Moses in

לְהַבֵּשׁ לְנִשְׁבָּרֵי־לֵב ׃רָא לְשְׁבֵּים דְרֵוּר וְלַאֲסוּרֵים־פְּקַח־קֵוֹחַ׃

the Law and by the customs of their fathers. The hungry traveller was thus allowed to assuage the pangs of hunger. To these simple and unlettered men everything was quite clear. You may eat for your own satisfaction but you should not reap anything to take away with you. That was what God meant when He had Moses write that you should not take a sickle to your neighbour's corn. To take and eat with your hands was not working.

That was not how the Pharisees saw it. It did not dawn on them that being triumphant at the sin committed by another was, in itself, questionable. They had him, if not him directly at least they had him through his disciples. They had him. His disciples might be common people; they might be ignorant of the Law, but they were his disciples and if they broke the Law then it was his fault.

Clearly it was his fault. If he were a teacher then he would have taught them. If he were a prophet then clearly he would have known what they were doing before they did it and would have warned them. They had him. He was no Messiah, no Teacher, no Leader and no Prophet. And if he were none of these then he must be a charlatan. He was a pretender who deceived the people who were foolish and naïve and who, in their ignorance, had put their trust in him instead of those who by long and arduous study were qualified to teach to Israel God's Law. They had him. It was their duty, their God-given duty, as they saw it, to challenge and to expose him. He was a deceiver and clearly in the enemy's camp, a servant of Beelzebub no less and a danger to all good men and women.

"Look what your disciples are doing!" demanded the senior Pharisee, puffing a little from his exertions to catch

31

לְהַבֵּשׁ לְנִשְׁבְּרֵי־לֵב ;רָא לִשְׁבוּיִם דְּרוֹר וְלַאֲסוּרִים־ פְּקַח־קָוֹחַ:

up without seeming to use undue haste on a Sabbath day. They all accused him with self-righteous indignation and some outrage which was not all put on.

"Why are they doing what it is not lawful to do on the Sabbath?" added another, his face suffused with anger mixed with not a little triumph as well. The trap they had longed themselves to set had been sprung, though as yet they were not aware they themselves were its victims.

To the tortuous minds of the Pharisees the disciples were obviously guilty of at least four separate infringements of the laws regarding the Sabbath. In plucking ears of corn, they were reaping. In rubbing them to remove the husks they were threshing. If they blew on the contents of their hands to blow away the chaff they were then winnowing and, finally, if they picked out grains of corn to eat they were sifting. To such pettifogging depths had the study of the Torah sunk under the rule and hegemony of the rabbis and lawyers of the Pharisees.

He could have pointed out that Moses, in forbidding the use of a sickle to cut the corn, was, in so doing, forbidding reaping. Therefore what the disciples were doing was clearly not, by Moses' implied definition, reaping. He could have referred to their own rule that since an ear of corn weighed less than half a fig this could not be carrying a burden on the Sabbath. He could have argued that it was permissible to lift an ox or an ass that was trapped, fallen into a pit, on the Sabbath and so free it from its danger. He did none of these things. Instead He gave two examples, one from Scripture and the other from common sense and common practice. Neither could be argued against.

"Have you not read what David did when he and his companions were hungry and in need? In the days of

לְהָבֵשׁ לְנִשְׁבְּרֵי־לֵב זָרָא לִשְׁבֻּיִם דְּרוֹר וְלַאֲסוּרִים־ פְּקַח־קָוֹחַ ׃

Abiathar the high priest, he entered the house of God and ate the consecrated bread, which is lawful only for the priests to eat. And he also gave some to his companions." The incident in the Book of Samuel should have been decisive and clear to the Pharisees, but the gentle irony in the Lord's question, "Have you not read," must have fired the bitter jealousy which is "as cruel as sheol [hades]".

They had indeed read, but their reading had been on commentaries about the Scripture and they had allowed tradition to interpret it for them. So jealousy had become a rage that demanded vengeance which would not be pacified with gifts nor with any ransom. They who had read everything any Jew could possibly read! How dare he say to them, "Have you not read?"

How easily may human gifts be perverted; the love of learning be turned into the pride of accomplishment; the love of religion turned into bigotry. And bigotry it was that made them insensitive to the clear teachings of the passage in the History of David their hero king. They ought to have realised, but they did not, that they too were eaten up with jealousy, their minds blinded by anger, fuelled by malicious prejudice. David was the anointed King of Israel; he ought to have been enjoying the privileges which had once been his, of leading Saul's men of war. But Saul, eaten up just as they were with jealousy, was hunting him to take his life, his judgement clouded with bloodthirsty anger.

So too they were hunting the Prophet from Nazareth to destroy Him utterly. They should have realised, but they did not, that He too was the Lord's anointed, descended from David on both His mother's side and that of the man Yosef the carpenter who was supposedly His earthly father. The records of the genealogies could easily have confirmed that. They should have known, but

לַחֲבֹשׁ לְנִשְׁבְּרֵי־לֵב זָרֵא לִשְׁבֻיִם֙ דְּרֹ֔ור וְלַאֲסוּרִים־ פְּקַח־קֹ֑וחַ׃

they did not, that He was great David's greater Son, born in Bethlehem, born of a virgin, their true King and, like David, a king in rejection.

There was no excuse for their blindness. No excuse for not understanding the glaringly simple analogy. There was no excuse, for even they agreed that the Scripture could not be broken; it was the final answer. There was no excuse for not seeing that the Scripture put concern for human life and even for the well-being of animals above that of ritual observance. The God of compassion was well aware of the weakness of the human frame and had made the Sabbath for man, whereas the Pharisees would have turned that on its head and have man made for the Sabbath.

To seal the argument, as if in obedience to another of the Law's requirements, that of two witnesses, the Lord made one other pointed remark. He directed their minds to the glaringly obvious fact that before their very eyes, every Sabbath, in Jerusalem, the priests worked. In offering the sacrifices, attending on the altar, sounding the trumpets and seeing to the many other matters required for the smooth running of the religious ceremonials of the Temple, they worked. He said, "Haven't you read in the Law that on the Sabbath the priests in the temple desecrate the Sabbath and yet are innocent?"

Having said this His concluding remarks could not have been more calculated to inflame their indignation and their hatred: "But I tell you that one greater than the Temple is here. If you had known what these words mean: 'I desire mercy, not sacrifice', you would not have condemned the innocent. For the Son of Man is Lord of the Sabbath."

Not knowing what to say, in disarray and lost

לְהַבֵּשׁ לְנִשְׁבָּרֵי־לֵב ;רָא לִשְׁבוּיִם דְּרוֹר וְלַאֲסוּרִים־פְּקַח־קוֹחַ׃

completely for words, the Pharisees, with loss of face slunk away, jealousy and anger boiling inside while trying to maintain an expression outwardly of dignity and of decorum. He caught up with the disciples who, amazed at this crushing defeat of the best of Jewish thinking, fell back in silence following their Lord respectfully but fearfully too. For even they, dull as they often were of understanding, felt the hostility and the sheer outrage of the other party. Where it might lead they knew not but they were afraid. Where it would lead the Lord knew only too well and a deep sadness fell over Him as they made their way a short distance to another of the synagogues.

(You can read about Jesus and His disciples in the cornfield in Matthew's Gospel, chapter 12.)

3

Prisoner of Faith

Several events had coincided to stir up something of a hornets' nest. The new prophet from Nazareth, Yeshua ben Yosef, had caused consternation and a great deal of indignation among the folk in Jerusalem. That is, the folk who were anyone that really mattered. The priests were grinding their teeth in anger and the Pharisees had their deep suspicions about someone who taught openly and in the synagogues without any recognised qualification. The common people, some openly, some secretly, depending on their degree of dissatisfaction with the regime of the priests, approved. They smiled with glee, some of them, while others laughed openly and a few brave souls baited the priests and their minions for their venality and rapaciousness.

In the general confusion a few had pretended to help but, by giving an extra slap to already panicked oxen, had created more. Some tried to pick up the wicker cages containing doves but, as if by accident, allowed them to fall open, releasing a flock of frightened birds. Sparrows too were somehow released to join in and to make matters worse. With a flurry of wings all these made their way to safety.

The men who ran the stalls or who changed Roman and Greek coins for Jewish ones, the only currency acceptable in the sacred precincts, scrabbled on the ground for coins. This money-changing was done with

לְהַבֵּשׁ לְנִשְׁבָּרֵי-לֵב ؛ רָא לִשְׁבוּיִם דְּרוֹר וְלַאֲסוּרִים־ פְּקַח-קוֹחַ؛

immense profit for the priests who controlled all this buying, selling and choosing. Now passers-by saw wealth scattered over the ground and ran to scoop it up or to winkle it out of cracks in the stones of the pavement. Some returned the money; some allowed it to stick to their fingers or in pockets of their garments or in their money bags.

So unusual and so shocking had been the sudden eruption of the unknown man from Galilee into the precincts of the Temple that confusion ensued. Panicked by the equally panicked animals and birds, the vendors and money-changers too ran about squawking louder than the sacrificial beasts and birds they had been in charge of. A few, more collected than their colleagues, had gone off to the rooms of the chief priests to tell them of the unique and terrifying happenings. So they had discharged their responsibility and turned the worry for it over to those who really counted. They returned, full of self-importance and indignation at their loss of revenue, to the ruins of their stalls and tables.

Shouts for order mingled with shouts of indignation and outrage, and the frightened bellowing of oxen, the bleating of sheep and goats and the flurry of wings caused more panic and confusion. Little boys clapped their hands in delight or screamed with fear. Men and beasts ran this way and that while other people looked on open-mouthed at this unprecedented sight. Very few, except the priests themselves and those who worked for them doing the actual selling, expressed disapproval though some felt that the uproar was in bad taste and a desecration of the solemnity of the Temple.

Meanwhile, Yeshua from Nazareth, who had been the cause of all the trouble by driving out the sacrificial animals and overturning the tables of the money-

37

לַחְבֹּשׁ לְנִשְׁבְּרֵי־לֵב ׀ רָא לִשְׁבוּיִם דְּרֹור וְלַאֲסוּרִים־ פְּקַח־קֹוחַ׃

changers, left the scene. He made His way through the temple court and out into the old city under the vast arches which spanned the triumphal ascent into the House of the Lord God of Israel.

Far behind ran two representatives of the High Priest. These were younger priests sent by the authorities to demand an answer for the desecration and to investigate the reasons for it. They were also to bring, if possible, its prime mover back to the Temple to answer charges. Such was the shock and the horror at what they saw as the sacrilege of the Galilean, the cause of the trouble, that they forgot their priestly dignity and hurried after their quarry with unseemly haste.

Usually conscious of the dignity of their priestly calling, they would not have dreamed of hurrying, in such an undignified manner, with the skirts of their robes in disarray, getting in everyone's way and seriously out of breath. Normally they would have avoided the dust, the dirt and the noisy, cheerful, quarrelsome, colourful and mercurial crowds thronging the streets of the old city, the city of David. This was where the Galilean was apparently making for, and so they pursued Him.

They tripped, they barged, they pushed their way through the crowds. They came into violent collision with donkeys, with camels and with oxen. The animals, not being aware of the social and religious standing of the men they came into contact with, were not impressed. Nor, for that matter, did they recognise any social or religious pecking order other than that established with horns and with hooves, so it was with these that a few who were quick enough retaliated to the unexpected collisions. One priest was kicked, to the delight of the people sitting in the shade, by a donkey and went off limping. The other got into a serious shoving match with

לְהַבֵּשׁ לְנִשְׁבָּרֵי־לֵב זְּרָא לִשְׁבֹּּּים דְּרוֹר וְלַאֲסוּרִים־ פְּקַח־קְוֹח:

a particularly large and malodorous camel. It was a match in which the priest came off second best, again to the delight of the crowd. The animals only obeyed their drovers because they, as is the habit of drovers the world over, carried and knew how to use whips and goads.

Bitterly resenting these, it gave the animals a certain bovine satisfaction to be able to retaliate against the dominant humans and even, for a moment to earn the approval of the drovers who used them cruelly. The young priests, however, retired from the unequal fray and made their way with bruised bodies and even more damaged dignity, to their seniors. On the way they met some of those same seniors and poured out to them their tale of woe and injury.

They did not get much in the way of sympathy, for the older men, having preserved their dignity and their self-control, were only interested in answers to the questions: Where? Why? Which way? What does He look like? The crowds, seeing that the fun was over, went back to their own business and the serious calls of commerce or physical labour. One or two still tut-tutted that those who ought to have been examples of rectitude and dignity should have allowed themselves to have been the chief actors in such an indecorous display.

The less flustered, but still angry Priests found Him who was the cause of all the fuss, sitting with His disciples and some bystanders in the courtyard of the house of one of His sympathisers. The interrogators made their entrance with a dignity which owed more to self-importance than any consciousness of their real role in the community. A fountain played its watery dance near the entrance and the calmness of the prophet from Nazareth made a strange contrast to their angry demeanour. The crowd made way for them to approach

39

לְהָבֵשׁ לְנִשְׁבְּרֵי־לֵב זְרָא לִשְׁבֻיִּם דְּרֹור וְלַאֲסוּרִים־פְּקַח־קֹוחַ׃

Yeshua and He smiled a welcome. It was a smile with no malice, no triumph, nor any patronising superiority in it. It was a smile that invited friendship and dialogue; not recriminations, nor angry words. It was a smile which, though slightly disconcerting to those who had come for a confrontation, was not answered. It gained no friendly response. Rather it was taken to be all the things it was not.

The disciples were still thinking about the verse from the Psalm: "The zeal of Thine house hath eaten me up." New ideas were opening up in their minds as a result of the events of the day. The Priests, on the other hand, made their attack a direct one.

"You drove out the sheep and the oxen from the Temple," they accused, and went on: "You overturned the tables of the money-changers. You should know that it is necessary for the sacrificial animals to be ones that the Levites have inspected and passed as fit for offerings. If it were not so people would offer the lame and the blind for sacrifice. How can you be so ignorant of the Law?" They spat out the words at Him contemptuously.

He lifted His head and looked at them quizzically, as if to say, "Well! What about it? Are you sure you know what you're talking about?" Taken aback, the senior of the priestly officials demanded: "What miraculous sign can you show us to prove your authority to do all this?"

They expected that this demand would leave Him without words, unable to give the sign which was expected of any true prophet. What they did not expect was the answer they got. It both infuriated them and confused them. It was, it seemed, ridiculous in the enormity of their misunderstanding, and impossible unless He were what He had already implied He was. Disciples, priests, some Pharisees who had joined them

לַחֲבֹשׁ לְנִשְׁבְּרֵי־לֵב לִקְרֹא לִשְׁבוּיִם דְּרוֹר וְלַאֲסוּרִים־פְּקַח־קוֹחַ׃

and the bystanders, did not know what to think. Some wandered away, deciding that the conversation was too rarefied, too much above their simple understanding of things to bother with. The disciples puzzled over it but they were not to understand until much later.

They meant Him to justify His actions somehow. They expected to bring Him down to their level of hair-splitting law juggling. He looked at them again until most dropped their gaze before his silent, open and solemn challenge. After a pause he looked round the crowd once more and said: "Destroy this temple and, in three days, I will raise it up."

Wintry smiles were wiped from faces, the expressions to be replaced by incredulity and ridicule. They thought He was referring to the massive building on the Temple Mount in Jerusalem. They thought His mind was on the temple built for them by Herod, miscalled 'The Great'. They laughed and the senior one shook his head, replacing the look of horrified unbelief with the previous bleak smile. He remarked, "It has taken forty-six years to build this temple, and you are going to raise it in three days?"

It had not been an attempt on His part to mislead them, nor to play semantic games. Rather He was giving them a chance to question what they did not understand and to ask what He meant. Had they done so, He would have been able to lift them from the material earthly temple which was the focus of their minds and of their lives, to the heavenly and the divine. He would have been able to show them the Salvation of Israel and of the world, which was His mission.

There was nothing more to be said. They walked away and the expressions again changed to grim thoughtfulness. Some barely hid a grimace of disgust at

41

לַחֲבֹשׁ לְנִשְׁבְּרֵי־לֵב ;רָא לִשָׁבוּיִם וְדִרוֹר וְלַאֲסוּרִים־ פְּקַח־קוֹחַ׃

what they thought was an incredibly stupid remark. Only one or two beside the disciples looked thoughtful. They had to make their report to the High Priest and, depending on what they told him, he would decide, when, where and how to bring about the downfall and the arrest of this man who so defied all civic decency and all religious sentiment.

In fact there was no move on the part of the Temple authorities to arrest Him. Rather they placed a careful watch on Him. Their spies and a host of self-important tellers of tales reported His every move and His every word. They did so, not without embellishments, of course, for what teller of tales does not like his story to sound more plausible and exciting? As far as Caiaphas the High Priest was concerned, and as far as his father-in-law, Annas, was concerned, it was better that others did their dirty work. Their method was that of manipulation through half-truths and carefully edited accusations.

Their minds began to work with the cunning that had brought them survival over the years in the hazardous world of Roman and Jewish politics. Herod, superstitious, cruel and suspicious, seemed a likely tool. In the end it was the Pharisees, respected by Herod Antipas with a certain religious awe, who were to prevail upon him to do something about the Baptist. If the Baptist were to be taken out of the picture then perhaps Yeshua's support would decline accordingly.

Beneath the surface the ramifications of the events of the day had wider repercussions. Like ripples caused by a stone dropped into a pool, groups which had never, as yet, heard of Yeshua, became aware of things they had hitherto accepted unthinkingly as part of the natural and ordered fabric of society. The social differences were already there, of course, just as they are in every society.

לְחָבֹשׁ לְנִשְׁבְּרֵי־לֵב גָרָא לִשְׁבֻיִם דְּרוֹר וְלַאֲסוּרִים־פְּקַח־קוֹחַ׃

The Pharisees despised the common people. They openly ridiculed and sometimes vilified the priests who were of the opposing sect of the Sadducees. The chief among the priests basked confidently in the political power they exercised. They played power politics with the Governor, and with Rome, and through the wide-ranging network of Jewish business men and bankers whose economic tentacles reached from one end of the empire to the other and even far beyond to regions barbaric or civilised, they exerted enormous influence.

The common people themselves often made fun of the Pharisees with their care about dress, avoiding contamination, and their scrupulousness over washing and food. They resented the priests, some of whom, as well as making a very good living, seemed to be over-friendly with the Romans. The Romans were bad enough, but definitely at the bottom of the heap were the despised tax collectors. They, for their part, did not care, as long as they made money from collecting the taxes; however disliked, they had the Roman army to back them and they were getting rich. In their eyes that was all that mattered.

And now, at last, someone had dared to voice this reality which had, as part of its injustice, a market in the sacred precincts of the Temple. The greed and the venality of the priests was the real desecration of Israel's most sacred spot. Now it had been expressed, out loud, in no uncertain terms and the glaring injustices, the vast divisions in what should have been a united nation and the hypocrisy of those who claimed to know the Law, were made plain. He had put into words what they all felt but which few were able to express. Made into a "House of merchandise" – that summed it all up.

There was one man, however, a member of the ruling

לְהַכֵּשׁ לְנִשְׁבָּרֵי־לֵב וְרָא לִשְׁבוּיִם דְּרוֹר וְלַאֲסוּרִים־ פְּקַח־קוֹחַ:

Council, but a man considered by some, at best as being
too honest for his own good, or at worst unreliable, which
amounted to the same thing. Filled with perplexity he
paid Yeshua a visit one night. He had seen the
miraculous signs, he had heard of reports of others. He
believed the evidence and that brought him face to face
with a serious problem. If the evidence of the signs was
true then clearly the prophet from Galilee was a man sent
from God. If he was a man sent from God then He ought
to be believed and accepted.

Few, if any, of his fellow Pharisees accepted such
reasoning. They would have called it simplistic or would
simply have given way to anger. They would have
pointed out that he paid scant heed to the observance of
the Sabbath and they would have argued that if he were
really from God then he would have become a Pharisee.
Though Nicodemus had reasoned so himself at one time
he felt that there were serious flaws in the arguments put
out by his brother Pharisees.

On top of all this, here in the capital, he had
committed, what to many was sacrilege, so he deserved
to die. Attitudes were hardening and there were already
those who regarded the Galilean prophet with deep
suspicion, even hostility. But were they right?
Nicodemus allowed his mind to roam over the stories of
the prophets of old. Even David had not been beyond
the judgement of God. Nathan the prophet had been
sent to him with God's words to rebuke and to warn of
punishment for his adultery and murder: "You are the
man ... Why did you despise the word of the Lord by
doing evil in His eyes? You struck down Uriah the Hittite
with the sword and took his wife to be your own."

So what if Yeshua had actually come from God to
rebuke and to make public the venality and the sin of the

לְהָבֵשׁ לְנִשְׁבָּרֵי־לֵב זְּרָא לִשְׁבֻוִים וְדֹר וְלַאֲסוּרִים־פְּקַח־קוֹחַ׃

priests and the whole Sanhedrin in this worse sacrilege of making money out of the service of God? Was he himself not also involved? He was a member of the Great Sanhedrin and so any decisions made by that body were his decisions. Even though he did not agree with them and had spoken against them, there was still his own sense of guilt. In this matter he had not spoken up; it was a custom which had gone on for years and it was to his shame that he had not seen it for what it was.

Most of the leading Pharisees were in agreement with the practice. The prophet Malachi, in his day, had warned against bringing blind and sick beasts for offerings. The fact of making money had been glossed over. Perhaps they had seen it but had chosen not to notice. Perhaps *he* had seen it and had chosen not to notice and to expose it. It was a deeply troubled Pharisee who came to the house where Yeshua from Nazareth was lodging and joined Him on the rooftop where, traditionally, the prophet's chamber was built.

'Nicodemus' was a name which meant 'people conqueror'. In his case it did not apply to a tyrant but to someone who rose above the views and opinions of the populace and of his own social, religious and economic group. Such was the man who came that night to seek out the Prophet from Galilee and to find out more about Him.

"No one could perform the miraculous signs that you are doing if God were not with him," he began. The stars above them seemed to come closer as if to listen attentively to the answer which was ready on the Teacher's lips.

"I tell you the truth, no one can see the kingdom of God unless he is born again."

It was not the sort of answer Nicodemus had

לְחַבֵּשׁ לְנִשְׁבְּרֵי־לֵב זָרָא לִשְׁבּוּיִם דְּרֹוֹר וְלַאֲסוּרִים־ פְּקַח־קֹוֹחַ׃

expected. He was at first startled, then mystified.

"How can a man be born when he is old? Surely he cannot enter a second time into his mother's womb to be born?"

It was not an answer he readily understood. It soon became apparent that the man he saw as sent from God, had a profound understanding of human psychology and of the Scriptures. As He gently chided him for being a rabbi and not knowing the words of the Prophet Ezekiel, He was opening up to him heavenly realities. Ezekiel had written: "I will sprinkle clean water on you, and you will be clean. I will cleanse you from all your filthiness and from all your idols. I will give you a new heart and put a new spirit in you."

It was not whether Yeshua was a prophet or not that was at issue. That was clearly answered by the signs and by the fulfilling of the Scripture. What was important was that Nicodemus himself should be born into the Kingdom of God and learn to distinguish the earthly from the heavenly. So the Teacher who was a carpenter taught the student who was a rabbi. The teacher of Israel learned many things and life was never the same again for that one man. It is never the same for people when they learn the heavenly realities which Yeshua has to teach them.

His days in the capital were, for a time, at an end. It was time to move on, so, followed by His disciples, He travelled eastwards to the Jordan.

(You can read about the cleansing of the temple in Mark's Gospel, chapter 11, also John chapter 2.)

4

The Shadow of Machaerus

The disciples knew how John had announced Yeshua as the Lamb of God who was to take away the sin of the world. In the world, not just Israel; there were so many things which were totally new to their thinking. There were so many things they did not understand. There was so much to learn, so much to try to understand. Some of it, they had been told, they would understand finally, at a later date – sometime in the future.

Then John had spoken about Yeshua as someone whose sandals he was not worthy to unloose. When Yeshua asked for baptism, John had demurred and argued that it should be the other way round, but Yeshua had insisted saying, "thus it is fitting for us to fulfil all righteousness." Another difficult thing to puzzle about and to hope to understand. Perhaps sometime, things would finally be made clear to them.

They were making their way to the Jordan. People were saying that John too was baptising nearby. Yet John had indicated Yeshua – implying that they should follow Him. As they reached the river, many things were on their minds. As well as the relations between the Baptist and their Teacher, there were the recent events in Jerusalem. Perhaps He really was preparing to rally Israel to Himself and to announce Himself as their Messiah.

If He was going to do this and cast out the hated and despised Romans then the Zealots would flock to Him and so would many others. The rejection of Him by the priests and by most of the Pharisees was clearly apparent.

לַחֲבֹשׁ לְנִשְׁבְּרֵי־לֵב ;רָא לִשְׁבוּיִם וְּרוֹר וְלַאֲסוּרִים־ פְּקַח־קוֹחַ:

The Herods were friends of Rome and could not be expected to support a rebellion. These were stirring times they were living in, and not a little frightening.

They were just a few miles north of the point at which the river flowed into the Dead Sea. Not far to the north John too was baptising, in Aenon near Salim. It was an opportunity too good to miss. The Pharisees had seen to it that their spies reported to them every move made by the Prophet from Galilee and those of John. They watched and they waited and, just a little while after the scenes in Jerusalem, the two were close together, just a few short miles apart.

As was often the case, different schools of thought and differing shades of opinion existed. Each one thought its own interpretation the right one. Each one was eager to argue its case with the others. There was no shortage of argument in Judea that summer. Bathing the body, washing the hands, washing and purifying of cups and plates – all were a minefield for the aspiring Pharisee, yet many enjoyed making the minute points of argument and looking at every relevant case. They looked also at many things that were not relevant and there were endless sayings about how this rabbi or that teacher interpreted this custom or that ordinance.

The Pharisees, in particular, held these things to be of great importance. The endless arguments went on and on. They were yet to hear the words of rebuke spoken by the Prophet from Nazareth.

"Woe to you, scribes and Pharisees, hypocrites! For you cleanse the outside of the cup and dish, but inside they are full of extortion and self-indulgence. Blind Pharisee, first cleanse the inside of the cup and dish, that the outside of them may be clean also." This would be later when their opposition and plotting was soon to bring about His arrest and execution.

The disciples of John were less scrupulous in their washings and purifyings. John, as the announcer of the

לְהַבְּשׁ לְנִשְׁבְּרֵי־לֵב ;רָא לִשְׁבוּיִם דְּרֹוֹר וְלַאֲסוּרִים־ פְּקַח־קֹוֹחַ׃

Messiah and whose forerunner he was, was concerned rather with the true cleansing which was a change of heart and mind. Washing dishes and washing one's hands had, of course, a practical use, but to insist on such scrupulous ritual observance of the mere physical was to lose sight entirely of the more important spiritual aspect of life. This was the great mistake of the Pharisees and the point at which their legalism broke down most seriously. The body may be important, but it is only the dwelling place for the soul and the spirit. These are what really matter.

The Pharisees who came in a group to talk to the disciples of John would have loved to argue these things but this, though to them serious, was merely a pretence; an excuse to bring out other ideas. It was to be an opportunity, not so much to argue the rights and wrongs of certain cherished practices, but to put an idea into the minds of John's disciples and into the mind of John himself; if that were possible. They had been well briefed; their minds aspired to bigger game and worked with masterful cunning.

Disastrously for them it was to turn to the Baptist's greatest triumph, though none but he and the greater Teacher he served, would have seen it as such. After some talk with the disciples of John they sought out the opinion of the master, the Baptist himself. It was to be a masterstroke, a chance to insert a wedge between John and the One to whom he had borne witness. On a human level it was brilliant. On a human level it ought to have worked so that suspicion and even enmity between the two might have arisen. To some eyes, they might have been seen to be possible rivals. It was the similar manner of the preaching and the similar manner of the practice of baptism by immersing the repentant candidate under the water which put the idea into the minds of the Pharisees. They could not understand that between the two, John and Yeshua, there was the

לְהַבֵּשׁ לְנִשְׁבְּרֵי־לֵב זָרָא לִשְׁבֻּים דְּרוֹר וְלַאֲסוּרִים־ פְּקַח־קוֹחַ׃

relationship of servant to his Master, of pupil to his Teacher and of worshipper to his God. To attempt to drive a wedge between them was as impossible as getting the priests to give up their lucrative business in the Temple, when even as the Pharisees journeyed to Jordan, the priests were making up their losses and putting up fresh stalls to sell doves and to change money into Jewish currency acceptable to the Temple authorities.

At last came the opportunity as the conversation drifted from one aspect of washing to another. The leading Pharisee and the oldest among them looked across at John and, in mock seriousness and with what seemed like deep respect, said to him: "Rabbi! He who was with you beyond Jordan, to whom you have testified – he is baptising, and all are coming to him."

The question hung in the air between them. The disciples of John suddenly began to have doubts. Why, they thought, did John continue to baptise? Why did Yeshua baptise? Were they at odds and even rivals for the hearts and minds of the people? Had their teacher changed his mind, without telling them, regarding Yeshua from Nazareth? Was John the prophet foretold by Moses or was it Yeshua? For his part John's mind seemed far away, somewhere else, not in this world.

He smiled as if at some inner blissful vision and then turned to his questioners, the smile fading and turning to sadness. He shook his head slowly in a gesture of rebuke at their ignorance and their unbelief. The wind from the east, from the desert, stirred the leaves and the rushes at the river's bank. The men who had come with confident glee in the expectancy of causing dissent felt an answering shiver of doubt go through their minds.

John's reply was one of the most remarkable speeches ever made by human lips. It showed a vision and a devotion such as few can even imagine and an obedience to the heavenly vision that few among servants of God down through the ages have ever

לְהַבְשׁ לְנִשְׁבָּרֵי-לֵב קְרָא לִשְׁבוּיִם דְּרוֹר וְלַאֲסוּרִים- פְּקַח-קוֹחַ:

achieved; "A man can receive nothing unless it has been given to him from heaven. You yourselves bear me witness, that I said, 'I am not the Christ,' but, 'I have been sent before Him.' He who has the bride is the bridegroom; but the friend of the bridegroom, who stands and hears him, rejoices greatly because of the bridegroom's voice. Therefore this joy of mine is fulfilled. He must increase, but I must decrease."

To the great ones of this world, these words would mean little; or if they did try to understand them they would have seemed ridiculous. What else is there but Power, Wealth and Success, as this world counts success, wealth and power? That is how they see it; that is how they saw it then. There was more, and the words lingered on in the minds of disciples and bystanders alike.

They made a particular impression upon John the disciple, who wrote them in his Gospel. Whether he heard them as reported by another, or whether, for some reason, he was there on the day they were spoken, he it was who recorded them for us so that we too may be inspired by them to give up all the tawdry goods sold in Vanity Fair and to seek the true wealth which is laid up for us in heaven. To risk martyrdom and death, not in deeds of violence nor of great destruction but in gentleness, in kindliness and by faith in God and obedience to the Lord to whom John bore witness.

Perhaps some few of the Pharisees saw, with surprise, the meaning of the words, for even some of that strict and proud sect bowed the knee eventually to Yeshua from Nazareth. Marriage and the wedding were subjects often found in the Law, the Writings and the Prophets. Had not God Himself performed the first marriage in the Garden and had He not brought Eve to Adam to that first marriage bed? Thus was not God Himself there acting the part of the friend of the bridegroom? Also was not the Lord God the husband of Israel and was there not one day to be a great marriage feast when God eventually

לְחַבֵּשׁ לְנִשְׁבְּרֵי־לֵב ‍זָרָא לִשְׁבוּיִם דְּרוֹר וְלַאֲסוּרִים־פְּקַח־קוֹחַ׃

set up His Kingdom upon the earth? All these things the Rabbis taught, showing that the union of a man and a woman was a sacred and blessed institution. So John was the bridegroom's friend and those who had ears to hear understood that the bridegroom was that same Yeshua to whom he had pointed as the Lamb of God who was to bear away the sins of the world.

"He must increase but I must decrease." We humans glory in success, we despise failure. We covet power and wealth and engage every faculty we have to acquire them. If we cannot get the substance then we strive for the trappings of power and we strut and posture before our fellows enjoying the pomp and the pageantry, the applause of the crowds and the envy of lesser mortals.

So we deceive ourselves, for all this: the empty titles; the rewards; the money, whether gotten honestly or dishonestly; the admiration of others who do not matter, and the power to flaunt ourselves before the mob, is but "such stuff as dreams are made of". We deceive ourselves, for time gives way to eternity and, leaving it all behind, we shall be in danger of plunging headlong into the noisy fear-filled dark for an eternity of remorse and regret, to "weeping, wailing and gnashing of teeth".

John reached heights sublime as he counted himself only worthy to decrease so that his Lord should increase. But, being only human, he was not to know, until he experienced it, the pain of that decreasing before he could be elevated, through his death, to his reward in Abraham's bosom. And that death too being a means of decreasing even more. He saw far off, as Daniel saw, afar off, "a stone, cut out without hands," which was to become a great mountain and to fill the whole earth. He saw the "mighty put down from their thrones, and the rich sent empty away." He saw, and others too would catch the vision and work and die in view of that great and glorious day.

He was to be tested to the very limits of his

לְהָבֵשׁ לְנִשְׁבְּרֵי־לֵב זְרָא לִשְׁבּוּיִם דְּרֹור וְלַאֲסוּרִים־ פְּקַח־קְוֹחַ׃

endurance, yet he was to emerge from that testing purified and victorious. He would waver, as we all waver, but his was the far greater testing, and he was to emerge in triumph to join that triumphal procession leading out of Hades, out of the grave, and leading up to the throne of God Himself in the third heaven. A triumphal procession led by the victor, Yeshua from Nazareth, God's own anointed, God the Son.

(You can read about John the Baptist in John's Gospel, chapters 1 and 3. The other Gospels are briefer in their references.)

5

Issue of Blood

She had been widowed young after only a few years of marriage and then had taken on other responsibilities which had filled up her life. As a young widow she would have been expected to marry again but instead she had taken on the running of the olive groves and the flocks her husband, considerably older than herself, had left her.

She had never re-married. She had not even considered it. Her parents were older and not in good health. It had not bothered her. It had been her duty to care for her parents and that she had done. They had no other children and she herself was childless. She had thrown herself into their welfare and looking after their business interests, as well as nursing them in the recurring bouts of illness that came upon them with increasing frequency.

They had left her provided for and she lacked nothing. Nothing within reason, that is. Indeed, with her careful management the value of her holdings increased. Men who thought they could take advantage of her because she was that unusual thing, an unmarried woman, soon found that they had taken on a shrewd business brain and her checking of accounts was meticulous, as was her memory. The servants she employed either in the house, on the land, or in the shop, had no cause for complaint about their wages, for she knew how to be generous to those who worked well and

54

לַחְבֹּשׁ לְנִשְׁבְּרֵי־לֵב ﬩קְרָא לִשְׁבוּיִם דְּרוֹר וְלַאֲסוּרִים־פְּקַח־קוֹחַ׃

faithfully. In their turn they knew that nothing would be overlooked and that she kept watch on even the smallest of details.

As the grief at the loss of her parents began to recede, she found she started once more to take an interest in life. She even began to take an interest in men and enjoyed their company though, there again, she would not be patronised by those men who thought women foolish and not able to hold intelligent conversation nor to argue about the Law as well as any rabbi. Only those men of equal intelligence and whose minds were not hemmed in by custom so they could not entertain fresh and exciting ideas held her attention and were welcome in her company. With older men; men of comfortable middle age, she was at ease. She made it very plain that fortune hunters would get short shrift, and short shrift they got. As she went about her daily household and her numerous business activities she met several respectable gentlemen and enjoyed their company and their conversation.

During those days when she nursed her parents and managed the businesses, the people of the town began to call her 'Gevirah' or 'Mistress'. Some called her Sarah, not that she was a mother in Israel but that she ruled her home and work as a princess or great lady. They laughed, a gentle respectful laugh, that she was these things and 'Nevat Bayith', the 'Keeper of the Home', as well.

She was circumspect and well aware that some of her male friends and acquaintances took more than a passing interest in her. The realisation excited her, though she was not some young girl who was likely to lose her head over the flattery of personable males. Her business interests and the daily domestic tasks of her household brought her into contact with many men and she learned

לְחַבֵּשׁ לְנִשְׁבְּרֵי־לֵב וְרָא לִשְׁבוּיִם דְּרֹור וְלַאֲסוּרִים־ פְּקַח־קֹוחַ׃

quickly how to keep some at arm's length, while
encouraging, just a little, those honourable and
interesting ones with whom she could develop
acquaintance into polite friendship.

Simeon the Tailor looked forward to the times when
she passed his shop or when they could discuss the price
of cloth which she sold him. She kept ahead of her
competitors but still made a profit, though not an
excessive one. The profit was not all on her side but she
was able to put work his way through the network of
business contacts and family friends – often the lifeblood
of any successful small business. If she passed his shop
on the way to the market, whether for business or for
pleasure, he looked forward to being able to pass the
time of day with her. These meetings gave the
opportunity to open up a conversation which could be
continued at a later meeting whose purpose was,
outwardly, that of buying and selling cloth.

"Would you make up some coats for the family of my
friend Elisabeth," she asked him, much to his delight, one
day. Not only was the business welcome but such an
order, clearly a charitable venture by the lady he was
coming to respect and for whom friendship was
beginning to develop into something deeper, would give
them an excuse to meet and to talk on other things. The
idea was not expressed, but each knew that the other
welcomed it and had hoped for it to happen.

It was not acceptable for a virtuous woman to be
talking overmuch in public with men; though over a
matter of business hours could be pleasurably spent on a
variety of topics. It might even be possible, depending
on the time of day and the state of the weather, to offer
the lady some refreshment. Simeon wondered how he
might do this without being unseemly and offending the

לְהַבֵּשׁ לְנִשְׁבְּרֵי־לֵב זָרֵא לִשְׁבוּיִם דְּרֹיר וְלַאֲסוּרִים־ פְּקַח־קוֹחַ׃

lady's honour. It would certainly be legitimate to discuss the state of trade, the likely weight of the olive crop that year, the rapaciousness of tax collectors and to observe the progress of his apprentices.

After she had made it clear that the choice of cloth was hers since she was paying for the garments, they were able to spend a pleasant half-hour pulling out rolls of cloth and checking their texture, colour and suitability. He was holding up a heavy woollen cloth when she commented that his apprentices seemed to be proving diligent and their skills improving more rapidly than might have been expected.

She complimented him on the care he took over the education of the young men. He in turn quoted the rabbi who said, "Let a man always teach his son a cleanly and light trade; and let him pray to Him whose are wealth and riches."

She had laughed and replied in kind: "It was good that your father had you taught the skill and craft of the tailor." She smiled at him and her eyes twinkled with humour and a little mischief as she added, "For have not the rabbis taught, 'Let not a man bring up his son to be a camel driver, nor a donkey driver, nor a barber, nor a sailor, nor a pedlar, for their occupations are those of thieves'?"

They laughed together, at ease in one another's company and enjoying the shared banter. He continued, on a more serious note. "It is right that every boy should learn a trade."

She agreed, saying, how else then would he be able to support a wife and a family? The idea had been there; it had been there these months, lurking just beneath the surface of her consciousness, ready to emerge in an unguarded moment such as this. She reddened and

לְחָבֵשׁ לְנִשְׁבְּרֵי־לֵב זָרָא לִשְׁבֵּים דְּרֹור וְלַאֲסוּרִים־ פְּקַח־קֽוֹחַ׃

knew that Simeon had seen the slight rise in her colour. Tactfully he turned away, wrinkling his forehead as if in deep thought. He wanted to spare her embarrassment, but she knew and he knew and, somehow, the shared experience brought them closer. They had both been uncertain of the feelings of the other but now they were sure and could go ahead, allowing their friendship to grow into love or they could remain close, enjoying one another's conversation and company.

In her heart of hearts she knew his interest in her was more than friendship. He too had sensed that her visits to his shop and workroom were often subtly contrived, though he dare not have admitted that to himself for certain. An exultation filled them both and they began to view themselves, dared to view themselves, in a role more than that of friends. They dared to think in terms of husband and wife, of wife and husband.

Quickly she brought herself back to reality. There would be many days yet before she could say or do anything openly to admit the growing affection between them and to admit publicly, or even privately, to him that it was there and it was real, reciprocated and good. Slyly she asked: "What about girls then, ought they to learn a trade? Other than the care of the home?"

He looked a little puzzled and thought for a moment. "I ought really to have thought more about that," he admitted, and went on. "It is really a deeper question than it would seem or that most people, indeed most of the rabbis, would care to admit."

He frowned and she, realising they had spent longer in discussion than was really seemly and that the apprentices were grinning again and eyeing the pair of them, suggested that he think about it and that they could discuss it at some future time.

לְהַבֵּשׁ לְנִשְׁבְּרֵי־לֵב זָרֵא לִשְׁבוּיִם דְּרוֹר וְלַאֲסוּרִים־ פְּקַח־קוֹחַ:

"You have the measurements," she pointed out,
"perhaps I shall call by in a few days' time to see how the
work is progressing."

His face lit up and he nodded eagerly. "There should
be something to see for your inspection just as soon as
you like; perhaps the day after tomorrow?" he suggested.

Turning to his apprentices he said, with mock
severity, "And some people I know have more than
enough to get on with, without grinning behind the back
of their master and employer at valued customers and
friends."

The apprentices hurriedly bent their heads back over
their work, but the grins lingered on their features and
they were happy that their master, a very good master
and likeable man, seemed likely to find happiness,
having been tragically bereaved some years before.

There was a lightness in her step as she hurried off
about her business. She was going to check on her olive
groves and the sheep she had purchased and given into
the keeping of a shepherd, a steady man who she knew
she could trust with her wealth. She was looking forward
to arriving home again.

Not a vain person, she still took much pride in her
appearance and was looking forward to examining
herself in her mother's mirror. She wondered how she
would look on the arm of Simeon the Tailor. Adding her
holdings to his and having then two houses they could
rent one. They would be rich. She did not believe in fate,
not like the Greeks and the Romans, yet for all that to so
count up her possible future blessing was not good.
However, it did not seem wrong to examine her
appearance in her mother's mirror. It had been one of
her wedding presents, a special gift from her father.
There was something exciting in the thought of seeing

לַחֲבֹשׁ לְנִשְׁבְּרֵי־לֵב זְרָא לִשְׁבוּיִם דְּרוֹר וְלַאֲסוּרִים־ פְּקַח־קוֹחַ:

herself in a bride's mirror.

The next day seemed to drag on for longer than the few hours of its real duration. She was eager to make her way once more to his shop and he for her visit. However, she lingered a little so as not to seem too eager. It seemed natural for him to be sitting outside, but she guessed he had been looking out for her. They smiled and it was as if her heart turned over.

"I'm not a young girl," she thought, "but I am acting like one." They inspected the progress of the work and she expressed herself well pleased.

"Your friend, I hope she likes the coats." He was hesitant; this was delicate ground and she was a lady of modesty. She would not want to make a fuss or display of her charity. He guessed this was a charitable gift for a lady in poor circumstances.

He went on: "But they are all for boys and for one man. Are there no girls and does she not have one for herself?"

She looked at him and inclined her head in agreement. "I wondered about that," she said slowly. "Elisabeth has boys, young as you see, and her husband is ailing and cannot always work hard though he does his best. The boys do need coats; it can be cold at nights, but if I wait before giving them it will be her birthday in a few weeks and perhaps if you make her a coat too the whole lot could be a present. And she would not think I was patronising her."

"I will make her up a coat myself, if you will permit it. You choose the material and the pattern and I will work on it; it will be special for her birthday."

They looked at each other and smiled a shared conspiratorial smile. So it was agreed she would pay for the boys' and the husband's coats and he would make

5 Issue of Blood

לְהַלְבֵּשׁ לְנִשְׁבְּרֵי־לֵב זָרֵא לְשָׁבֻיִם דְּרוֹר וְלַאֲסוּרִים־פְּקַח־קָוֹחַ־:

Elisabeth a coat himself and not charge as long as she chose the material and the pattern. After some hesitation she agreed, but suggested she do some embroidery on the coat so that it would be really feminine. Thus, working together, a new dimension entered their relationship and deepened it yet more.

After some more discussion he persuaded her that he might be able to give Elisabeth's husband some light work and some deliveries which would not be too taxing for him.

"It will do him good to get out with a purpose," she agreed. "It will give him some of his self-respect back and with it more confidence."

After that they discussed work for women. They agreed that to be the mistress of her household and to educate her young children and her daughters, gave a woman plenty to do and a position with status in life.

"But," she added seriously, "a woman like Elisabeth who has children and a sick husband may find it useful to have a skill, not just domestic or to do with children."

He nodded. "I have been thinking about all this. It seems to me that women can and do perform lots of skills. You yourself have business interests which you take care of better than many men. There is Abigail, truly a 'Father's Joy'. She works as a perfumer and has a friend who is an apothecary, growing and prescribing herbs for healing."

They nodded their agreement and he added that a woman who has had her own household must find it hard to serve another woman, especially if she once had higher standing in the community. She glowed inside, with a pleasurable warmth, that he could be so sensitive. The more she knew him the more she found him the gentlest, most sensitive, and kindly of men. The more

לַחֲבֹשׁ לְנִשְׁבְּרֵי־לֵב ׃רָא לִשְׁבוּיִם דְּרוֹר וְלַאֲסוּרִים־פְּקַח־קוֹחַ ׃

time they spent together the more she realised that he adored her.

"And would you want your girls to serve an apprenticeship alongside callow and irresponsible youths like my apprentices in there?" He nodded and pointed with his chin towards the workroom where the youths quickly wiped the smirks from their faces and bent hurriedly over their work, showing a sudden enthusiasm for what had not been given very much attention since she had arrived.

"Oi! Oi! I do not work those youngsters hard enough. I am too soft. Perhaps I should expand and get an overseer who would shout at them from time to time." He shrugged his shoulders and made a face.

She laughed. "And you would then rebuke your overseer for being too harsh with the boys and give them extra money to go out and buy fruit or sweetmeats in the market. You see," she said, "I know your character and I think, in spite of all you say, your apprentices will turn out to be excellent craftsmen, for they have an excellent master."

He felt the warmth of her approval and changed the subject, liking to stimulate her mind, knowing that she would respond with wisdom. "The rabbis – some rabbis" he corrected himself, "do not agree with us. They see study as a skill which people ought to acquire if they can."

She did respond, as he had expected, with the shrewd common sense which is the true wisdom: "I have heard one say that he would leave alone every trade in the world for the study of the Torah because a trade is only valuable in this world, but the Torah is valuable for this one and the next."

He nodded and looked at her quizzically. "But you do

לְהַבֵּשׁ לְנִשְׁבְּרֵי־לֵב זְרָא לִשְׁבּוּיִם דְּרוֹר וְלַאֲסוּרִים־פְּקַח־קוֹחַ׃

not agree with that?"

"No! It seems to me mistaken as well as pretentious."
His face showed interest and he murmured for her to
go on and explain.

"God, they say, adorns every trade with beauty. But I
have heard it said, I think by the Great Hillel, 'Fair is the
study of the Torah, if accompanied by worldly
occupation: To engage in them both is to keep away sin'."

He nodded enthusiastic agreement. "Yes indeed! The
study of the Law is for all – for ordinary folk as well as for
rabbis, and for women as well as for men. But there must
be more do you not think?"

She was not sure what he meant, but the conversation
was becoming more and more interesting. "Yes!" she
agreed, "everyone ought to study the Law but then we
might all be rabbis. As to the value of a craft skill then I
am sure it must do things for a young person, but I am
not quite certain what, so I would like to hear what you
have to say."

There seemed to be two strands to the discussion. He
took up her first point about the Torah. "I remember,
some years ago now, four or five perhaps, there was a boy
from Nazareth. His parents were distraught; they were on
their way back from Pesach in Jerusalem. They could not
find him and had to return to the city, where they found
him attending the public lectures in the Temple courts.
He had been there for three days and was listening to the
rabbis and asking them questions; very intelligent
questions by all accounts."

"I have heard that too," she replied, "but few boys do
that or take the study of the Torah that seriously."

He agreed and added, "But what if that were the
pattern, that all, girls too had that opportunity to hear and
to question the rabbis. Does not the Law tell us: 'And

לְהִבָּשׁ לְנִשְׁבְּרֵי־לֵב יִרָא לִשְׁבֻיִם דְּרוֹר וְלַאֲסוּרִים־ פְּקַח־קְוֹחַ ׃

these words, which I command thee this day shall be in thine heart. And thou shalt teach them diligently unto thy children and shalt talk of them when thou sittest in thine house, and when thou walkest by the way, and when thou liest down, and when thou risest up.' This is for all Israel, not just for the few whose families are wealthy enough for them to allow their sons to attend the schools." There was an enthusiasm in his voice, conviction rang in its tones and a fresh light came to his eyes.

"I agree with all you are saying. I can see the difficulties too, but they are not insurmountable. But what about the trade skills we were talking about? If we agree that the Law is most important and is the true basis for education then where does skill of hand, of eye and of brain come in?"

His smile widened. "I think you hit on it earlier in the conversation about the need for girls to have a wider range of skills. At first there must be the chance to try out many crafts and then to decide on what is best and most suitable for the child or young person. After that they specialise on one craft so as to master it thoroughly."

"And!" she interjected, not allowing his enthusiasm to run away with him.

"And! Ah! And!" He thought for a moment, then, gesturing with his hands and fingers, asked, "Would you not agree that to acquire a skill needs long practice and may test one to the limit?"

She nodded her agreement; he went on: "Now then, to master that skill requires also the skill of patience. This is developed, the more so as the apprentice can visualise the finished product in the raw material and understand the uses for the various tools. So! It must be that the materials of one's trade and the tools of that trade

לַחֲבֹשׁ לְנִשְׁבְּרֵי־לֵב זְרָא לִשְׁבֻוִּים דְּרֹור וְלַאֲסוּרֵים־פְּקַח־קֹוחַ :

themselves impose a discipline as well as the skill of hand, eye and brain, necessary for a successful performance of the tasks of the trade. The young person copes with failure, with frustration, and develops qualities of self-control, patience, imagination, rationality and they grow in respect and self-confidence. Thus they mature and become adults able to make a useful contribution to their community." He spread his hands in a sort of QED gesture inviting her response and agreement.

And so they found more and more a shared interest in so many things. They delighted together in con-versation and the joy of pushing an understanding of so many matters they had long considered important to further limits. Indeed they found that by wrestling with matters in discussion they increased the clarity of that understanding.

But it was not an intellectual companionship they shared. Both were conscious of a rapidly growing tenderness and fresh delights simply in one another's company. Each time they spent together they parted with regret but with a feeling of pleasure that soon they would meet again and continue their shared enjoyment one of the other. Both felt an increasing lightness of heart and a youthful spring in their steps.

She smiled to herself as she savoured the thought that Simeon made her feel eighteen again. Better still, the feeling of youthfulness, of being a young girl falling in love for the first time, was delightfully enhanced by the wisdom of years and the confidence of her widowhood and the friendship she shared with him.

The joy merged into excitement and their souls danced on the fringes of bliss, for there was an added piquancy brought about by the stirrings of sexual attraction and the possibilities of its satisfaction. Only

לְחָבֵשׁ לְנִשְׁבְּרֵי־לֵב ۚ קְרָא לִשְׁבֹּיִם ۟ דְּרֹור וְלַאֲסוּרִים־ פְּקַח־קֹוחַ ׃

possibilities though, for that had to be kept severely under control, and the likelihood of marriage was something too serious and too grave a step to be considered lightly. They were no longer eighteen but they knew that if their friendship should develop that far they would have much to enjoy together. It was much that would be lasting and deep, for which the sexual would be the summit, the pinnacle, the capstone and its consummation in its intense mutual pleasure.

It was not to last. On all horizons there may be clouds. They may start as but a speck, far off, but grow to fill the sky and to cast their gloom over the whole world of sense and of experience. There came a morning when the sun shone less brightly. The speck on her horizon; and on his, had he but been aware, became more threatening. The atmosphere took on an ominous deadness, as before a storm. Day followed day and the threat grew worse.

The spring was gone from her step and her brow grew furrowed with worry. She seemed distracted in her manner and did not always follow his conversation so readily. At times she lost the thread of an argument even when she had initiated the subject herself. He could no longer make her laugh merrily with his gentle teasing. Nor did she respond with little jibes of her own, recalling incidents, special little events, which only had meaning for themselves. Events they were and shared experiences about which they could smile or shake their heads in amused, wry mockery of themselves.

She did not mean to forget, but the fear and the worry was crowding out the shared amusements; the laughter ceased; drowned as it were in a pool of sorrow. Her visits to his shop grew fewer. Though her longing for him was as great as ever, he was not to know that and, sadly, he

לְהַבֵּשׁ לְנִשְׁבְּרֵי־לֵב זְרָא לִשְׁבֹּיִם דְּרֹוֹר וְלַאֲסוּרִים־ פְּקַח־קֹוֹחַ׃

concluded that she was tiring of him. Perhaps, he thought, she finds me dull and slow. He had been entranced by the quickness of her intellect and, modest man that he was, delighting in her as he did, assumed that he could not match her with his more ponderous mental processes.

This was not in fact the case; as man differs from woman, so their thinking differed. His more on a logical step by step to an inevitable conclusion; hers able to go off on a wider artistic and creative journey down byways of thought that would not occur to all but a few.

But she could be mercurial and sometimes she got away from the point of a discussion, even falling into irrational imaginings. Such flights of fancy were in danger of distracting the process of rational argument and he was able to redirect her less profitable musings and bring them back to the matter in hand. Thus they complemented each other and ideally worked together in solving problems and in exploring ideas the Greeks had long ago abandoned for mere intellectual games and scoring of mental points.

Their Jewishness enabled them to look at a problem seriously with a humour that did not lose sight of the arguments and a reliance on the universals and the absolutes given them by God's Holy Law, the Torah.

She had known that he would notice. He always noticed any change in her mood; he was sensitive to her as no one she had ever known was sensitive.

"It's nothing," she had insisted, "just some woman's problem; it will clear up soon."

He looked at her uncertainly; he knew it was something more, something serious, but he understood too that she did not want to talk about it. It hurt that she would not confide in him, but he also realised that some

לַחֲבֹשׁ לְנִשְׁבְּרֵי־לֵב יָרָא לִשְׁבּוּיִם דְּרוֹר וְלַאֲסוּרִים־ פְּקַח־קוֹחַ:

matters were best shared among women or even kept
private and he respected her need to be private about
this. However, the feeling of unease would not leave him
and over the weeks and months it seemed as if their
relationship was undergoing a change. She smiled, but
the smile had about it the look of a painful grimace. She
laughed, not so often, and the laughter was forced. They
teased and joked but the teasing was mechanical, often a
repeat of things they had shared in times past and the
freshness had gone.

The menstrual flow that should have dried up did
not. The haemorrhaging continued and got worse. There
were times when it seemed to get better, but it would
come back worse than ever. She grew weak; she felt
listless and dull. Her visits to Simeon's shop became a
duty rather than a pleasure and the passion had dried up
in direct inverse proportion, it seemed, to the increase in
the bleeding. She felt dirty and her attendance at
Synagogue ceased for she recognised that she was
'unclean'.

On one occasion he had pleaded with her. "Miriam!"
His voice was gentle; concerned; full of hurt, hurt for her
rather than for his own loss. "Please let me help you.
Whatever it is, even if it is secret, you could share it with
me. I could help," he added desperately, "I can advise. I
know physicians and I know rich and influential men
who know physicians. I will go with you. I'll do
anything." His voice broke and she could see that the
tears were ready to come to his eyes, full of longing, full
of hurt and concern as they were.

Her hurt was as great, greater even. She had to be
strong when she felt so weak and foolish. She had to be
hard when her heart was breaking and she longed to
surrender herself and seek solace in his arms.

לְהַכֵּשׁ לְנִשְׁבָּרֵי־לֵב זָרֵא לִשְׁבוּיִם דְּרוֹר וְלַאֲסוּרִים־פְּקַח־קוֹחַ׃

"You can't help," her voice did not betray the despair she felt and which gnawed at her stomach like a vile rodent fastened to her and eating her away with sickness and with sorrow. "It is a woman's thing; a man would not be able to understand. Anyway," she continued, "I am to see a physician who knows about these things. I have already tried one but his astringents do no good. This other one is wiser, more skilled, and more experienced." And more expensive, she added to herself.

He felt hopeless and emotionally drained as he left her and turned for home. He had no idea when or even whether he would see her again. She was changed and had become as a stranger to him. Yet for all that he loved her, as he had known he had loved her for a long time. He was certain that she loved him and in his despair told himself that all would be well one day and that she would come back to him.

He tried to talk to his friend Yeremyahu who was a rabbi and had some knowledge of medicine. "How can I advise unless I know what is wrong?" asked the medical rabbi. "I do know doctors who might be able to help but they are very expensive and cures are few and far between. I have to tell you, Simeon my friend, that there is very little in the way of hope for her." The rabbi watched sadly as his friend of many years walked unsteadily back to his business.

Some of the physicians she visited were sympathetic, honest too, and warned her that very little could be done about her disease. Astringents might have effected a cure but they did not. If any relief came at all it was only temporary and the haemorrhaging returned as bad as or worse than before. And the physicians still wanted their fees. They had lives to lead and families to keep and could not be expected to work and to give of their

לַחֲבֹשׁ לְנִשְׁבְּרֵי־לֵב זָרֵא לִשְׁבֻּיִם דְּרֹור וְלַאֲסוּרִים־ פְּקַח־קֹוחַ׃

expertise for nothing. So she paid, and paid, and paid.

She was fully aware of the folly of some of the remedies offered. Among the more ridiculous and more ineffective of the nostrums was the eating of a corn of wheat found in the dung of a white she-ass. She felt foolish and revolted at what was plainly a quack remedy with the forbidden but widely practised reciting of magical incantations. These were frequently passages from the Torah. Even more demeaning was to have to sit astride holes in the ground where vine twigs and leaves smouldered while having to read some of the more meaningless magical formulae.

She despised herself for submitting to these degrading performances, yet so desperate was she that submit she did in the hope that something, anything, might happen to improve her condition. Nothing did. Rather she got worse.

Her income was rapidly being eaten up and her hitherto meticulous care for her holdings began to slacken. She no longer cared, for the disease made her listless and sapped her energy. Her hair turned grey and she began to think seriously about abandoning her homeland for the gentile and for the Greeks who also had renowned, and some said, successful physicians.

She sold her lands and houses and, in a last desperate effort to find help and a cure took ship for Alexandria. It was not just an abandonment of her homeland. Nor was it simply a rejection of Jewish doctors and medical practice. With a feeling of horror but determined, at whatever the cost to seek for an ease to her suffering, she turned her back also on Israel and on Israel's God. She felt she was an apostate and the horror of that decision filled her with fear. Yet she persevered and there was part of her that felt that God had let her down.

לְהַבֵּשׁ לְנִשְׁבָּרֵי־לֵב קְרָא לִשְׁבוּיִם דְּרוֹר וְלַאֲסוּרִים־ פְּקַח־קוֹחַ׃

Happiness and fulfilment had been within her grasp and yet they had been cruelly snatched from her. It was not only her own happiness which had been destroyed. Others too had to suffer because she could no longer care for them. Her tenants and her servants and all those who depended on her bounty and upon her for employment had to fend for themselves. No longer was she there to shield them from the cold rigours of the world's cruel callousness.

At times such as this when she thought about her less fortunate friends, she thought also about the plans she had been excitedly making in her imagination for the blissful time when Simeon would ask her to share his life and his household. Poor dear Simeon! Her eyes would fill with tears and she would give way to sobs which wracked her whole body, already weakened by suffering and disease. How dare God allow her poor Simeon to be deprived of his happiness! Such bliss, such joy, so many possibilities for good had been theirs.

They would have fed the starving, clothed the naked and would have housed the homeless. But now! Now! Nothing! Only suffering and deepest sorrow and regret that ate at her soul and embittered every aspect of her life. But even in such despair it was his suffering and not hers which gave her the greatest sense of hurt and remorse.

From Alexandria to the famous island of Cos. She submitted to the heathen rites of the Greeks for she felt that she had no other option. The Greek doctors were invariably kind and gentle with high standards of professional ethics and practices derived from their founder Hippocrates. However, they also charged money. How could they not? And how, she thought, could the

5 Issue of Blood

לַחֲבֹשׁ לְנִשְׁבְּרֵי־לֵב זְרָא לִשְׁבֻיִם דְּרוֹר וְלַאֲסוּרִים־ פְּקַח־קוֹחַ׃

poor, the downtrodden and the oppressed, ever find justice in this world? She had seen rich men and women bloated with good living seeking relief from their self-induced sicknesses. She had seen young and old, men and women too, addicted to wine and to strange potions which gave dreams while taking away real life in sleep and listlessness.

She had seen battle-scarred men with severed limbs or the blind and fearfully disfigured, begging in the streets, abandoned and forgotten by the great ones who had led them to victory or to defeat. The end was always the same: disease, mutilation and a living death, eking out a desperate and dirty existence in the gutter while the great ones responsible for their wounds ate off gold and silver and grew fat on the spoils they would not share and the injustices they created.

With the last of her money and a loan from a sympathetic Jew she managed to buy a passage back to Joppa and from there she managed to join travellers returning to her home town. Fearing to show herself to Simeon and ashamed that he might get word of her return, she took lodging in the house of a relative who allowed her to live in one room, thinking that he was, by so doing, a good and charitable person. He had in fact bought up much that had been hers at far less than its real value, and so she found herself living, on sufferance, in what had once been hers.

By this time she was not able to walk far, and tired very easily. For a month or two she spent her days sitting or reclining in her room or on the terrace outside. However, her distant cousin who owned the property soon objected to this as her ragged appearance seemed likely to give the place, or himself, a name for meanness and for poverty.

לְהַבֵּשׁ לְנִשְׁפֵּרִי־לֵב זָרָא לְשַׁבְּתִּם דִּי־לוֹר וַלַאֲסוּרַים־פְּקַח־קְוֹחַ׃

How he found her she did not know. Find her he did. Word somehow had got back to him that she had returned and was living in obscurity and shame, depending on the charity of a cousin. The news hit him like a blow in the stomach. He felt a sudden elation that however changed her circumstances, there might at last be a chance for them to be at least friends once more.

In spite of the elation he felt at the possibility of seeing her again, there was also a dread that whatever had taken her away from him, off on her travels, was not cured and that she would still push him away from her. It was a dread of what he might find. He only vaguely comprehended the reason for it. Everything seemed so unfair. It made the whole thing worse, for he could not dismiss from his mind the idea that she found him unattractive and wished really to be rid of him.

His shop and workshop was, of course, like so much in the commercial heart of the town, a centre for gossip. She had not long made her weary way back to the region than someone thought they saw her and reported the fact to her spouse who told a workmate, who then asked Simeon if he knew she was back. Simeon did not, but made enquiries among her relatives and received, not only the assurance that she had indeed returned, but information as to where she was living.

He debated within himself whether he ought to seek her out. Perhaps it would only annoy her and she wanted to be left alone. But then he thought that it did not matter; if she turned him away then she turned him away and he would be no worse off than before. At least if he knew her whereabouts, he would be able to obtain news of her and, so to speak, keep an eye on her.

Unbeknown to her he had seen her cousin and made it plain that, though she did not want anything to do with

5 Issue of Blood

לְהַבֵשׁ לְנִשְׁבָּרֵי־לֵב ֶֿרָא לִשְׁבוּיִם דְּרֹור וְלַאֲסוּרִים־ פְּקַח־קֹוחַ׃

him, he still took a very sincere and personal interest in her welfare. He insisted that the cousin look after her and get a woman in to help her with washing and cleaning. He paid for these services himself, for the cousin was as tight-fisted as he was jealous of his reputation. Simeon did not wish to be named and Miriam thought that the woman came by the good offices of her cousin. The cousin did not enlighten her.

At last he decided he must see her. Several times he had walked as far as her lodging, then, misty eyed, he had turned back unable to bear the rejection with which he feared she would treat him.

He knocked at the door. It was slightly ajar and a tired voice, devoid of life and hope, asked. "Who is it? Who's there?"

"It's me, Simeon," he replied and begged her to let him in.

She opened the door and stood in the gap not exactly welcoming, nor sending him away. She just stood there, apathetic and tired. She gave him a wan smile and weariness showed in her face and in every line and in her posture. How old was she now? He cast his mind back and calculated. She must be forty or more and he was sixty. What a long time it had been.

Like a tongue-tied boy he found words stumbling out without any control nor with any order: "I had to see you. There might be some hope. How tired you look, but you are still beautiful."

His remarks sounded foolish and insincere. He wanted to say, "I love you," but he could not, dare not. He paused, looking into her eyes; those eyes which had been so full of life and laughter and which had delighted him so much, that they were the last thing he saw as he went off to sleep and the first thing he saw as he woke in

74

לְחַבֵּשׁ לְנִשְׁבְּרֵי־לֵב זְרָא לִשְׁבוּים דְּרוֹר וְלַאֲסוּרִים־פְּקַח־קוֹחַ׃

the morning. He wanted to take her in his arms and to make better whatever was wrong by the sheer force of his will.

"Yeshua! Yeshua of Nazareth – " He tried again but still it was as if her presence had robbed him of the ability to think and to talk rationally. She shook her head at him, a gesture reminding him of the old days when she had shaken her head in mock exasperation when he had seemed to fail to make sense of something he wanted to explain, or had got something wrong. She smiled again and there was something of the loving glance and tenderness he had known before she was struck down with the affliction.

"Why don't you start at the beginning and tell me all about it," she said gently. Then she went on, seeing his anxiety and need, "Why don't you come in. I'm sorry to have kept you waiting outside."

The room was sparsely furnished. He sat on a stool and she on the couch which was her bed at night. She added some fuel to a small brazier and went to a cupboard.

"You will take some wine," she asked but assumed his agreement, for she also brought out cups and a flask of water. "It is poor stuff, not what we were used to."

Then, as if angry with herself for allowing sentiment to soften her, as she poured the wine and added the water in a mixture of two of water to one of wine, she said abruptly: "You were saying something about Yeshua from Nazareth. I wonder if anything much good can come out of Nazareth, but go on anyway and tell what you were trying to say."

Her manner had changed; it was as if, by harshness of speech, she was trying to compensate for the almost tenderness she had allowed to creep into her voice a

לְהֵבֵשׁ לְנִשְׁבְּרֵי־לֵב ָנְרָא לִשְׁבוּיִם דְּרוֹר וְלַאֲסוּרִים־ פְּקַח־קוֹחַ :

moment before.

"He has healed people," he started lamely. "He commands the demons and they leave the afflicted. All diseases are subject to Him, people come to Him and He heals them. Lepers, the paralysed, people with useless limbs; they have all been restored by Yeshua. He is not like the rabbis; He will take no money but He is full of love and goodness. Some say He could be Messiah." He did not think he was doing very well. She too had heard of the miracle-working Nazarene and had wondered, but had lost all hope and had given up the possibility of ever finding a cure for her affliction.

"So! This Yeshua of yours, what else has he done?"

Her question was sarcastic, like a severe adult to a foolish child. He felt like a foolish child but he had seen some of the miracles and he believed, and he longed that Miriam too should come to know Him. He ploughed on though it was heavy going, for she was full of cynicism.

"He made water into wine at a wedding in Cana . He cured the son of one of Herod's top officials, just spoke the word. That Centurion who lives nearby, he who built the synagogue, He healed his servant. Both those were done without Him even seeing the sick people concerned. He just spoke the word and they were healed at that very moment when He spoke."

In spite of herself she was impressed. This was very different from the healers she had experienced over the past twelve years. However, all the cynicism boiled up to the surface.

"I have seen people healed," she said, and her lip curled in contempt at the charlatans and the ignorance she had encountered. She felt contempt too for her own gullibility and her anger was directed away from her at Simeon.

לְחַבֵּשׁ לְנִשְׁבְּרֵי־לֵב זָרָא לִשְׁבוּיִם דְּרוֹר וְלַאֲסוּרִים־פְּקַח־קוֹחַ׃

"The Greeks in their Asclapia get people to rest but encourage them to have dreams in which they say the god appears to them. The doctors interpret the dreams but the result is the same. Some revolting broth or a course of massage and all for what? For nothing! Nothing at all! Unless it is the fee they charge and that certainly is not nothing.

"Oh! Then there's the Syrians." There was mockery in her voice. "They dance round a sick person shaking a rattle and going red in the face. They are supposed to be driving out the evil spirits. And that isn't all!" Her voice rose with indignation. "Our rabbis stroke their beards and walk round you quoting bits of Scripture they do not understand, then they prescribe some useless potion and charge a bigger fee than all the others put together.

"They are all charlatans, actors playing the part of doctors. At least they are good at the acting and at charging for the performance. All any of them care about is what people think of them and how best to rob their patients of their money while making the poor fools believe they are doing them good."

She sank back exhausted on the couch; her anger had worn her out and she breathed deeply as if the room had suddenly become close, the atmosphere hot, the walls confining.

"Oh yes! I've seen people healed alright. I've seen travelling physicians gather a crowd about them with a man beating a drum. When enough people are gathered he starts the performance and tells everyone what a great man he is and how some god or another has given a special gift of healing. Then someone appears walking with sticks crying that he needs the help of the great doctor. It's an accomplice, of course. The doctor goes to him and lays his hands on him and the man throws away

לְהֹבֵשׁ לְנִשְׁבְּרֵי־לֵב זָרָא לִשְׁבֻיֹם דְּרֹוֹר וְלַאֲסוּרָים־ פְּקַח־קֹוֹחֵ ׃

his sticks and starts to leap about and to sing. They do it very well because they have practised it so many times. Then all the fools rush up to him to have his hands put on where it is supposed to hurt, and to give him their money of course," she added.

She slumped on the couch and sobbed. "I've seen them healed, the fools, and I have been a fool myself."

A few moments and, in spite of the tears, she turned to him with a little of the old mischievous smile on her face.

"I dread to think what some of those potions are made of," she said, and hid her face again in her hands.

"He really does care, this one, Yeshua."

She was not going to give in so easily. There was bitterness and anger of twelve years to get out of her soul and she was not sure she wanted that; it was just about all she had to live for, to be angry and bitter, and to hate the world. To sit in the darkness of her room and cry to herself and avoid the light of the sun shining outside in the street and the noise of the children playing, and the dust and the dirt and the crowds, all busy, all with so much to live for when she only had her regrets.

"Don't they all," she replied with a snort of contempt. "They care alright. They care about the way people look up to them, as men of great wisdom and skill, when really it is all put on. They care about their reputation and they care about how they can persuade their patients' money into their money bags before they hurry off to the next town to gull the fools there. Oh yes! They care alright!"

He tried to interpose with his observations of Yeshua from Nazareth.

"Don't you talk to me about doctors and healers," she spat out at him like an angry cat. "I have tried them all and they are all charlatans and rogues, with not a caring

לַחֲבֹשׁ לְנִשְׁבְּרֵי־לֵב ׃רָא לִשְׁבֹיִם֙ דְּרֹ֔ור וְלַאֲסוּרִ֖ים־ פְּקַח־קֽוֹחַ׃

bone in their bodies! I have had my fill of them and I wish them all to perdition!"

She looked so angry, her face still pale but filled with raw emotion, that he stepped back towards the doorway. He had never seen her like this. This was not the Miriam he had known; she had changed. She was Miriam but a different Miriam – one who could hurt, like a cornered animal; it seemed she wanted to lash out with her claws and scratch someone.

He tried another ploy. "Have you heard of the Baptist?" he asked her anxiously, not wishing to be the victim of her anger. She nodded wearily, wishing now she could end the conversation. How dare he come to her like this with his naïve talk about some Messiah! She did not reply but looked at him, tiredness showing in the sag of her cheeks and the drooping posture she assumed on the couch.

He leaned forward on the stool as if to infuse interest and energy into her with his gaze and with his enthusiasm. "He called all Israel to repentance and then he said that Yeshua was to be the Saviour of us all. He said he was not worthy to untie His sandals. He said that Yeshua was the Lamb of God – you know – like the Passover or like the Scapegoat on the Yom Kippur."

She looked up at him questioningly, not taking in what he was saying, too weary to think about it; just wishing he would leave.

"Look, the Lamb of God, who bears away the sin of the world," he quoted the Baptist's words, but she had become lethargic and could not take them in or see their significance for her or for her situation.

The next day there was a storm. It was a storm they had not experienced before and even the oldest inhabitants had not experienced its like. He had called

לְהַבֵּשׁ לְנִשְׁבְּרֵי־לֵב יְרָא לִשְׁבֻיִם דְּרוֹר וְלַאֲסוּרִים־ פְּקַח־קוֹחַ׃

on her again and was trying again to tell her about
Yeshua the Carpenter. Sometimes she listened but at
other times she seemed to grow weary, or it may have
been that his arguments became tedious to her.

"We talked of Him once," he reminded her. "When
he was twelve. The family had been to Jerusalem, for
Pesach it was. He had stayed in the city while the rest of
their party were travelling back to Galilee. They could
not find him and had to go back to the city and look for
him. Don't you remember? We remarked how strange it
sounded. They found him with the rabbis in the Temple
courts. He was listening to them, asking questions,
intelligent, discerning ones."

Memory came back to her of that conversation
during happier times. Seventeen or eighteen years ago,
an age it seemed, and yet as the memories became more
vivid, almost as if it were yesterday.

"*That* Yeshua?" She indicated the question with her
voice, her eyes widening with curiosity.

"Yes! *That* Yeshua!" he confirmed, nodding at her. He
continued, "He has been telling everyone about the
Kingdom of God. He has disciples who follow Him.
They sit at His feet and walk with Him along the way."

He paused, a wistful expression on his face and
longing in his eyes. His faraway look changed to an
anxious one as he turned to her.

"If He healed those others He can heal you." His
hand went to his mouth, concerned that she would take
offence or that he had overstepped the bounds where
good, helpful advice becomes bad, intrusive and
manipulative. His fears were not realised, but neither did
she respond as he had hoped.

"I cannot go to a Messiah," she stated. "I have
betrayed my nation and my God; I have been in Greek

לְהַבֵּשׁ לְנִשְׁבְּרֵי־לֵב קְרָא לִשְׁבֻוּיִם דְּרֹור וְלַאֲסוּרִים־ פְּקַח־קֹוחַ׃

temples, Egyptian temples, Syrian shrines and I have sought healing from them all. They are no better than our rabbis and now I can go to no one. Soon I shall die."

Her head sank onto her breast and all hope was extinguished from her expression. "Some of them mean well." Her thoughts had returned to her travels. "There was this slave in the Aesclapion on Cos. He was trimming the lamps and said to me that whether I dreamed or not I should tell the doctor that I had dreamed of snakes. If I did that, he said the doctor would think I had had a good dream and would get better.

"He thought to cheer me up but it showed me what hypocrisy it all was and how they were really all actors. Some people were not really ill at all. They were fat and overfed or they had too much wealth and were like spoiled children running after fresh experiences, then bored with them. Such people would go to the Aesclapion just to be made a fuss of and have people listening to their imagined woes. They were all spoiled children and it was all so false. Some people are ill and they really do get better. Perhaps they would have got better anyway; perhaps being convinced they were, made them better. There must be enough of those for people not to see through it all."

She had actually heard some things about Yeshua. Most people were enthusiastic, but she had seen and experienced enthusiasm before and was not convinced it would last. Already there were those among the Pharisees who spoke against Yeshua and she heard other stories about how He was making Himself unpopular in some exalted quarters.

She did not let Simeon know that much of what he said was not news to her. Part of her was too apathetic to explain. Another part wanted to listen then to weigh and

לַחֲבֹשׁ לְנִשְׁבְּרֵי-לֵב זָרָא לִשְׁבוּיִם דְּרוֹר וְלַאֲסוּרִים- פְּקַח-קוֹחַ׃

to sift the evidence so that she could come to her own conclusion and not be pushed into anything by the enthusiasm of others. Though Simeon had thought he was telling her a fresh tale about the Official of Herod's administration, she had in fact picked up from gossip in the market place and from casual conversations overheard in the household, a lot more than Simeon had told her. As he left her to return home, she thought it over in her mind.

Yeshua was perhaps a prophet, one of the old prophets like Elijah, who had had no formal training yet was sent by God. But then the Baptist had been like Elijah in the way he lived in the deserts and the way he dressed. She had heard about the official from the court of Herod and how he had gone to Yeshua and spoken to Him as if He were an inferior. Socially, of course He was, and yet He had mildly rebuked the official, reminding him of his unbelief. The man had changed his attitude in a moment and called Yeshua 'Lord', begging Him to come and to heal his child. Then on top of all that Yeshua had calmly told him: "Go your way, your son lives." Simeon was right, though she did not easily give up her cynicism over doctors and those who claimed to possess healing gifts. Yeshua did care; He was kind and compassionate and He healed anyone who came to Him. He had healed the gentile centurion's servant. Many Jews would not have had anything to do with him even though he had built a synagogue.

She wondered whether God cared much for those distinctions: Jew, gentile, Greek, Roman, barbarian; what did any of it matter, one God had created them all. The centurion had said that he was not worthy that Yeshua should come under his roof. Was anyone worthy? She pondered on it for a bit and it seemed to her that if no

לְהַבֵּשׁ לְנִשְׁבְּרֵי־לֵב ; קְרָא לִשְׁבוּיִם דְּרֹוֹר וְלַאֲסוּרֵים־פְּקַח־קוֹחַ :

one was worthy and that if Yeshua did concern Himself with them anyway He really was from God, for only God could forgive and He would reach out to all His creatures. Israel just had special privileges, that was all. The rabbis had got it all mixed up; they thought they were better than anyone else, but they were not.

She sat lost in thought and the clouds cleared from the sky. The storm that had come on so suddenly had cleared long ago as spectacularly as it had started. Now, in the late afternoon, the sun shone down, filling the town with light and gladness.

Opening her door she peered out and saw the world fresh and bright. Dare she, she wondered. Dare she go to Yeshua? She had betrayed Israel's God, but then so had Gomer the daughter of Diblaim, and her husband had bought her out from the slave market. Hosea had become an object lesson to the nation, for they too were unfaithful and He still loved them just as Hosea loved Gomer.

What if Yeshua had been a rabbi, she thought. Would He have behaved the way He did? She thought not and remembered the party of women crowded round the fruit stall in the market. They had come to gossip and the conversation had turned to the prophet from Nazareth.

"He's only a carpenter," exclaimed one of the women when the name of Yeshua had been mentioned. Another had argued forcibly that none of the prophets were special; they came from all levels of society. Amos was a country bumpkin while Isaiah was plainly an intellectual. Jeremiah had been too young for the prophetic office and yet God had told him He had chosen him. Jonah had obviously been well-off but he had been lazy and bigoted.

לַחֲבֹשׁ לְנִשְׁבְּרֵי־לֵב זְרָא לִשְׁבוּיִם דְּרֹור וְלַאֲסוּרִים־ פְּקַח־קֹוחַ׃

Then another woman had told how He had changed water into wine at a wedding and asked what did they think a rabbi would do. She had laughed and said, "If there were any Pharisees present I'm sure they hurried off in embarrassment."

The others agreed, knowing how everyone would have felt if there was not enough wine at a feast they had given. They could not think of a greater embarrassment and wondered how it had happened. The narrator, eager to continue her story raised her voice somewhat.

"He gave instructions to the attendants who were serving the feast," she said, "as if He were the ruler of the feast, yet He did it so quietly that no one knew and no one was embarrassed. It was like," she hesitated, "well, like He had thought of everything. He knew just what He would do, but spared everyone's feelings."

She looked round at her audience, but she had their attention and she continued. "There were six stone waterpots there. He told the attendants to fill them with water up to the brim. They did and then He said, 'Draw some out now and take it to the master of the feast.' He was surprised and said they had kept the good wine until last." She paused and looked round. "It was just as if He were one of the old prophets, like Elijah or Elisha, or," her eyes widened at the enormity of what she was about to say, "or as if He were Moses himself."

The women drew in their breath audibly and thought about this. Had not Moses foretold that God would, "raise up unto thee a Prophet, from the midst of thee, like unto me, unto Him shall ye hearken."

One of the other women nodded sagely. "The men from Jerusalem challenged the Baptist so; they asked him if he were the Prophet, but he said he was not."

Another interrupted her and added, "John said that

לַחֲבֹשׁ לְנִשְׁבְּרֵי־לֵב ָרָא לִשְׁבֿוּיִם דְרֿוֹר וְלַאֲסֿוּרִים־ פְּקַח־קֿוֹחֵ׃

Yeshua was mightier than he and that he was not worthy to untie Yeshua's sandals. He must be the Prophet, or Messiah – or both," she added lamely.

Some seemed to agree; others looked doubtful. The stallholder had been eyeing the group with increasing frustration and challenged them. "Ladies, I have the sweetest figs and the most luscious melons you will find anywhere in this market or any market in the land. You are turning customers away from me you are such a crowd. Why do you not do yourselves a favour and buy some of my fruit? Your families will praise you for being ladies of discernment who only feed their families on the best."

One lady muttered as she hurriedly made her departure from the gossiping group, "or who only feed their families on the most expensive."

"I have the best, the ripest of fruits for your enjoyment," he wailed.

The other ladies also hurried off, making excuses or muttering under their breath that it might be the ripest but it would likely be overripe by the time they got it home and their families would not thank them for that.

Miriam was thinking about Messiah. What would He do, she thought. Would he turn out the Romans like so many said they wanted? Or would He be a man of peace and allow the injustices to go on in spite of what the Prophets seemed to say about Him. Perhaps, she thought, there might be two Messiahs. She had heard it said that some rabbis leaned to that view: a kingly Messiah and a Priestly Messiah. Somehow that idea did not ring true, but then if He really were to turn out the Romans He would also get rid of a lot of the priests in the Temple who made money out of the animals for sacrifice which they sold to the people and were guaranteed to be

לְחָבֵשׁ לְנִשְׁבְּרֵי־לֵב גְרָא לִשְׁבֻּיִם דְּרוֹר וְלַאֲסוּרִים־ פְּקַח־קוֹחַ׃

Levitically clean and pure.

What did the priests do with the Temple tax? she wondered, the half shekel which every Jewish male was supposed to pay into the Temple treasury. She did not think it was used to feed the starving, to clothe the naked or to alleviate the suffering of the sick, the downtrodden or the widows. She shook her head in puzzlement. The priests insisted that only Jewish money could be acceptable so they made extra money out of the money-changers they licensed to deal in foreign currencies.

She had gone out again, wondering whether she might not take Simeon's suggestion and try to see if Yeshua were in the town or if there were news of Him. As if by design of some power other than herself, some influence which knew her innermost thoughts she overheard another woman holding forth. She was a large woman in every sense of the word and her voice carried, penetrating above the chatter and the hum of market noise and talk and the shouts of hucksters drawing attention to what they had for sale.

"My husband works for Rabbi Alexander," she announced as if he held some important post in the rabbi's household. Miriam allowed herself the beginnings of a giggle deep inside her but quickly stifled it, so that she could hear more. He probably prepares the vegetables for the cook, or empties the night soil, she thought. Something of the old mischief was returning to her thoughts, something of the younger, less bitter and cynical Miriam was surfacing again.

The woman, confident that folk were listening, went on in the same loud and dogmatic tone: "That prophet from Nazareth is a disgrace," she said indignantly. "Rabbi Alexander says he ought to have been arrested."

"Do you mean that riot in the Temple?" prompted

לִלְבֹּשׁ לְנִשְׁבְּרֵי־לֵב זְרֵא לִשְׁבוּיִם דְּרֹוֹר וְלָאֲסוּרִים־ פְּקַח־קֹוֹחַ׃

another woman who was clearly the large woman's accomplice in the act.

"Yes, I do," she replied. "Disgraceful, so it was! He drove out the animals for sacrifice, overturned the tables of the money-changers and dared to call the Priests thieves and robbers! Can you imagine it? Fancy talking to the Priests as if they were common criminals!"

Not all the women were sympathetic to her view. Just because her husband was steward of some rabbi's household did not make her an expert on all matters theological or liturgical.

"They are," said an opponent, "robbers and rogues. Those money-changers are a disgrace, and they charge for every coin they change." She folded her arms in a gesture of defiance to the large lady who drew herself up to her not inconsiderable height before answering.

"Do you expect them to work for nothing? Esther, you should know better; they have a living to earn and they do a necessary and valuable service for the Temple and for the community."

Her adversary did not feel up to rational argument but was not going to give in easily. "Thieves and rogues," she insisted, "bloated with living on the earnings of honest and poor ordinary people." She huffed her indignation against life's injustice, turning her back on the conversation and walking away before the other woman could reply.

The large lady, determined to regain the initiative and the attention of her audience, laid on her indignation with wide eyes and horrified shakes of her head. "In the very Temple itself," she pursed her lips in horror at the thought. "Such shouting, such screaming; money all over the floor, you never saw such sacrilege! Terrible! Terrible!"

לַחֲבשׁ לְנִשְׁבְּרֵי־לֵב ׀ רָא לִשְׁבֻיִם דְּרוֹר וְלַאֲסוּרִים־ פְּקַח־קוֹחֵ׃

Lost for words she glared at her acquaintances, daring them to contradict her, she whose husband was the steward of the Rabbi Alexander and so knew all about these things.

Miriam felt that some power greater than herself was impelling her now. She walked on through the crowded market, already feeling dazed and dizzy from her exertions. It did not take much to tire her these days. "Do not make my Father's house a den of thieves." That is what they had said Yeshua had told them. He had done what many Galileans wanted to do and had said the sort of thing they would have liked to say had they dared.

She would see the carpenter. She made up her mind and resolved to keep in touch with events by asking the neighbours when they heard whether he was back in the town. He had left that morning early or even the day before, but she was tired; oh so tired. Wearily she trudged through the dusty street back to her room and lay down.

Meanwhile the boats that had gone with Yeshua over the lake had returned, fleeing before the storm and seeking shelter alongside the fishing jetties. Simon Peter's boat with Yeshua and His other disciples was still away and there were fears that they had been overwhelmed by the storm.

"No boat could live in that wind," muttered more than one old grey beard. They shook their heads and spoke of the up-and-coming prophet who was now lost to the nation. Even those who had mistrusted Him now saw Him as a hero or one who, maybe, promised to show the people the way to better things.

The next day Simeon called on her again. Again her heart leapt for joy but she strove valiantly to hide her elation at his presence and merely peered at him

לְהַלְבֵּשׁ לְנִשְׁבְּרֵי־לֵב זְרָא לִשְׁבֻּיִם דְּרוֹר וְלַאֲסוּרִים־ פְּקַח־קוֹחַ:

questioningly. At last she asked him in and listened to him again as he told how Simon Peter's boat had returned with everyone safe and sound and with tales of the deliverance of the demon-possessed man of Gadara and the miraculous calming of the storm.

" 'Peace! Be still.' He just got up and commanded the winds and the waves." Simeon shook his head at the wonder of it. "The wind stopped, just like that, immediately, the moment He commanded it to." His enthusiasm seemed to have no bounds now. "He really is Messiah, He must be! No one could do such things were He not the Anointed One of God."

Miriam began to tire of his company. These days he seemed to have but one thing on his mind. She had agreed in herself that she would go and see this Yeshua, but it was only to see. She did not know what she would do when she did see Him and she did not want Simeon to push her into anything she might regret.

Still suspicious of healers and still convinced that by her association with the pagan priests and doctors and the idols they served she had put herself beyond the pale of Israel and that Israel's Messiah might, indeed probably would, reject her. Why should He want anything to do with me," she thought, but still determined to go out to find where He was staying and see what went on.

Simon Peter's house seemed to her the most likely place to start, but she did not think she would be able to spend all day traipsing round the city looking for Him. She tired rapidly these days and felt that death was not far off. She thought about Simeon. "What does he see in me?" she mused. "My hair has gone white with fear and worry. My face is haggard and I look twenty years older than I really am. I am an old woman in all but years and I am no use to anyone. I would be better off dead," she

לְהָבֵשׁ לְנִשְׁבְּרֵי־לֵב זְרָא לִשְׁבֵּים וְדֵרֹור וְלַאֲסֹורִים־ פְּקַח־קֹוחַ׃

concluded sadly and the tears began to flow as they so often did these days. She rocked herself as she tried to nurse herself in her misery, suffering and self-pity. She saw no hope, no light, no future; not for herself and not for her poor dear Simeon.

As she rocked, and pondered, and wept, she heard a young voice singing outside. Opening her door a crack, she saw a young woman across the courtyard. It was one of her cousin's many daughters. Married now a year she was visiting her mother and sat, the baby in her arms, cradling him and gazing entranced with fondness and the delight of motherhood, as she sang. The baby was obviously to be named Hosea, 'Salvation', for her song, which she made up as she went along, was of hope and of Israel's coming deliverance.

> Hosea! Sleep in peace.
> Hosea! Dream of peace.
> Hosea! You shall be our peace
> When Messiah comes.
>
> Full of mother's milk,
> Soon you will awake,
> Awake to Israel's peace.
> Awake to Israel's dream.

It was a pretty song, for the girl had a naturally musical voice and put into it all the longing of the nation for its deliverance from the tyranny of foreign overlords, from oppressive tax collectors and from the lies and petty tyrannies which fall worst upon the poor. The voice had all the warmth of mother love, of hope for the wonderful new life which had emerged from her womb, and for a better tomorrow and a better world for the little one to

לְהָבֵשׁ לְנִשְׁבְּרֵי־לֵב זְרָא לִשְׁבוּיִם דְּרֹור וְלַאֲסוּרִים־פְּקַח־קֹוחַ׃

grow up in, free from suffering, pain and death, and free from the oppression of money and of power.

The girl's long dark hair had come loose and hung down, framing her head and the baby asleep on her breast as a picture of all the hopes and simple joys which time and human nature inevitably betray. The tears stung Miriam's eyes and she thought of the disillusionments to come, the hurts and the disappointments for both mother and child. As she did the girl began to sing again.

> Hosea loved by Mummy.
> Hosea loved by Daddy.
> Precious little baby
> Loved and cherished
> By us all.

With all the tenderness that only a mother can give her young baby she gently rocked the child and hummed the tune she had made up for him. Miriam thought: Hosea meant 'Salvation' and Yeshua was really Yehoshea, 'Salvation of the Lord' – so was Yeshua, the carpenter, really 'Jehovah's Salvation'? Was He truly Israel's deliverer? And if He was, then could He also deliver her? She would see, she would see. She had to find Him first. But then it occurred to her that if God was God and if God intended her to, then she would and if He did not, if He rejected her for her unfaithfulness, then she would not; and that would be that.

She went out into the light. Out into the day and the warmth of the sun and it seemed that fresh strength came to her feeble limbs and straightened her aching body. She walked through the market square and down towards the lake where the fishermen's houses were built

לַחֲבֹשׁ לְנִשְׁבְּרֵי־לֵב ;רָא לִשְׁבוּיִם דְּרוֹר וְלַאֲסוּרִים־ פְּקַח־קוֹחַ׃

on the lakeside and where she hoped that she would come upon Yeshua and would have her questions answered one way or another.

Pausing to rest by the jumble of houses hard by the Synagogue, she heard the noise of people. A crowd was slowly flowing through the narrow street that led from the lakeside towards the Synagogue. It ebbed and flowed and eddied and swirled like the lake itself. It shouted and called out to itself and quarrelled and chattered with excitement as it pushed itself into the narrow street. Someone running ahead, a boy hardly more than a lad, stopped to catch his breath near where she leaned on a wall of a house.

"What is happening?" she asked, "what is going on?"

The lad answered respectfully for he saw a white-haired lady, already, to his immature mind far gone in age, and he was, as all Jewish boys were taught to be, respectful to his elders. "It's Yeshua the carpenter of Nazareth," he blurted out. "He's coming this way to the house of Jairus the ruler of the Synagogue. I am to take the news that He is coming."

"Why?" asked Miriam. "What is it that Jairus wants with Yeshua the carpenter?"

"Didn't you know?" asked the boy in surprise, "His only daughter is ill, could be dying. They think the prophet from Nazareth might be able to save her if He comes along quickly, but the crowd are holding Him up; there are so many of them and the streets are narrow. Some people are getting nearly crushed against the wall."

A moment of panic took hold of her. If there were such a press of people then how would she in her weakness get to talk to Yeshua? It would be impossible to get near Him unless he were on her side of the street and even then, with so many people crowding about, it

לְהָבֵשׁ לְנִשְׁבְּרֵי־לֵב זְרָא לְשָׁבֵיִם דִּרוֹר וְלַאֲסוּרִים־ פְּקַח־קוֹחַ׃

could be dangerous. She grimaced and thought, what if she were crushed? What if she were killed? Would it matter? She could hardly be any worse off than she was and of the after-life she only had confused ideas. Better to risk the crowd and try her best to get near Yeshua.

At least they were moving slowly and though He might be in a hurry to attend to the sick girl, He could not move fast because of the crowd. That, in a way, gave her a better chance of attracting His attention or of just reaching Him. Another thought came to her. Did she need to attract His attention, did she need to talk to Him? Surely He, if He were Messiah, would know what was wrong with her. Maybe if she could just touch the fringes on his over garment, that would be enough. "Just a touch," she thought. "I ought to be able to reach out to him and just touch the fringes of His garment, that will be all. He won't want to be bothered with me, but if I can reach out to Him I shall get better." Her heart was filled with hope and her stomach felt empty and fear filled her as she watched the crowd to seek for her opportunity.

As the crowd began to edge past her she saw Yeshua. She had not seen Him before and was disappointed, for she had expected to see a tall, imposing figure of a man, but what she did see was just an ordinary one. The words of Isaiah came to her: "And when we shall see Him there is no beauty that we should desire Him."

The man anxiously accompanying Him was imposing – a man used to command. But it was clear that in all that excited crowd where people showed the whole range of human emotions from fear to enthusiasm to extreme uncertainty, only Yeshua had complete control of Himself. Around Him were some of the disciples and they too seemed to border an area of calm and perfect self-control. The big man with Him could hardly control

לְהָבֹשׁ לְנִשְׁבְּרֵי־לֵב זְרָא לִשְׁבֹּיִם וְדְרֹור וְלַאֲסֹורִים־ פְּקַח־קֹוחַ׃

his impatience and his extreme anxiety. He pushed against the crowd who, at the most difficult moments seemed intent on stopping and blocking the way.

Nearer and nearer they came. It seemed as if the Prophet from Nazareth moved, or was moved by the press of the crowd, towards the side of the street where, anxiously, she waited. He had almost passed her and she almost despaired, desperate that He should not pass by without giving her the chance to touch Him. She reached out, and as she did so, He stepped back to avoid a woman in the crowd who had stumbled and almost fallen. She stretched between two men who looked as if they had come straight from their fishing, and as she did so His backward movement brought her reaching hand onto the tasselled corner of His garment.

It was as if the world stood still and as if a silence descended on the universe. The noise of the crowd, the wailing that was starting up from the house of the ruler of the Synagogue, even the crying of the birds and the barking of dogs was stilled. She was numb, her mind a blank.

Then the consciousness that she was healed thrust itself upon her. She was no longer tired but it was if her whole being, not just her body, throbbed and pulsed with life and energy. A power had been infused into her through that simple touch. She stood up straight and the lost years fell away from her. Their disappointments, their hurts, their despair were all gone. This was the negation of all the negative things that had assailed her. This was life where there had only been death, its vacuum sucking out the life and hope, the strength and the purpose. If her hair did not regain its original black it no longer felt lank and lifeless. Her limbs were no longer full of aches and pains, but supple and ready to stride out

לַחֲבֹשׁ לְנִשְׁבְּרֵי־לֵב ־נָרָא לִשְׁבֻּיִם דְּרוֹר וְלַאֲסוּרִים־ פְּקַח־קוֹחַ׃

to a new, fresh existence; a life full of possibilities or opportunities and of love.

The goings on around her had been blotted out in the silence of the miracle; but now sound and sight returned and she looked to see the crowd pressing round the Prophet, the disciples trying to clear a way for Him. Jairus, with despair written in anguish on his features and desperation in his hands raised imploring towards the Carpenter-Prophet, stood impatient and fearful.

"Who touched me?" The voice was gentle yet it carried an authority that had to be obeyed. Peter and others of the disciples remonstrated with Him.

"Master! The crowd is pushing and shoving," they said, perplexed, "and you say, 'Who touched Me?' "

He smiled gently with a certain wistfulness, and said: "I perceive that power has gone out from me. Someone touched me."

The disciples stood bewildered by the sudden halt in their slow progress towards the house of Jairus. Miriam, though He had not called her or even looked at her, knew that He knew. She knew He was challenging her and willing her to come forward. She had to step out and be seen, be known to have been the one to reach out to the Prophet who was the centre of the concourse.

She stepped forward, hesitantly, then with greater confidence, beginning to realise the full majesty of her Saviour, she fell to the ground, kneeling in the dust with bowed head before Him. For a moment they formed a tableau as dramatic as any in that emotionally charged scene.

"Daughter!" He addressed her, "Be of good cheer; your faith has made you well. Go into peace."

He was dismissing her – sending her, not away, but into peace. She did not understand what He meant by

5 Issue of Blood

לְהָבֵשׁ לְנִשְׁבְּרֵי־לֵב זְרָא לִשְׁבֻיִם דְּרוֹר וְלַאֲסוּרִים־ פְּקַח־קָוֹחַ׃

that but understanding came as she felt the 'peace of God which surpasses all understanding' suffuse her soul and lift her spirit. She turned away as the crowd moved on and the noise from the ruler of the Synagogue's house grew louder.

They made room for her as, in a daze of wonder and of happiness she made her way back not at all as she had come. She made her way back until confronted by a familiar and welcome figure, who took her into his arms, the tears of joy streaming down his face.

(You can read about the woman's healing in Mark's Gospel, chapter 5, and in Luke chapter 8.)

6

TEARS OF SORROW AND OF JOY

The two processions were approaching one another as if they had arranged to meet at the gate of the town. 'Pleasantness' was its name, Nain, but that could also be read as 'afflicted', as one leading the procession from inside the town most certainly was. They were readying themselves, forming up before the gate, waiting until all was in order before moving off. The other had started just after first light that morning and had travelled the long road, some twenty-five miles from Capernaum.

It would take but a few minutes for them to meet, to converge where more than two roads met outside the walls of the small country town. It was to be more than the convergence of two processions of people; one wailing its lamentations, the other in earnest deep discussion interspersed with that humour which is never far from the Jewish mind, and less serious talk. It was to be a meeting of contrasts, a meeting of fruitfulness and joy.

Neither was aware, as yet, of the other, for the stone walls of the fields and the fig trees and the olive trees hid the one from the view of the other. The mourners were hidden still inside the walls and the others deep in argument and in thought upon the weighty matters which were being considered and expressed. Only One knew where they were headed. He was the One who had chosen the path and who had, long ago, before time

97

לְהָבֵשׁ לְנִשְׁבְּרֵי־לֵב זְרָא לִשְׁבֻּיִם דְּרֹור וְלַאֲסוּרִים־ פְּקַח־קֹוחַ׃

began, arranged this meeting.

His joy at the earnestness of the disciples and of the great crowd, which had followed Him from Capernaum that morning, was tinged with a deep sadness. If one of His suffered, so did He, with a sympathy which no mere human mind could share, nor plumb its depths. He was "A man of sorrows and acquainted with grief." Much of that sorrow was His very own, for He knew the ruin which human wickedness had made of the loveliness of the Creation, which was His also. Much of the grief was His very own too, for the terrible things which He was going to have to undergo in order to put things right and to "restore that which he did not take away."

In men such matters become remote – abstracts; from which we remove ourselves to a distance, to try to understand them and in trying, all too often, rationalise them. His was the sorrow too of sensing it as His own; of truly 'suffering with' and feeling, as if they were His own, the burdensome sorrows of a world crying in the minor key of pain and suffering, of the bitterness of loss and of the emptiness of bereavement.

The procession moving southwards was an apparently ragged one constantly in flux. It was both excited and controlled but with the controls, not of constraint, but of respect for others and an all-pervading love of humanity. The excitement was generated by the wisdom with which the Prophet from Nazareth taught them. Some, in the front of the crowd, had gone ahead of Him and walked backwards so as not to miss the gracious words which proceeded from His lips. Many crowded around Him but not too close, out of respect for such a teacher; they kept a distance out of reverence for His person. All were anxious to drink in the things He taught, for He taught them not as did the scribes and other

לְהַבֵּשׁ לְנִשְׁבְּרֵי־לֵב זָרָא לִשְׁבֻיִם דְּרוֹר וְלַאֲסוּרָים־פְּקַח־קוֹחַ:

religious teachers of the Jews. Many were anxious to ask the questions which burned in their hearts. Should one, from the rear of the crowd of disciples and other followers seem particularly anxious to ask something then the crowd, as if by common consent, parted to allow him access to the Teacher.

Some who had been with Him since early that morning could not have said why they followed, but simply knew that each moment was precious. There were, of course, the disciples, fishermen and other common folk, who went with Him everywhere and who, sometimes, went off in pairs to announce the coming of the Kingdom. They eagerly stored away, in their receptive minds, the words He spoke, though at that time there was much that they did not and could not understand. Those things would fall into place and be ordered by understanding later on.

They all loved the way His lucid and simple explanations cleared up so many points of difficulty in an understanding of the Torah which the arguments of the scribes, the lawyers and the Pharisees seemed only to complicate further. Indeed those learned men loved to argue in such a convoluted way that they seemed to prove things the opposite of what a simple man would make of the text.

The Teacher thus made Scripture, the Law, the Writings and the Prophets available to the ordinary folk of that time and place. It would be their task, later to make it all available to the whole wide world. How apt the words which some had spoken: "Never did any man speak like this man," and, "He does all things well."

There were so many questions to ask, so many pithy sayings and intriguing illustrations. There were so many beautiful stories, so full of meaning, and meaning within

לְהָבֵשׁ לְנִשְׁבְּרֵי-לֵב זְרָא לִשְׁבוּיִם דְּרוֹר וְלַאֲסוּרִים- פְּקַח-קוֹחַ׃

meaning. There were glorious, wonderful truths, truths which could set men free. They followed Him, not as sleep-walkers, nor as men in a trance, nor as those in the ecstasies of the worshippers of the pagan gods and goddesses. They followed Him. They followed Him as men who drink at the very springs of life; as men who are satisfied but must take again and again the living water, knowing they must give it out, longing to give it out. To give it out to others, so that they too might taste its sweetness and so slake their terrible thirst.

They did not know it; they could not be aware; but the Teacher whose words were their joy and their very life force, knew. He knew where they were going and why. He so controlled the pace, even as he talked and answered questions, that this procession of disciples and followers must soon encounter another.

It was another of a different sort. It was another where sorrow and lamentation contrasted starkly with the eager questioning and the rapture of knowledge newly gained, which prevailed among the followers of the Teacher.

Most of the Teacher's followers had learned of or had even been present at the strange encounter with the Centurion at Capernaum. They had marvelled at how the Teacher had healed the Roman Officer's servant. He had merely spoken the word, responsive to the Centurion's entreaty, and the servant had been raised up from his sickness. Shortly they were to witness another such marvel, for sickness and death were vanquished enemies at the Word of the Teacher.

There may have been a few, motivated at first by curiosity alone, who had followed Him from Capernaum. But their ardour, if curiosity had not turned to something more, something firmer and more lasting, would have

לְהַלְבִּישׁ לְנִשְׁבְּרֵי־לֵב זָרָא לְשָׁבוּיִם דְּרוֹר וְלַאֲסוּרִים־ פְּקַח־קוֹחַ׃

cooled, inversely as the sun grew hotter and the road got harder. It was about twenty-five miles from Capernaum to Nain. The shadows were lengthening as they approached the little town and though looking forward, perhaps to finding somewhere to rest, yet they still were full of eagerness to learn more, to question yet more and to witness yet more. They were indeed to witness something more, something very special and a joy which was different though having its source in the same abounding love, as their joy.

Late afternoon was fading into evening, and evening was the time when funeral processions set off on their last sad journey to the place of burial. The other procession from the north was on the road approaching the gate. Flutes played a dirge and voices wailed: "Alas, the hero! Alas, the lion!" At the head of the procession a woman, her head covered and her face obscured by her veil, supported by her friends, with slow, dragging and weary steps, led the way. Many people of the city had joined her that evening as the sun dipped beneath the western horizon.

It was held by the Rabbis, that to stop for a funeral and then to join the procession and to follow it to the cemetery, was a religious duty and one which conferred great merit. Indeed people ought to stop their business to follow a funeral to that last resting place. Even the business of study, that most sacred of all duties, according to the Rabbis, ought to cease in order for the scholar to follow this obligation and so pay respect for the dead and for the living who mourned.

She who led the procession had little money, for though they had been content they had also been poor. She had scraped together all she could in order to pay for the flute players, for the mourning women whose loud

לְהַבֵּשׁ לְנִשְׁבְּרֵי־לֵב זְרָא לִשְׁבֻּים דִּרוֹר וְלַאֲסוּרִים־ פְּקַח־קוֹחַ׃

wails filled the air with sorrow and despair, and for the man to make an oration. In her desolation she had determined that she would not be shamed before her neighbours and that her only son, her delight and the support of her old age, should have all honour and respect shown to him as she had shown and he had shown love in their lives.

He had been a loving and a more than dutiful son, giving up his ambition to study in order to be the man of the family, so she would give him honour in death as he had honoured her in life.

The previous day had been spent sitting with her back to the body. She had left only briefly to go to a neighbour's house for a bite or so of food, offered with kindly and gentle insistence, so that she could keep up her strength. She had come as a young bride to this house, barely sixteen. She had come to this little house and it had been, for her, a palace. It had been Ehud's house and it had been her house. Everything in it and about it spoke to her of the presence of both her Ehuds, and now she was alone.

It seemed lonely and empty without the sound of their voices, their laughter and their discussions with their neighbours and friends. Always they had enjoyed making their house a place where neighbours, friends and strangers were welcome. They had not simply been mindful of the injunctions of the Law about hospitality, but they enjoyed to share the little they had with other people.

The little house she had always dreamed of as a little girl and to which her Ehud had brought her as a girl bride now seemed the house of a stranger. As a littler girl she had played at keeping house for Ehud and later, of having his children. She had made a little pretend house

102

לַחֲבֹשׁ לְנִשְׁבְּרֵי־לֵב קָרָא לִשְׁבֻיִים דְּרוֹר וְלַאֲסוּרִים· פְּקַח־קוֹחַ׃

and had sat her dolls round the table. Then she had gone to fetch Ehud and, taking him by the hand, had shown him her pretend house and the 'children' and had told him that it was their house and these were their babies. He was the 'daddy' and she was the 'mummy'.

Some of the boys would have laughed, but not Ehud. Ehud had never laughed at her or mocked her; he had only laughed with her, and what laughter they had shared! Ehud might have been embarrassed to be playing with a girl but, if he was, he did not show it, but had helped her give the dolls their food and then put them to bed. He had gently squeezed her hand and said, "We have a nice house and nice children, don't we?"

He had been eighteen when at last they had married. Ehud, her Ehud, had been all she ever wanted and day by day their happiness grew and their love deepened and matured. As he had gently and lovingly squeezed her hand when they had played with the dolls, so every day he would take her hand in his great big hand and draw her to him to kiss her. He would smile down at her with such gentle devotion and such tenderness, with such love and such pride in his little wife.

As the memories of the sheer joy of living and of shared love flooded her memory with painful reminder of loss she thought how many were not blessed with such joy. So many marriages, it seemed, lost their sparkle, their excitement and their joy in the mental and physical shared oneness. The fruit of that oneness, Little Ehud, had also been a delight. She would have liked a dozen children, all of them little Ehuds, but they had one and he was loved the more because of it. Big Ehud took their little boy with him when he went off to tend the vines, the trees or the sheep, of richer neighbours. Little Ehud

לְהָבֵשׁ לְנִשְׁבְּרֵי־לֵב זְרָא לִשְׁבֻּים וְלִרוֹר וְלַאֲסוּרִים־פְּקַח־קָוֹחַ׃

adored his father and went with him as often as he could. His father's eyes lit up whenever they turned to his son and he taught him all the skills he himself had learned from a child.

At night, by the light of a lamp, they read from a roll of the Law and recited together the Shema: "Hear O Israel, the Lord our God is one Lord." At Passover the boy had learned to take the part of the eldest son and to ask his father, "What mean you by this feast?"

Together they tended the single olive tree they owned and the row of vines. They boasted that these vines bore the finest grapes in all the world; but not to anyone else for that would have been an arrogance that did not enter their minds. Little Ehud, as everyone now called him, went off clinging to his father's hand, holding onto just two of his fingers or with his hand completely enveloped in his father's large hand.

"I'm going to work today with Daddy," the boy would announce to his mother proudly. And she would reply, "Well I had better make you up a big parcel of food, for you will have to work hard and both of you will have to keep up your strength."

His eyes would watch her delightedly as she wrapped bread, raisins made from their own grapes, onions, and some green leaves, a skin bottle of goat's milk and some cheese for them to take. If he was lucky and they were in season, she would smile mischievously and put in some of the figs from their fig tree which grew against the wall of their house.

"Be sure to let your daddy have a couple of the figs," she playfully admonished, "don't eat them all yourself!"

Off they would go, her tall strong husband and their little boy showing all the vigour and the happiness she had ever wanted in a son of hers. He even had his own

לְהָבֵשׁ לְנִשְׁבְּרֵי־לֵב זְרָא לִשְׁבֵים וְדְרֹור וְלַאְסוּרִים־פְּקַח־קָוֹח׃

tools: a pruning knife and a little spade, so he could work alongside his father. The skills of pruning the trees either to increase fruitfulness or to inhibit disease, had become second nature to him before he was eight. By that time he was attending the elementary school attached to the synagogue in the town. He had begun to learn short passages from the Torah while very young before going to the school. Once started he showed a remarkable aptitude for his studies and learned to read the Torah for himself very quickly.

With red eyes and, from time to time wracked with sobs, she allowed her mind to float through the avenues of the past – through scenes of such exquisite happiness that they hurt; and now that they were both gone, such desolation that the pain was intensified a hundred times, or so it seemed.

She would sometimes smile sadly through her tears, then the pain would return and she would collapse moaning in an agony of loss. She watched as the scenes unfolded before her eyes. She watched and saw her little boy come running home to her.

"Mummy! Mummy! I can read! I can read!" he announced and flung himself into her arms. When her Big Ehud had come in from his work her son had also run up to him proudly to tell of his day at the school and the wonderful things he had learned. They were so proud as he ran off in the mornings to the school and as he ran home again to tell them more of the knowledge he had acquired. Big Ehud even waited, putting off his own departure so that he could wave goodbye to his son or walk a little way along the street with him.

The avenues of time grew misty with tears and dissolved in sadness. She wept for that older grief when her Ehud, her husband, had been taken from them. Her

לַחֲבֹשׁ לְנִשְׁבְּרֵי־לֵב זְרָא לִשְׁבֻיִם דְּרֹור וְלַאֲסוּרִים־ פְּקַח־קֹוֹחַ׃

world had collapsed then – but bit by hit she had managed to build it up again. Not as it had been, for the house no longer rang with his voice and her bed was empty and lonely. His body had lain where Little Ehud's body had also lain, but an hour ago. Now she wept for both of them, lost to her forever.

Little Ehud he had remained, for he took after her in stature though like his father in all the skills and in the humour which kept their house full of laughter from morning to night. So, in a sense the grief she felt for the loss of her husband had been alleviated somewhat by the kindliness, the skills with animals and with plants, and the gentleness her growing son showed to all and sundry and to her in particular. As Big Ehud had abounding energy and a wonderful love and admiration for her, so his son made up to her in many ways the loss of a husband as he turned out to be more and more like his father and grew into an ideal son, dutiful and kind.

She had been warmly cocooned in the love and the devotion of her two menfolk, in their loving adoration. They ate together, went to the synagogue together, read the Law together, went to the markets together when the men were not working, and went for long walks together in the surrounding countryside. Together they breathed in the sweet perfumes of the flowers and listened to the joyous birdsong. Together they delighted in the green hills, the groves of olives, the corn waving in the wind and the ever changing moods of the Sea of Galilee. And together they delighted in the company of one another. Such bliss was life for the little family in Nain.

Her Big Ehud had been taken from her but Little Ehud, just coming into manhood, took up his father's mantle. He too had shed bitter tears, for was not the most wonderful man in the whole world taken from him

לְהַבֵּשׁ לְנִשְׁבְּרֵי־לֵב צָרָא לִשְׁבֻּיִם דְּרוֹר וְלַאֲסוּרִים־פְּקַח־קוֹחַ:

too? He had walked with his mother, supporting her frailty before the bier to the last resting place for the body. He fully shared his mother's distress, but gave up his ambitions to become a teacher of the Law and loaded his father's tools into a bag; and he had gone round looking for work in order to support his mother and to be to her a comfort in her widowhood.

Landowners and those who kept flocks gladly employed him, for all knew that Little Ehud lacked none of his father's skills and none of his commitment to his work. Yitsak ben Yehudah, one of the richest, knowing how straitened the circumstances of the widow would be, and knowing too the integrity and the skills of Little Ehud, had sent for him and actually offered him work. Yitsak ben Yehudah was a good man but he was no fool and he knew how well Ehud ben Ehud could work.

After a trial period Yitsak had said to him: "You may be but a lad Ehud ben Ehud, but you are nearly as good as your father was. I will put your name round my friends for I have never seen a man so devoted, and the Law says that we should honour our father and our mother. Of sons, no woman could ask for a better."

So, if a vine-dresser was needed or someone to prune the fruit trees or to see to a sheep that was ill, they called for Little Ehud. Once more the little house had regained its merriment though never as before; a sadness and a burden was always present just inside the door. It was, however, warm with love and again it held a welcome for others of the bereaved and many found comfort within its walls. Once more the widowed mother had begun to feel secure and comforted. Once more she felt something of the love she had felt for her Ehud when as a little girl they had fed and put her dolls to bed. No one could take away those precious memories and she kept

לְהָבֵשׁ לְנִשְׁבְּרֵי־לֵב זְרָא לִשְׁבוּיִם דְּרוֹר וְלַאֲסוּרִים־ פְּקַח־קוֹחַ׃

them to herself, going over them in her mind in the dark lonely hours of the night.

She was drained, empty, all emotion gone, too tired and too weary to cry any more; yet she cried, gently, quietly to herself, barely a moan. It seemed almost that this was not really happening to her, that she was seeing someone else through her eyes but a someone who was also herself. She watched herself, who was not herself. She saw a frail, dazed, prematurely aged old lady at the head of a funeral procession. She heard, as afar off, from a long way away, the mourners and the sound of the flute.

Then, suddenly, as if she had gone inside and closed a door, the sounds stopped; a few uncertain notes from the flutes and they ceased playing too. Slowly coming out of her bemused state, she watched, as out of the other procession, there stepped a man. Everyone else stood, as if fixed to the spot. Even the sighing of the wind in the trees seemed muted out of respect for something about to happen. It was as if all the world were somehow in awe.

He seemed just an ordinary man; on the surface that is. Neither his clothes, nor his looks, nor his bearing, at first seemed in any way out of the ordinary. Yet he was not ordinary. The crowd who had followed Him along the road from Capernaum were stilled; all their eyes were fixed upon Him. So unusual was it for a funeral procession to be stopped that they too who mourned and who followed the mourners, were also riveted to the spot and they too had their eyes fixed on Him. He seemed just an ordinary working man, yet He was not an ordinary man. Many that day would have insisted He was special, unique, different from all other men.

There was about Him an aura of authority which had

לַהֲבֹשׁ לְנִשְׁבְּרֵי־לֵב לִקְרֹא לִשְׁבוּיִם דְּרוֹר וְלַאֲסוּרִים־ פְּקַח־קוֹחַ׃

stopped the two lines of people in their tracks. There was that about Him – that authority which caused none to make any protest at His actions. Indeed He acted as if it were His right and that custom and common practice should give way in His presence. Yet for all that His very presence commanded that respect; there was no suggestion of arrogance. In anyone else, the High Priest, even the governor, or, above him, the Emperor, such actions would indeed have been arrogant. But in Him there was no such thing and He acted as if all that He did were perfectly right and natural.

His pace was without hurry, yet determined. He was both a warrior going out to battle and a loving, caring friend who brought comfort and compassion. His manner was all gentleness, yet there was strength and authority. Such authority as she had never known in a man. It radiated from him out to her and to the crowd who, mute, gazed with wonder and a sense of mounting awe. She knew too that this man, who was more than man, understood and felt, with perfect understanding and with perfect feeling, her own grief and hurt as if it were His own.

As His gaze fixed itself upon her, she felt her heart leap, as it were, with fresh emotions of love and wonder too. It felt as if her burden of grief were being slowly, gently but surely lifted from her and she felt light of heart for the first time since he, her world, had been struck down. She lifted her head to face those lovely eyes full of compassion, and she heard His words: "Do not weep," He said. And, in obedience to that loving command, her tears dried up and she felt a small flower of hope begin to blossom at the very centre of her being.

He understood it all, she realised. He understood with a perfect understanding. Her bleak misery at her

לְהָבֵשׁ לְנִשְׁבְּרֵי־לֵב זָרָא לִשְׁבֻיִם דְּרֹור וְלַאֲסֹורֵים־ פְּקַח־קֹוחַ׃

twofold loss, her tragic future, He knew it all and understood the contentment, the excitement and the laughter of her past. He knew all about her husband, her son and her love and she could begin to rejoice in the knowledge that He knew.

Awareness that this ordinary man was no ordinary man flooded her being and she wanted to fall at His feet and plead for her son to be restored. He smiled lovingly at her and she realised that He knew that too. If she had loved and did love then this man was Love. If she had served her neighbours, her friends and those two very special people in her life, then she knew too that He served who was Lord of All and who ought to be served.

His love reached out to her and to the crowd gathered in that dusty open space in the cool and the twilight of that evening. His love reached out beyond them to the whole of the wide world which was not wide enough to contain His love, for He was Love. It even encompassed Caesar, his Senators, his bureaucrats and his servants and those mighty dread legions which held the empire in thrall. It reached out to the tax gatherers, the thieves, the brigands, the harlots, the most humble and the most despised of people. Far beyond them it reached out to and encompassed the birds and the beasts, the fish and the creeping things. It reached out to the seas, the mountains, the plains and the deserts, for this was His world; He had made it and would make it again.

His hand stretched out to the bier. The crowds stirred, some with interest, some with a mere curiosity to see what He would do and what would happen. The majority were expectant, for they sensed that a mighty miracle was to take place, but as yet they did not understand; their vision was still clouded by the miasmas

לְהָבֵשׁ לְנִשְׁבָּרֵי-לֵב זָרֵא לִשְׁבוּיִם דְּרוֹר וְלַאֲסוּרִים- פְּקַח-קְוֹחַ׃

and the dust of earth. One or two were shocked and surprised that a holy man should defile Himself with such a touch – for it meant that, like those who carried the bier, He would have to wash Himself and remain ritually unclean until the next day. His touch and His words exuded power. His voice was one of such gentleness yet few could doubt the authority it carried. The last of the afterglow lit the scene as the clouds seemed to lift a little and the clouds over their understanding also lifted.

There was a gasp of wonder from those at the front of the crowd and from some a gasp of horror as he that had been dead began dazedly to sit up. Many now craned themselves forward to see the wonder and to marvel at another miracle. All cast about in their minds as to what this signified and who this was who could do such mighty acts. The disciples had seen His miracles before, but this was an even more powerful confirmation that He must be the promised Messiah. There were speculations among the others and mutterings from those at the back who had not actually seen what had happened and were asking their friends nearer the front to explain to them. Conversation grew and a murmur and babble of talk increased.

Some began to speculate: the Teacher from Nazareth was more than a Rabbi. True, they said to themselves and to each other, some rabbis have had healings in answer to their prayers or by the recitation of the sacred Name. On the other hand never had anyone witnessed anything quite like this before. Was He not a powerful prophet of God? Was He not in the tradition of Elijah and Elisha? They were men of God who had cleansed lepers and who had raised the dead. Others insisted that this was indeed Elijah come again at the end time and

לְהַלְבֵּשׁ לְנִשְׁבְּרֵי־לֵב זְרָא לִשְׁבֻיִם דְּרוֹר וְלַאֲסוּרִים־ פְּקַח־קָוֹחַ׃

who would bring in the reign of Messiah. Yet others insisted that He must be the promised Messiah, for no one could do these miracles unless he were the Anointed of God. Several said that He was not Elijah nor the Messiah, for Messiah would come in great glory and this man was just a carpenter.

"No!" they said, "He is the prophet like Moses come to confirm the Law and to whom Israel should listen, who was promised by Moses." So the arguments went on and the noise rose in pitch, but was quickly stilled as if He had once more commanded attention, but He had not spoken.

She looked, in amazement, joy and with a growing song of praise in her heart that Israel's God should do this for her! She knew with certainty though she did not properly understand, that Messiah would bring the dry bones of Israel to life and that her son who was alive and well, standing awkwardly at the side of the bier, was a foretaste of that great miracle which was to come. One day, perhaps very soon, Messiah would bring Israel again to life.

It was now clearly, blindingly obvious, to her at least, that this was He. The loving hands had reached out and the young man, her son and her delight, had stirred and sat up. The men carrying the bier had set it down upon the ground the moment He had reached out to it. He gave them no command but they acted as if He had, and had obeyed that unspoken word to rest their burden at His feet. They had then stood back, embarrassed that they seemed almost to intrude upon a scene so intimate and so private. The crowd too, suddenly stilled, drew back a little in awe and reverence after that first gasp of wonder.

He had spoken, but few had heard Him, so quiet and

לְהָבֵשׁ לְנִשְׁבְּרֵי־לֵב זְרָא לִשְׁבוּיִם דְּרוֹר וְלַאֲסוּרִים־ פְּקַח־קוֹחַ׃

so gentle had been His tone. Only the mother and the men who had carried the sad burden of death had heard, and perhaps those in the forefront of the crowd whose hearing was more acute than normal. Though spoken with gentleness and in low tones the dead had heard. The authority of the words had echoed and had pierced through the dark shadows of the halls of death. They had reached and were heard in that happy place where the souls of the righteous rested in Abraham's bosom, and where all was contentment and peace, waiting for that glorious resurrection of the just at the time appointed by the Father.

"Young man, I say to you, arise!" There was some small stress on that last word but on its utterance, the powers of death were robbed of their prey and he that had the power of death was impotent to resist that gentle command from the Prince of Life. He, and they, could but look on with malevolence, scheme for revenge, and wildly imagine they could yet defeat the Lord of Life. The soul had fled to the paradise of the saints and, at His word, flew back instantly to the dead body it had inhabited, the tent it had dwelt in, those few brief years upon earth. It flew in an instant through those dark corridors echoing with the wails, the lamentations and curses of those condemned for ever to the outer, noisy, hideous, fearful darkness.

The body, its vital forces restored, came back to life, to health, and to strength. It revived to a health and strength and a vitality it had not known even in the vigour of its young manhood before disease had wasted and struck it down. "Young man, I say to you, arise!" – With one simple but wonderfully potent word every vital function was restored better than before, for that is the way with God that His kingdom increases and grows for

לַהֲבֹשׁ לְנִשְׁבְּרֵי־לֵב זְרָא לִשְׁבֹּיִם דְּרֹוֹר וְלַאֲסוּרִים־ פְּקַח־קֹוֹחַ׃

all time and for eternity.

The hands that had snatched the young man from death reached out again in his bewilderment, and drew him forward. Such gentle, loving hands; such gentle loving eyes fixed themselves on him and all fear and bewilderment was gone. They lovingly turned him to face her whose bitter tears of grief and loss were now turned to tears of joy, of relief and of such exquisite wonder. By the strength of His arms they fell into each other's arms: mother and son, son and mother, together again.

The fondness of His expression was that of a father for his dear children, as indeed they were. He brought them together and looked on them with love as, soon, on one sadder and more awful day He would again bring together a mother and a son, a son and a mother: "Here is your son! Son, here is your mother!"

The son enveloped his mother, his strong arms around her dear, frail shoulders. They wept together for love, for gratitude, and for happiness. It was a happiness that is seldom given for men and women to know on this earth, a happiness reserved for the bliss of heaven.

It was infectious, that happiness. Like a cloud of sweetness it flowed outward and the men and women who had followed the funeral to share the grief of the bereaved widow, now shared her joy. The crowd who had trodden the long road from Capernaum felt it too and felt the tears sting their eyes for wonder and for happiness. They turned to each other and nodded wisely, glad that they had witnessed all this.

"God has visited His people," they said. The rest agreed or remarked that, "A great prophet has risen up among us."

They made their way back to the town, the townsfolk

לְהַבֵּשׁ לְנִשְׁבְּרֵי־לֵב ;רָא לִשְׁבוּיִם וְרֹיֹר וְלַאֲסוּרִים־ פְּקַח־קֹוחַ׃

mingling with the men and women who had travelled
that momentous day from the north by the Sea of Galilee.
They invited them into their homes and made them
welcome and they rejoiced that the prophet from
Nazareth had visited them and had done this great
miracle among them.

(The basis for this story can be found in Luke's Gospel, chapter 7.)

7

Prison and Suffering
I must decrease.

They came for him just as evening was falling. The sun was dipping down beyond the Judean hills to quench itself to darkness in the wine dark sea. They came as he had just finished his baptising and as he had spoken his last words of encouragement to the poor and his last, forbidding words of warning and of judgement to the rich, the powerful and the arrogant.

The soldiers came for him, as he had known they would, sooner or later, with their masks of regimented brutality and disciplined strictness. They came for him where desert streams and pools of water blessed the atmosphere near Jordan and where the ground sprouted trees, desert cacti and shrubs. It was a place where goats browsed on the leaves and where camels fed on the thorny bushes. It was a place where men grew tough and leathery in the scorching sun. It was a place of loneliness which had been transformed by the crowds who came to see and hear the Baptist and, for some, to obey his message and to prepare themselves for the Coming King. It was a solitary place where a man might be alone with God.

The spies, both the professionals employed by Herod Antipas, and those who reported to him, each with his own hidden agenda, had given Herod's men clear directions. There were plenty who would have told

לַהֲבֹשׁ לְנִשְׁבָּרֵי־לֵב זְרָא לִשְׁבֻיִם דְּרֹור וְלַאֲסוּרִים־פְּקַח־קֹוחַ׃

anyone where the Baptist was and what he was doing. It was no secret, but Herod had to find a use for the spies he trusted; they would not exaggerate nor twist the truth. They had served the Tetrarch for a long time and their survival was tied to his. The Baptist did nothing that was hidden; all was open and honest as far as he was concerned. But that is not the way of governments; that is not the way rulers and kings, even petty tetrarchs, do their thinking. Theirs is a cynical and twisted way of thinking; they trust no one; believe no one, so they are in a state of semi-paranoia. They trust no one and believe no one because they too are untrustworthy and rely on lies to keep themselves secure. To them the truth is not what it seems and everyone has guilty secrets to hide.

Rather afraid they were, those soldiers, of the Tetrarch. The superstitious awe in which John was held, even by Herod, as well as by the common people, unnerved them. It was in this unsettled mood and with some trepidation that they came to arrest the Baptist. They were not always brutal or callous men, these soldiers of Herod. They were called upon to do brutal and callous things from time to time, but to each other they were loyal. They had a fierce devotion to their wives and children, for many of the older ones had families. To these they were kindly men; generous and indulgent to a fault. Children were especially close in their affections and a hard-bitten senior decurion, a sergeant, playing with his own and his neighbour's children was a sight to be seen.

On duty they simply did their job. They learned early on not to ask questions. Questions were for their social and military superiors. They simply took their pay and got on with the job. In private these tough soldiers were often embarrassingly sentimental and could weep over a

7 Prison and Suffering

לְהָבֹשׁ לְנִשְׁבְּרֵי־לֵב זָרָא לִשְׁבוּיִם דְּרוֹר וְלַאֲסוּרִים־ פְּקַח־קוֹחַ׃

hurt to a sick pet dog or to one of the regimental children.

Herod was, in many ways, like his father, but without his utter ruthlessness. He could be cruel, but he was also scheming and sly and he was ever arrogant and, like the old Herod, he was drivingly ambitious. Unlike Herod the Great he had a lack of self-control. It was this which had lost Archelaus, his brother, his position in Judea and had earned him exile. He liked his pleasures and the current pleasure was Herodias, once the wife of his other brother Philip, and now his wife. Not his wife, however, according to Jewish law, for according to that he, and she, were adulterers. They had been named such, not by the priests but by the Baptist, which was why the sergeant and his dozen men were on their present task.

John had yet to plumb the depths implied in his own words that he must decrease. He was shortly to find out what they could mean in terms of degradation and suffering. He would be able to take comfort that the prophets, for the most part, had been there before him. The sad and sorry road, which he was about to be forced to tread, had been trodden by many servants of God before him. It was to be a road of suffering and tears, a road of rejection and loneliness.

As they were leading him away he began to realise how little he understood about the future. Certainly he had warned the nation and all who came to him about the Kingdom and had pointed to the Coming One who was its King, then and in the future. He had spoken about Him by inspiration as the Lamb of God who would "bear away the sin of the world". How was this to be? He had wondered what this meant for his cousin. A sacrificial lamb had to be slaughtered so that its death could take the place of that of the sinner, who, for his

118

לְהַבֵּשׁ לְנִשְׁבָּרֵי-לֵב רָא לִשְׁבוּיִם דְּרוֹר וְלַאֲסוּרִים- פְּקַח-קוֹחַ׃

sins, deserved to die. If He had to die how could He then bring in the Kingdom except by resurrection? Perhaps that was the key to it all and to that Kingdom's removal of the Roman yoke and that of their puppets, one of whom, Herod, now had him in his power. Would Yeshua save him? If so, when would He do so? The questions revolved round and round in John's mind as he walked away from all that God had called him to. They surged around the fragile walls of his understanding and the walls shook. They festered in his mind as the long night dragged on and that mind, once so strong, found in itself chinks and crannies of weakness.

The soldiers did not speak much. Soldiers did not talk to their prisoners, except to give orders. They were taught that familiarity bred contempt and a contemptuous prisoner would be a troublesome one. They were taught not to feel any sympathy for prisoners. To prevent this they were indoctrinated to keep quiet, to keep their distance and to act coldly and formally. There was danger in closeness; closeness could lead to sympathy and sympathy was a step along the path to disloyalty. Prisoners were enemies until proven otherwise and it was not for them to decide.

You did not want to feel sympathy for a man who might soon be imprisoned, beaten, even scourged and then crucified. Such sympathy would be misplaced. It would be especially misplaced if it was you that had to carry out the orders for torture or for execution.

It was not that executions like crucifixion were usual. That was the prerogative of the Romans. However, few really knew what went on in Herod's dungeons and those who did were not going to let on. That would have been more than their job was worth; it would have been more than their life was worth. Anyway such men that did such

לַחֲבֹשׁ לְנִשְׁבְּרֵי־לֵב גָרָא לִשְׁבוּיִם דְּרוֹר וְלַאֲסוּרִים־ פְּקַח־קוֹחַ׃

things for tyrants usually enjoyed their cruel craft and
kept it to themselves within their own tormented and
perverted minds.

They were, nevertheless, more than a trifle uneasy in
the company of such a prisoner as the Baptist. They had
expected there to be some trouble, but there had been
none. The Zealots were not present in any numbers
since they were not interested in a preparation of heart
and mind for the coming Kingdom, preferring, as they
did, direct action with dagger and with sword. The
soldiers, even the sergeant in charge, would be glad when
they handed him over to the sergeant of the guard at
Livias, Herod's fortress, and to the responsibility of the
Colonel commanding the troops there. For his part he
would be happy to get the prisoner in one piece and
relatively unbruised.

However, unease there was. This man was said to be
Elijah returned to the world to announce the Kingdom as
the prophet Malachi had forecast. What if he really were?
It seemed doubtful but you never knew and the idea was
a disturbing one. Elijah had called down fire from
heaven which had burned up the soldiers sent to arrest
him until, at the third try, the officer had grovelled before
the prophet. The less they said the better, so that nothing
could be misconstrued as disrespect. Like their supreme
master Herod the Tetrarch they were deeply superstitious
and not a little fearful, as they hurried with their prisoner
through the night.

One, however, among them, the youngest soldier,
could not restrain his curiosity. "Sarge?" he asked in a
nervous voice. He would have done better to keep quiet
like the older and more worldly-wise of his mates. The
sergeant did not bother to turn his head.

"Shut up!" he snapped.

לְהֵבֹשׁ לְנִשְׁבְּרֵי־לֵב זְרָא לִשְׁבֻיֵם֙ דְּרֹור וְלַאֲסוּרֵים־ פְּקַח־קֹ֑וֹחַ׃

But the youngster was burning with curiosity and sense could not prevail against youthful anxiety to be informed.

"Sarge?" he quavered again.

The sergeant did not turn, did not raise his voice, did not alter his grim facial expression.

"Shut up!" he repeated and added, "Report to me after!"

The other soldiers grinned to each other. Their knowing looks said, "He'll soon learn." The sergeant, they knew, like most sergeants, was not one for giving explanations. He could discuss at length with the other NCOs the quality of the wine they were issued with or the quality of the young recruits they were required to train and to lead these days. They would shake their heads and remark that things had not been so in their young days.

This particular sergeant was very much in the Spartan tradition, making one word do where others might have used several sentences. He was laconic to a fault. "Orders is orders," was his motto, and young soldiers who asked questions were likely to feel the weight of his fist. Military matters were simple. Sergeants obeyed the orders of the officers. They did not necessarily like the officers. In some instances they knew they could do a better job than the officers.

None of that mattered. It was a fact of life. If things went wrong then it was the fault of the officers. No one could blame the sergeants; they merely passed on the orders to the men and saw that they were carried out to the letter. You did not question nor did you argue. Arguing was for fools and he was determined to have no fools in any platoon where he was the platoon sergeant.

As for solders, it was his considered opinion that the

121

לַחֲבֹשׁ לְנִשְׁבְּרֵי־לֵב זְרָא לִשְׁבוּיִם דְּרוֹר וְלַאֲסוּרִים־ פְּקַח־קֹוחַ׃

best ones were the ones who always agreed with their sergeant and who only opened their mouths to say, "Yes Sarge!" in a loud voice before smartly doubling away to perform whatever task the sergeant had told them to do. Soldiers who questioned, or who, the gods forbid! started to think for themselves, were to be kicked and punched into submission and put on extra fatigues, until they learned and became soldiers who were not utterly useless, but ones on whom the sergeant could depend. Asking why? got in the way of military discipline and that was the reason for sergeants.

Sergeants were the backbone of any army, that was what all NCOs knew; any of them would tell you so. If you happened to be a Junior NCO you knew it too and believed it with every fibre of your being, because that was what you aspired to be one day. No one in his right mind wanted to be an officer. That meant responsibility.

Herod told the officers what he wanted. They had to interpret those orders into military practicalities, then they gave precise orders to the sergeants and the sergeants told the men. If things went wrong it was not the sergeants' fault, the orders had not been clear or precise enough. The officers were to blame. As for the troops, they just did what they were told; they did not think. They just marched. Usually they then marched back again. Rarely there might be a battle, and if there was then some soldiers got wounded or killed. That was the way of things; but gaps in the ranks meant promotion for some and more pay for many. It wasn't a bad life, all things considered.

They tramped on over rocks and patches of scrub where desert bushes grew or they passed areas of cultivated land where there was water. The paths they walked led, like the tributaries of a river, onto broader

לְהַכֵּשׁ לְנִשְׁבָּרֵי־לֵב זְרָא לִשְׁבוּיִם דְּרוֹר וְלַאֲסוּרִים־ פְּקַח־קוֹחַ:

roads, then through more desert landscape. After a few hours under the brilliant light of a full moon, they reached the fortress and gave the password to the sentries on the gate and then to the sergeant of the guard. The guard sergeant took a large ring with keys on it from his belt and signalled to the soldiers to bring the prisoner inside; where he was then taken to a cell and locked in. He would stay there until Herod sent for him to Machaerus.

Breathing a sigh of relief at having successfully brought his prisoner to the fortress and being now discharged of that responsibility, the sergeant dismissed his men for a well-earned rest. Not however before calling the luckless young soldier to stay behind and wait, at attention, on his pleasure.

"Not you! You wait 'ere till I've reported to the Officer of the Day!"

Turning to his colleague he lowered his voice to a comradely tone. Indicating with his thumb the hapless soldier, he said, "Keep an eye on 'im, will yer Ben. Make some use on 'im. I 'spec yer got some jobs need doin'?"

The guard sergeant grinned. "Better 'an that mate, the latrines could do wiv a wash out, an when 'e's done that 'e c'n scrub the messroom tables and then the floor. That is if yer takes yer time reportin' to the officer. Sergeants mess orderly'll find yer somethin' ter eat I don't doubt. I'll send one of the off watch guards ter roust 'im out."

The sergeants guffawed and leered at the prospect of the misery of the wretch who by then had realised the wisdom of the old saying that 'silence is golden'.

Three sons of Herod, miscalled 'The Great', had inherited each a part of his kingdom. The total was still less than the old Herod's original territories had been. The Romans did not like kings getting too rich, or too

123

לְהָבֵשׁ לְנִשְׁבְּרֵי־לֵב יָרָא לִשְׁבוּיִם דְּרוֹר וְלַאֲסוּרִים־ פְּקַח־קוֹחַ׃

powerful, or too interested in acquiring territory. 'Divide and rule' was their motto; so they divided the dominions of Herod on his death sometime in 4 BC. Later the ruler of Judea had been kicked out by the Romans. They did not like incompetent kings who might ruffle too many feathers. Ruffled feathers in politics all too often could lead to rebellion; and rebellions the Romans definitely deplored. So Archelaus had to go, and to Spain he went, where he was least likely to be able to interfere and rock the already unstable Jewish boat.

In his place they put a Procurator, more of a financial official, since the taxes from a province were all too important to Rome to be left in unsafe hands. Pilate was a member of the middle classes, the families who, though not aristocratic, had an important part to play in the Roman state since they ran the commercial world of Rome.

That left Antipas and Philip. Antipas ruled in Galilee west of the Sea of that name and Perea east of Jordan and south of Galilee, reaching down to the southern end of the Dead Sea. The territory to the east of Galilee was given to Philip. Though Antipas was certainly a chip off the old block, being despotic, cruel and ambitious, his brother Philip was not. Philip ruled his tetrarchy well. He went about doing judgement and justice and his citizens had a tolerably pleasant time under his rule; apart from Roman taxes and the hordes of tax collectors, that is. It was Herodias, Philip's wife, who wanted to be the wife of Antipas, who was the immediate cause of all the trouble. Not that she cared very much about those she inconvenienced on the road to getting her own way.

The old Herod had been brilliant at choosing the winning side. Caesar and Antony had appointed him king of Judea. When Antony got involved with the Queen

לְהָבֵשׁ לְנִשְׁבָּרֵי־לֵב קְרָא לִשְׁבֻיִם דְּרוֹר וְלַאֲסוּרִים־ פְּקַח־קוֹחַ:

of Egypt, Cleopatra, to do the lady a favour, Antony gave her some parts of Herod's kingdom. Herod never forgave them for this, though there was nothing much he could do about it at the time.

Immediately the lovers were defeated at the sea battle of Actium, Herod declared his support for the young Octavian, who later became the Emperor Augustus. Becoming part of the Augustan fan club ensured rich rewards, since Augustus, after the final defeat of Antony and the suicide of Cleopatra, needed a reliable ally in the eastern Mediterranean. Herod was that man and never looked back, politically that is.

People say that 'you cannot please everyone'. Herod tried and generally he was successful. Devious, despotic, cruel and treacherous he might have been but he knew on which side his bread was buttered and never wavered in his loyalty to Augustus. Clearly he was there to keep the Jews quiet and politically correct, which in those days consisted of pleasing the Emperor in Rome.

Though the Jews never actually got to like him, Herod did manage to build them a most magnificent temple. That at least kept the priests happy and, to some degree the Pharisees. Herod could be lavish when he considered it necessary and his building projects show just how shrewd and how lavish he could be.

Indeed, as well as cruelty, despotism and a bit of murder from time to time, his forte seems to have been building. It is one of those injustices in life that evil and unpleasant men are often also talented and successful. If you can call multiple murders of one's wives, one's sons and one's friends talent, then Herod had a wide variety of it. Augustus did say at a particularly bloodthirsty time in Herod's career that he would rather be Herod's dog than his son. After that, it is no wonder that the incident of the

לְחָבֹשׁ לְנִשְׁבְּרֵי־לֵב זְרֹא לִשְׁבוּיִם דְּרֹור וְלַאֲסוּרִים־ פְּקַח־קֹוחַ׃

Wise Men from the East and the babies in Bethlehem, failed to cause much of a stir. To Herod's court and to all who knew him it was simply business as usual. A few toddlers in a Judean village did not weigh anything in the scales of justice for such a man against his own survival.

He used his genius for building to please the Romans. This he did by enlarging some places and giving them Roman names. Julius, and Livia, are examples, but the magnificent port city of Caesarea was the chief. It was a Roman city, thoroughly paganised and with all the Roman entertainments, though perhaps not with quite the brutality to which the Romans were accustomed. Nor were the theatre shows quite so depraved as in Rome. Herod also had to look to Jewish sensibilities and even he had to walk a knife edge between the Jews and Rome, but he did so and he did so successfully during a comparatively long reign.

A man of Herod's violent and cunning character must also have been somewhat paranoid. He cannot have got where he did without making a few enemies. He was ruthless enough to make sure that his enemies, real or imagined, ended up dead or in prison. He also had to plan for untoward events which he could not control, such as the death of a friendly emperor and the succession of an unfavourable one. Indeed Tiberius, the heir apparent, was known to dislike Jews and religion in about equal amounts. If the Roman empire fell or the empire fell into the wrong hands then the king of Judea would possibly have to fight, though he would have preferred bribery, murder, and diplomacy or a combination of all three. However, if it came to fighting and the possibility of an invasion, then it was best to be prepared. Herod was prepared. All over his kingdom, especially at the borders, he built fortresses. These

לְהַלְבֵּשׁ לְנִשְׁבְּרֵי־לֵב ؛ רָא לִשְׁבוּיִם֙ דְּרוֹר וְלַאֲסוּרִים־ פְּקַח־קְוֹחַ؛

fortresses were also palaces.

Herod saw no reason to deny himself the pleasures of luxurious living; that is the privilege of the ruling class, even if under siege. All these were provisioned with silos of grain, cisterns of water and arsenals of all manner of weapons of offence and defence. It was not just the Romans who might take military action; they would be fairly sure to win in the end. However, Herod was surrounded by enemies: Syria, Arabia, Egypt, and Tyre all had rulers who, at any time, could turn out to be enemies, rivals or, more likely, false friends. Hence the need for fortresses.

Such a fortress was Masada where one thousand men, women and children were to hold out against the might of fifteen thousand professional soldiers of Rome under Silva, one of Vespasian's most able, resourceful and trusted generals. The Jewish war started in AD 66. Jerusalem fell and was destroyed in AD 70. Masada held out until 15th April in AD 73 when the Romans finally broke in and found that Eleazar and his defenders had all committed suicide rather than fall into the hands of their enemies. Only one woman and a couple of children, hiding in a storage silo, were left of the brave defenders of the fortress.

This was all in the future when John was taken to Machaerus, a fortress on the East of the Dead Sea, very similar to Masada, built on top of a towering precipitous mesa, a flat-topped mountain overlooking the country round about, rising sheer for hundreds of feet. It was both fortress and palace, and Herod Antipas had good reason to be there at the time.

Some time before, he had formed a liaison with the wife of his brother Philip. She was called Herodias and Herod was besotted with her. It probably added spice to

לְהַבְשׂ לְנִשְׁבְּרֵי־לֵב זְרָא לִשְׁבֻּיִם דְּרוֹר וְלַאֲסוּרִים־ פְּקַח־קוֹחַ׃

the affair that she was married to his brother. Family loyalty was never a strong point of the Herods. The adulterous relationship had outraged the moral sensibilities of many of the Jews. John the Baptist in particular had condemned it openly, publicly proclaiming that it was not lawful. As the last in line of the old Hebrew prophets John was true to his inheritance and was quick to condemn sin wherever, whenever, and in whoever he found it. Herod was not amused. His new wife was even less amused; she was furious. Who did this hedgerow preacher think he was to criticise her, the daughter and the wife of Kings and a royal Queen if ever there was one! In her own estimation that is; what other people thought she did not much care.

Herod Antipas had arranged to divorce his existing wife, the daughter of King Aretas, whose kingdom was to the East. She, however, heard about his plan and got leave from her erring husband to go and visit Machaerus. When she got there she did not stop for long, but skipped angrily over the border and back to daddy with her tale of outrage and of woe. Daddy was not amused and was preparing to fight. If a war started between the two petty kings then the Roman governor of Syria would have to intervene and then the Emperor would not be pleased.

Tiberius was not pleased most of the time; a glum, serious sort of man was Tiberius. Ever since his mother and the previous Emperor had stopped him marrying his sweetheart, Vipsania, he had been a bitter man. Had he married the girl things might have been different. Even into old age poor grim old Tiberius carried a torch for Vipsania. If for the sake of duty he had had to give up his sweetheart he was not likely to be sympathetic to a romantically inclined middle-aged Herod who adulter-

לְהִלְבֵּשׁ לְנִשְׁבָּרֵי-לֵב קְרֹא לִשְׁבוּיִם דְּרוֹר וְלַאֲסוּרִים- פְּקַח-קוֹחַ׃

ously married his brother's wife.

On top of all that it seemed that John, being the popular preacher that he was, might get ideas above his station; he certainly made a fuss about Herodias and that affected the people who listened to the Baptist. Herod could happily have killed John to get him out of the way and out of what remained of his hair, so to speak.

On the other hand he was not able to take the high-handed measures the old King Herod would have done. There were too many Romans looking over his shoulder and breathing down his neck. Anyway to murder John would possibly make him even less popular with the common people. Herod, like most kings at the time, did not much bother what the common people thought, but then if they started rioting, a favourite pastime for some of the more hot headed of the Jews, then again the Romans would feel it their duty to interfere. Rioting tended to get in the way of tax collecting, and what were provinces for if not to pay taxes to Rome?

Altogether whatever he did he would be unpopular and he hoped, if he kept John locked up in a dungeon for long enough, people might forget about him. If they did that then he might be able to bump him off quietly without creating much of a fuss, which to Herod's mind seemed much the best solution for some of his many troubles.

Herod Antipas was also, like many of his generation and like the Emperor himself, deeply superstitious. This was another reason for Herod's unease. Who was John? What was John? People seemed to disagree, including those who should have known: the priests and the Pharisees. Even they had lurking suspicions that he could be some sort of prophet and therefore to harm him might be to bring those responsible into disfavour with

לַחֲבֹשׁ לְנִשְׁבְּרֵי־לֵב ۚ זָרָא לִשְׁבוּיִם דְּרוֹר וְלַאֲסוּרִים־ פְּקַח־קוֹחַ׃

God. It was all very disturbing. Herod, like Pilate the Procurator, was not overly religious and had the veiled contempt for religion held by most of the Roman ruling and intellectual classes among whom he saw himself as belonging. Though they did not believe in the gods and goddesses, they did pay some regard to the outward ceremonies as bolstering the stability of the state and the empire. Without religion the common people might be left without a moral basis for their living and so dangerously anarchic. Moreover since, as a ruler, he admired strength, he had respect for the strict lifestyle of the Pharisees.

Some people said that Herod was actually influenced by the Pharisees and so that might have been another reason for his arrest of John. Other members too of the upper classes might have been glad that John was safely locked up. John was not one to spare the feelings of his hearers and when the Pharisees came to him he had greeted them: "Brood of vipers, who warned you to flee from the wrath to come? Therefore bear fruits worthy of repentance ..."

Of course the common people were delighted to hear the Pharisees so castigated and brought down to size. Disaffection, however, was not something the authorities viewed with content. Any unrest could lead to trouble, and trouble, any trouble, led to interference with the collection of taxes. That, of course, caused repercussions in Rome and the Senate. Disturbing breezes in the Senate caused cold gales in the corridors of power in the provinces.

Among those common people were plenty of Zealots with daggers hidden under their clothes, eager for an opportunity to strike at those who were the oppressors. As far as the Zealots were concerned the definition of an

לַחְבֹּשׁ לַנִשְׁבָּרֵי־לֵב זָרָא לִשְׁבוּיִם דְּרוֹר וְלַאֲסוּרִים־פְּקַח־קוֹחַ:

oppressor, or a collaborator, was a wide one: tax collector, Pharisee, priest; indeed anyone doing business with Romans or with those who supported Roman rule. That included Herodian rule or indeed any sort of rule except that of some imagined Davidic state long lost in the mists of time. And some people envied Herod his position.

Sometimes he regretted it, yet ambition drove him on and all day he plotted and schemed and all night he lay uneasily on his bed. From time to time he retired to one of his palaces to enjoy the luxuries and the fruits of his princely state; but even here he could not get what he wanted, and if he appeared to get what he wanted he became discontented with it. Only Herodias seemed to be worth it all even though her acquisition might threaten everything, making him realise how precarious his position was. And making him that much more desperate, too, to retain it.

Poor unloved Herod, strutting and posturing in his palaces. Poor weak, anxious Herod, full of doubts and uncertainties, frantic because whatever he did made the situation even more uncertain and precarious. Desperate, angry Herod, hoping that with John under lock and key and with Herodias sharing his luxurious exile in Machaerus he might buy a few days of peace. All he found was the certainty that he was but a man, a weak, confused, frightened man; a desperate man on a downward spiral of self-destruction and -delusion.

As tetrarch he was a man of power and yet this woman Herodias held him captive. He would never be sure of her love and devotion though later she was to accompany him in his exile. She held him in silken bonds of lust, of frustrated love and of fear of losing her. As a ruler he had control over the lives of his subjects and over such as John who now was confined within the few

131

לָחֲבֹשׁ לְנִשְׁבְּרֵי־לֵב זְרֹא לִשְׁבֻיִם דְּרֹור וְלַאֲסוּרֵים־ פְּקַח־קֹוֹחַ ׃

feet each way of one of the cells beneath, cut from the solid rock of the mountain. Yet John still had more control than he, the tetrarch, had, for John had control over himself and was faithful to his ideals. John had never sold his morals for that which kings think of as power. John had never prostituted his beliefs in compromising with the Romans or with the Jews. John was a man of integrity and honour and even Herod knew the Jewish proverb, though he wished he did not: "He that has no rule over his own spirit is like a city that is broken down, and without walls." John ruled his own spirit and Herod knew he did not have even a fraction of that strength of character.

Secretly he envied John with an envy bordering on respect. "He that rules his spirit is better than he that takes a strong city." Caesar had taken strong cities, so had Herod's father, yet John was better than them all. Antipas had strong cities aplenty yet the cities of his mind and spirit, of his emotions and his will, were lost and broken, given to the fierce gales blowing and tearing his unchained libido and ambition. Herod had everything, yet had nothing. John had nothing yet had everything. He had that strength that had taken control over his own soul and his own mind. John had everything, for he had taken on a superhuman task and had carried it out and completed it to the bitter end, even to the dungeon, and had kept his integrity intact.

"It is not lawful for you to have your brother's wife!" The Baptist's words still rang in his brain, and John had also mentioned some of Herod's other crimes against humanity in general and against his own people in particular. This had all served to work Herod up into a veritable lather of frustration, anger and vindictiveness. Now John was in a dungeon and he was still a thorn in

לְהַבְּשׁ לְנִשְׁבָּרֵי-לֵב רָא לַשְׁבֻוֹיִם לְשָׁבֻוּיִם דְּרוֹר וְלַאֲסוּרִים- פְּקַח-קוֹחַ:

the flesh, for whenever he was with Herodias he could not enjoy her. The presence of the man of truth under his feet, as it were, turned all his pleasure to ashes. John's presence was felt everywhere. Confined in about eight feet by eight feet he might be but there was nowhere that Herod could escape his reproachful words, his scornful looks, and his angry denunciations.

Was John the great prophet like Moses and promised by him? If he were then surely God would not allow him to be imprisoned. But then, that argument held little water, for few other of the prophets had escaped imprisonment or worse.

For ten months John languished in the solid rock of Machaerus, deep down beneath the luxuries of Herod's court. Overhead there was the tramp of the soldiers going about their many duties. Higher still the revelry of Herod's inner circle of friends, sycophants and hangers-on, the senior officers of the garrison and the officials of the court. For Herod was efficient and kept his finger on the pulse of all that went on in his kingdom. Indeed it was this efficiency and this watchfulness which brought to his notice another cloud which seemed to be gathering on the horizon of his happiness.

There was news of another prophet. Would there be no end to it? Maybe God, if there was a God, was punishing him for his treatment of John and sending another John to torment him. Maybe not; he would keep watch. This one, like John, was Galilean; like John also of comparatively lowly birth, an artisan, unschooled and ignorant, though wise, quick-tongued and shrewd. Oh, yes! Herod would watch.

Herod did not consider himself a cruel or despotic man. Circumstances often drove one to extreme measures, and to preserve his kingdom he had often to resort

7 Prison and Suffering

לַחְבֹּשׁ לְנִשְׁבְּרֵי־לֵב זְרָא לִשְׁבוּיִם דְּרוֹר וְלַאֲסוּרִים־ פְּקַח־קוֹחַ׃

to torture, to prolonged imprisonment, and even, if he could get away with it, to executions.

He just wished he had the free hand his father had enjoyed. To keep up the appearance of liberality he allowed John to have his friends to visit him. Strictly limited and under control, of course, but then one might learn things from conversations with visitors and there were ears in the dungeons of Machaerus which often heard things of value to Herod. Information was the difference between a well-run kingdom and one that teetered on the brink of anarchy.

A king always had to know beforehand if there were plots, discontent or the early rumblings of these things like distant thunder heralding a coming storm. If the storms were to be averted the king had to know who, what, where and when. So John's disciples, in their twos and threes, were allowed to visit him, while Herod's soldiers listened to the conversations and reported anything of significance back to Herod.

Of the many snippets of information they reported was that John was concerned about another prophet. A prophet in Galilee but who moved freely through Philip's domains, in Samaria, which Jews avoided if they could, and in Judea and Jerusalem. They reported that the prophet, one Yeshua, had fed five thousand in the deserts east of the lake of Galilee with a few small loaves and some fishes. Herod puzzled over this and dismissed it as the incredulous imaginations of the peasants who were all too liable to see the miraculous lurking behind every bush and shrub.

On the other hand, Herod himself longed to see a miracle done, as the prophets of old were alleged to have done miracles. Had not Elijah and Elisha, his successor, both brought down fire from heaven and had not even

לְהָבֵשׁ לְנִשְׁבְּרֵי-לֵב ‪:‬רָא לַשְּׁבוּיִם דְּרוֹר וְלַאֲסוּרִים-פְּקַח-קוֹחַ‪:‬

some of the rabbis brought healing to the sick through their prayers? Herod's superstitious mind stored all these things away and hoped one day that some prophet would do some real miracles so that Herod might perhaps persuade him to favour the Herodian cause. A few miracles might well serve to influence the balance of power in Palestine and Syria, even perhaps further afield. Ambition once fired has no limits it might not consume.

Feeding the crowds would serve very well in the Herodian cause. Though the Herods had managed quite well without popularity, it might yet serve them to have the might of popular support on their side. And then! What if armies could be fed miraculously? Imagination ran riot and ambition stretched further afield, though a defeat for his erstwhile father-in-law, Aretas, might be a pleasant thing to savour. On the other hand it would require some quite powerful miracles to challenge the legions of Rome. A Galilean peasant, however much of a prophet he might be, did not seem quite up to that. Not yet anyway. Herod was also a realist, but it was nice to imagine.

In the meanwhile realism had to prevail and common sense had to take precedence over ambition. It would be in his favour both with Rome and with the Jews and the common people if he were seen to be generous to John. The Romans were as bad as the Jews for doing things according to the law and being seen to do so. Also, of course, his guards could keep the information coming. He also needed facts, not what seemed to him superstitious fancies and tales that had grown with the telling.

When John had stated: "He must increase, I must decrease," he had made a sublime declaration and shown the extreme worth of his devotion; the true value of his

135

לְחָבֹשׁ לְנִשְׁבְּרֵי־לֵב זְרָא לִשְׁבוּיִם דְּרוֹר וְלַאֲסוּרִים־ פְּקַח־קוֹחַ׃

discharge of the task of being a forerunner for Messiah. Now the statement was being tested to the limit in the hot and foetid air of the cell carved out of the rock below the level of the flat top of the mountain. Even John's rock-hard constitution was being taxed to its limit and the psychological pressure was added to, though without intention, by the news brought by his visitors. Yeshua, to whom he had borne witness, was eating with tax collectors and sinners. He went from place to place and, if his disciples' accounts were correct, seemed to be enjoying favour with everyone. They hardly mentioned the growing hostility of the Pharisees and how they were dangerously finding common interest with the Sadducees against Yeshua.

While John sweated it out, often chained to the wall with little exercise and a very sparse diet, Yeshua was pursuing a rather different sort of path from the one he had followed. Or so it seemed.

Ten months in a dungeon under a fortress designed by Herod the Great is no picnic. Machaerus might have been a holiday camp for Herod and his chief ministers and military officers. It was nothing of the sort for the prisoners who sweated and dreamed out their despair day after tedious painful day. If a regime were calculated to break a man's spirit, this was it. Yet, for all that John did not break.

He must have come near to breaking, very near; but he retained his faith and never quite gave way to the despair which must have cruelly afflicted his tortured soul day after day after day. He had doubts. They scurried to and fro about the darker passages of his soul and led to fears and even darker thoughts: that all had been in vain. The jibes and taunts of some of the soldiers would have bounced off the tough skin of the mind of

לְהִבֵּשׁ לְנִשְׁבְּרֵי־לֵב זְּרָא לִשְׁבֻּיִם דְּרֹור וְלָאֲסוּרִים־פְּקַח־קֹוחַ:

the abstemious man of the desert who had come in the spirit and power of Elijah. To the unhappy man in the cell already worn down by doubts they were an added torture. They were knives which pierced the armour of his faith and let in the demonic nauseous insects questioning his mission and mocking the years spent in self-denial in the deserts.

Had it all been for nothing? Had it all been a waste? They taunted him. "That Yeshua, he's having a good old time," said one guard who had overheard stories about his teaching in Capernaum.

"He mixes with Roman Centurions and with tax collectors," said another and added: "That Yeshua, he's a traitor; thought 'e was a mate of yours?"

At first John had smiled to himself, but after months he began to wonder, and with wondering came the horrible doubts. They nagged at and tormented his brain until it seemed to be on fire with accusing pointing fingers of fear. Until it seemed to be eaten up with voracious worms of doubt which led on to worse fears and near-despair.

At last, when two of his faithful friends and disciples were with him in the cell, he charged them to investigate properly and, if possible, to ask Yeshua Himself whether He really was the Coming One, the Messiah. They were to wait for an opportunity and to ask bluntly: "Are You the Coming One, or do we look for another?"

The disciples went away troubled and not a little fearful, for they too now began to doubt and wondered about their own position and beliefs. It seemed as if things were caving in and coming all to nothing.

When at last they found the Teacher, He was not feasting with tax collectors or with other wrongdoers. Nor was He in the homes of Pharisees and those of the

לְחָבֹשׁ לְנִשְׁבְּרֵי־לֵב זְרָא לִשְׁבֻיִם דְּרוֹר וְלַאֲסוּרִים־ פְּקַח־קוֹחַ׃

rich, as some had reported Him to be. John had not turned away such people but neither had he welcomed them. Where he could, he had held himself aloof and had preferred addressing the common people.

There were mixed feelings among the followers of John. With some there was a strong puritanical and ascetic streak in their character. These were of the opinion that Yeshua from Nazareth ought to have been praying and fasting as soon as John was arrested, and should have kept this up until he was released. They did not understand the honour being bestowed upon the Messiah's forerunner that he should seal his ministry with his blood and go into the presence of the angels to a martyr's reward, as had many of his predecessors, the prophets.

It was a noisy but anxious crowd that surrounded Him. While the Tetrarch was tortured by doubts in the palace and fortress 3,800 feet above the level of the Dead Sea, the Teacher, Yeshua from Nazareth, had restored a widow's son to life, restoring him to his distraught and sorrowing mother, to her surprise and her everlasting joy. Surrounding Him were sick folk of all kinds. They had come for help in their afflictions. Others had come for answers to the questions that puzzled them about life, injustice and what they ought to do. Some were merely curious and, a few, were suspicious, thinking they had heard it all before. The Baptist's disciples took their places near Him and announced themselves as John's messengers. "John Baptist sent us to You, saying, 'Are You the One that should come? Or do we look for another?' "

He gave them no direct answer. He merely smiled and gestured to them to join in with them among His disciples. His manner was warm and welcoming though the smile had been one of understanding, of sympathy and, somehow, not a little sadness.

It was like the old days with John. People were crowding round and there were questions and answers

לְהֵבֵשׁ לְנִשְׁבְּרֵי־לֵב קְרָא לִשְׁבוּיִם דְּרוֹר וְלַאֲסוּרִים־פְּקַח־קֹוֹחַ׃

flying back and forth. From time to time, when the arguing and the questioning died down, sick folk came forward and were healed. Sometimes they came in ones and twos, but as the day wore on they came in increasing numbers. Then, as afternoon crept into evening, the sun having travelled in its great arc across the sky and nearing the end of its daily journey, the stream of lame, blind, lepers, deaf folk or those afflicted with demons and with nameless terrors, dwindled and the folk who had drunk in his words since the morning began to pack up and go home.

At times during the day He had stood and told stories to illustrate points He wished to make concerning questions He had been asked. At other times He had sat and received those who came to Him or He walked among them where the blind held onto the arms of their relatives and the paralysed lay on mats on which they had been carried. Lepers had held out imploring hands to Him and virtue with kindness had flowed out from Him to heal them all.

They were going home, though with many a backward glance at the One who had been the source of so much happiness and joy. Some laughed and cried, for wonderful things had happened to them or they had seen those wonderful things happening to their friends and their loved ones. There were longing and imploring looks as if, had they been able, they would have wanted to take Him with them. Lepers in particular gazed at Him with adoration and worship then down at their limbs and at their hands and feet where the fingers and toes had been restored and the ulcers and sores had healed.

At last, as dusk was closing in, he beckoned the two disciples of John and with a weary smile spoke to them.

"Go your way," He said, "tell John what things you have seen and heard; how the blind see, lame walk, lepers are cleansed and the deaf hear; the dead are raised up and the poor have the gospel preached to them. And

לַחֲבֹשׁ לְנִשְׁבְּרֵי־לֵב זְרָא לִשְׁבוּיִם דְּרֹור וְלַאֲסוּרִים־ פְּקַח־קָוֹחֽ׃

blessed is he who is not offended because of Me."

They got up without a word, wonder writ large in their eyes and also with many a backward glance, they made their way to the nearest village to find lodging for the night. The following days would find them on the long walk back across Jordan and south to the loneliness of the prison on the other side of the Dead Sea.

Men said later that the words they had been given were in the nature of a rebuke to John, reproaching him for his unbelief. Others who tell the story speak of kind compassion, of gentle support for a faithful follower suffering extreme persecution for his loyalty and of a few words which, in the most effective way, lifted the misty darkness of this world. Words which were to show John a glorious vision of the next, of the bliss of the age to come and of the peace and justice of Messiah's kingdom which he himself had been privileged to announce. They were words which were to sustain him in the dark hours yet to come when he would face the most bitter penalty for his uncompromising stand for truth and for justice and for God.

As the two disciples left with a fresh spring in their step, the Teacher stood and beckoned to Himself those who still lingered beneath the setting sun. They crowded round Him as he lifted up his powerful voice to deliver an oration. It was a speech for John. It was a funeral oration such as is given at the last rites of some great hero. It was a tribute to faithfulness to the very end and to an honest, tough and devoted follower and warrior for the Kingdom of God.

"What did you go out into the wilderness to see? A reed shaken by the wind? But what did you go out to see? A man clothed in effeminate garments? Indeed, those who wear soft clothing are in kings' courts. But what did you go out to see? A prophet? Yes! I say to you, and much more than a prophet.

"This is he, of whom it is written: 'Behold, I send My

לְהַבֵּשׁ לְנִשְׁבְּרֵי־לֵב זְרָא לִשְׁבוּיִם דְּרוֹר וְלַאֲסוּרִים־ פְּקַח־קוֹחַ׃

messenger before Thy face, which shall prepare Thy way before Thee.' Assuredly I say to you, among those born of women there is not a greater prophet than John the Baptist; but he who is least in the Kingdom of God is greater than he."

The remaining people, of whom there were still many, gathered together their things, collected playing or straying children, and, with reluctant steps as if willing the sun not to go down and regretting having to leave this sacred ground, made their way homewards.

The once blind stepped out rejoicing in the new confidence given them by the gift of sight. All experienced a new happiness in their hearts and a new joy in their loved ones. Whatever this new kingdom of God was, it was good, it was wholesome and it was joyful. It was serious too and there was a feeling of challenge, for all knew that John languished in Herod's prison and all suspected that he would not come out alive. Little did they yet appreciate that the road on which they had embarked might be one of suffering for them too; but the most astute among them realised it. They did not realise yet, however, the price which the One central to all this had yet to pay in order to set up His kingdom in the hearts and minds of men and women and eventually upon the earth itself.

(The Biblical quotations can be found in Luke's Gospel, chapter 7.)

8

The Living Dead

If it was God who allowed this to happen to him then why did He allow it to happen? Why did it not happen to some really bad persons? Why not to the tax collectors who could turn out a man's goods all over the road, then, when he protested, threaten him with arrest by the hated Romans and, to add insult to injury would hike up his assessment even more? They grew fat on the spoils of the poor. Always it was the poor upon whom the burden of taxation fell. Not on the rich senators and knights who formed the powerful joint stock companies in Rome who farmed the taxes. Not on the tax farmers in the locality who bid against one another in order to get rich contracts that were a sure way to wealth and a life of ease. Certainly not to their agents who actually collected the money from travellers from one region to another; or from those who took their goods, on the backs of a couple of donkeys, to market hoping that the weather stayed fine, and that people were in a buying mood.

The tax collectors themselves were treated with hatred and contempt. In particular by those who, like his uncle, saw themselves as leaders of the community and as examples of religious observance and of patriotic zeal. The tax gatherers soon got accustomed to the attitudes of their fellows and grew a thick skin against the jibes and the curses. More dangerous were the sikarii, bandits

לְחַבֵּשׁ לְנִשְׁבָּרֵי־לֵב זְרָא לִשְׁבֻּיִם דְּרֹוֹר וְלַאֲסוּרִים־ פְּקַח־קֹוֹחַ:

armed with daggers, who saw themselves in the tradition of the Maccabees fighting for Israel's independence. Freedom fighters they pretended to be but the reality was in another word: bandit, for that was what they were, and all they really succeeded in doing was making life harder for the common people. The rich man could afford a couple of muscle men as protection. A poor peasant could hardly do that; he just prayed that the robbers did not see him or were busy with other fish to fry.

Everything was taxed: the fisherman's catch, the farmer's field and the crop when he had reaped it. They would tax the rain if they could, but not even the Romans could work out a way to tax the rain or the air people breathed, or they would have done so.

Then there were the Romans themselves; proud, arrogant men so sure of themselves, as those by nature born to rule the world. All that proud military violence, yet they went in fear of the displeasure of their Imperator, grim Tiberius, in one of his many villas on Capri, surrounded by his praetorian guard, himself in fear of death or of revolution. On second thoughts it seemed that they had made for themselves their own punishments and they would certainly suffer in their Hades after they were dead. Caesar might bestride the world, yet the common man went in fear of bandits and tax collectors and was in awe of the rich and the influential.

Caesar could not protect the ordinary people fully, nor could he stop the rapacity of tax collectors, nor the random violence of bandits, whatever they called themselves. Did Caesar matter, he wondered; who really did control the world?

Everywhere there was fear and uncertainty; everywhere men extracted what little happiness they

לַחֲבֹשׁ לְנִשְׁבְּרֵי־לֵב זְרָא לִשְׁבוּיִם דְּרוֹר וְלַאֲסוּרִים־ פְּקַח־קוֹחַ:

could from this life and then went ... where? He no longer
knew. He was not so sure he even cared. What had he
done to deserve this living death? He had been a poor
man. All he had asked from life was to live with his two
donkeys, his few goats and chickens. To sell his produce
gained from the two small fields his family owned and to
find a wife and to bring up a family. If he could hide
some of his profits from the tax men then that had been
a bonus giving him much satisfaction.

His uncle was a big, strong man who prided himself
on his religious and social correctness. He was one of the
elders of the village, head of the family and an official of
the synagogue. True, it was only a small village and only
a small synagogue, but that made his uncle a big fish in a
small pond. All this was to his uncle's immense
satisfaction. Yet in spite of the bitterness he could not
blame his uncle entirely. He was not a bad man, just
normal, with all the normal prejudices and all the normal
assumptions. He believed many of these to be false, but
then he would; he was an outcast, and bitterly resented it,
so he would find fault with the present order of things.
As head of the family his uncle would have the say to
whom the fields and the little grove of olive trees he had
tended so passionately, would revert now that he was "as
one dead."

His speculation about the probable fate of the family
property tailed off with a sort of shrug of the mental
shoulders. The bitterness came back as he pictured his
uncle on the day the leprosy had been confirmed. There
had been shame in his uncle's demeanour. Not shame
for his self-righteousness, nor for his hard-heartedness,
but shame that the family name had been besmirched by
having a leper among them. It was an affront to his
uncle's respectability that he should have a nephew who

לְהַבֵּשׁ לְנִשְׁבְּרֵי־לֵב זְרָא לִשְׁבֻּיִם דְּרוֹר וְלַאֲסוּרִים־ פְּקַח־קוֹחַ׃

was accursed.

He heard the words as clearly as he had heard them that day five years ago: "No death without sin, no pain without transgression." He had continued with a sickening condescension: "Of course you may visit the synagogue on Shavat, but you will have to stay in the room set apart for lepers. You must be first in and last to leave." Then he had added, after a moment's thought, "It may do you good to hear the reading of the Torah, and the Prophets. Maybe it will please God to forgive you."

There was not much hope of the latter. There were stories about rabbis, noted for their holiness, who had prayed for the miraculous cleansing of lepers and who, apparently had been heard. As far as he was concerned that was all they were, stories, and not very good ones at that. There was one story, however, that had the ring of truth and yet it was a strange one. Why had God allowed the healing of a goy, a gentile Syrian and a pillager of Israel? He thought for a moment, its very strangeness gave it the ring of Divine certainty.

"Naaman," the account went, was "captain of the host of the King of Syria and a great man before his master ... " Then he thought of the "little maid." She had said to her mistress, Naaman's wife, "Would that my lord were before the prophet that is in Samaria."

Somehow the word of a little girl, the lowest slave of the wife of the great general of the King of Syria's armies, came to the exalted man's ears, and from him to the king. It was all too strange and too improbable not to be true. He thought how possibly the last sight of her home, as she was led away captive, was her house burning and the mutilated bodies of her family abandoned for the dogs to eat in the dust of the road. He shook his head. This little Hebrew slave girl was more noble than any of them.

לְהָבֵשׁ לְנִשְׁבְּרֵי־לֵב נְרָא לִשְׁבוּיִם דְּרוֹר וְלַאֲסוּרִים־ פְּקַח־קוֹחַ :

How could she seek the well-being of such enemies?
And yet she had. Even the words, "before his master,"
that was the king; and then, "before the prophet." It was
as if the Scripture put the prophet living quietly in
Samaria on a par with the mighty monarch. It seemed he
was.

Neither king could cure leprosy, yet the prophet had.
Or had he? In reality he had merely told the general what
to do. It must have seemed like a fruitless journey, a wild
goose chase. First to the King of Israel, who throws a
tantrum and tears his clothes, arguing that the King of
Syria was trying to make a diplomatic incident so he
could have an excuse for going to war.

Then he gets sent to a house, not a very imposing
house by all accounts, in the suburbs, and the prophet
did not even open the door to him. He treated him like a
beggar. But then Naaman was a beggar; like himself he
was a leper. Nor was the instruction to "go and wash in
the Jordan" so very impressive. He puzzled for a moment.
As he thought about the story there appeared far more to
it than one would have supposed. Everything seemed to
be stood upon its head. The conqueror becomes a
suppliant, the kings with all their power are powerless;
the weak, the downtrodden whose lives are given them at
the whim of a spoiled noble lady have the deepest insight
into the reality of things and the greatest wisdom. Then,
as the story unfolded, and Naaman is about to go off in a
huff, a couple of his slaves, "came near and said, 'My
father, if the prophet had bid thee do some great thing,
wouldest thou not have done it? Much rather then, when
he says to thee, wash and be clean.' "

It seemed all to be about slaves knowing and slaves
doing what the men of power could not do. Perhaps
there might be hope for him, he thought; but then,

לַהֲבֹשׁ לְנִשְׁבְּרֵי־לֵב ָרָא לִשְׁבוּיִם דְּרוֹר וְלַאֲסוּרִים־ פְּקַח־קוֹחַ :

probably not!

He had attended the synagogue a few times but it had been a bitter experience. It was the pity in the looks of those who had once been his neighbours and friends that drove him away finally and for good. Some people treated him with horror and shrank away from him, but most were used to seeing the odd leper begging by the roadside. Now he was one of those despised and rejected people who lived out a half-life in the dust and the dirt, creeping away into holes and clefts of the rock to sleep and sitting begging by day.

He went about with his hair in disarray and, like a person in mourning, with the bottom half of his face hidden in a fold of his garment. He was not in mourning for a loved one but for himself. It was his own death which his manner and the arrangement of his clothing proclaimed. Not to mention the more distressing signs of leprosy which were all too obvious on his wasted body.

He was supposed to be repentant too, as if he had committed some enormous sin. The rabbis all agreed that leprosy was because you had sinned. Had not his uncle quoted the received teaching among those who claimed to have studied the Law? He grimaced again. His own case had led him to doubt everything and it had also taught him to treat everything with cynicism. Find out where and how a man is advantaged and you will see the motive for his opinions, he thought to himself. He had long ago worked that one out. It was true in the case of his uncle who did no real thinking of his own; he did not study for himself but listened carefully to what the rabbis had to say and then paraded the majority opinions as if they were his own.

Naaman had been a sinner, an enemy of Israel and of God. It seemed right and proper that he should be

לַחֲבֹשׁ לְנִשְׁבְּרֵי־לֵב זָרָא לִשְׁבֻיִם דְּרֹור וְלַאֲסוּרִים־ פְּקַח־קֹוחַ׃

leprous. And again came the question: why me?

One young rabbi, standing out of reach, out of harm's way, so as not to risk defilement, had argued with him and, like one of Job's three friends, had tried to make him see that his affliction was the result of sin.

"Leprosy," he had argued, "is a father of uncleanness." It was caused, he explained patronisingly, as if to a child, by sins of the mouth. He had known that. Had he not, in his youth, also studied under the rabbis and had even travelled south to Jerusalem to sit at the feet of the great teachers? Not a lot of good did it do him, he thought. He still got leprosy, for all his attempts at learning.

Paradoxically enough he had learned more and grown wiser through his own meditating on matters and seeking out conclusions for himself. As for the young and earnest rabbi, well, he supposed he was doing his best, according to how he saw that best. That was all anyone ever did and it was not a very good best. Fat chance of him being a rabbi now. Even if he were to be rid of his leprosy then he was not at all sure he wanted that any more. He had no certain conclusions, no sure answers any more. One day he might, he mused, but then he would be dead.

He wondered if he had been cursed by someone. The idea was ridiculous and he dismissed it angrily. It was a superstitious idea, the sort of idea which might fix itself in the minds of gentiles or some of the more ignorant of women. Even the proud Romans wore amulets and charms against the evil eye. Some Romans of the nobler sort pretended not to be superstitious; they even pretended atheism but he knew that even they cast hurried, nervous glances over their shoulders, and paid their dues before their household gods and at the temples. No nation was free from superstition. Only the

לְהַבֵּשׁ לְנִשְׁבְּרֵי־לֵב ;רָא לִשְׁבוּיִם דְּרוֹר וְלַאֲסוּרִים־ פְּקַח־קוֹחַ:

Jews were not afraid, because they feared Jehovah with a noble fear. They could look anyone in the face knowing that the man who "feared the Lord," feared nothing else.

That brought him back to the thought of Messiah. One day He would make Israel the head and not the tail. One day, perhaps; one day? Perhaps! Perhaps never!

He shook his head in a silent dialogue with himself. Maybe God just did not like him. But no sooner had his mind framed the thought than he knew it was unworthy and foolish. But if he dismissed it then what was there? A God who might, or who might not, make Israel great again as she had been in the days of David and Solomon. Who might or who might not; probably not! – since David and Solomon had all been a very long time ago. And even the rabbis could not agree on the nature of Messiah, who He was, or what He was.

Nothing made any sense any more, nothing fitted. It was like one of those Roman tessellated floors in one of their villas which an earthquake had thrown up and had scattered the bits that made it, so all you had were lots of little squares of coloured pottery and no key as to how they fitted together.

In the meanwhile he could go on walking, from one begging place to another, dragging out a tortured, dull existence with one day very much like the last. If he killed himself there would still be nothing. Perhaps all life was really death. But to kill oneself, that was unthinkable; it was the ultimate shame and would end in that dark place under the earth, sheol – an even darker, duller, more painfully tedious, tormented existence than that lived upon the earth. He shuddered; there had to be something better than this. But what?

Maybe there was no God at all. No Jehovah who had led the children of Israel out of bondage. No Almighty

לַחֲבֹשׁ לְנִשְׁבְּרֵי־לֵב זְרָא לִשְׁבֻוּיִם דְּרוֹר וְלַאֲסוּרִים־ פְּקַח־קוֹחַ׃

who had defeated the hosts of Egypt and brought
Jericho's walls tumbling down. No burning bush, no
Law, no Messianic hope, and Israel was just a pretence, its
imagined uniqueness and its vaunted special calling a
delusion of disordered minds. No! That could not be,
that truly was the road to madness; and he was not mad,
not yet. He was not yet ready for mental, as well as
physical destruction.

It was then that he remembered that the psalmist had
said: "But as for me, my feet were almost gone; my steps
had well nigh slipped. For I was envious at the foolish,
when I saw the prosperity of the wicked."

"Yes," he thought, "it is the wicked who prosper. The
Romans, the Herods, the rich priests, and the Pharisees."

Then there were the tax collectors who, like
loathsome parasites fixed themselves on the bodies of
the poor and, vampire-like, sucked their life from them.
There were the successful traders, the merchants who
dealt in the luxury goods only the rich and the Romans
could afford, who encouraged luxuriant decadence.
These were the wicked who prospered in the world. And
if these prospered, then what sort of a world was it?
Whose world was it? Another insoluble problem faced
him and he did not think he would ever be able to find
an answer. Not in this life anyway, and afterwards it
would be too late.

The Torah said that because God cared about the
poor, the fatherless and the widow, then His people
should do so too. But all around him he saw poverty,
suffering and misery. He saw violence, cruelty and
exploitation. Something had gone seriously wrong. Of
that he was sure. Even more to the point, did God care
about the leper? It seemed as if He did not. What else
was there but despair?

לְהָבֵשׁ לְנִשְׁבָּרֵי־לֵב זָ֫רָא לִשְׁבֹּיִם֙ דְּרֹור וְלַאֲסוּרִים־ פְּקַח־קֹֽוחַ׃

The psalmist had gone on to say words which every leper and every poor oppressed man or woman could say with perfect truthfulness: "Truly I cleansed my heart in vain, and washed my hands in innocency. For all day long have I been plagued, and chastened every morning ... When I thought to know this it was too painful for me. Until I went into the sanctuary of God. Then understood I their end."

Maybe the psalmist had understood their end, but he did not. He grimaced cynically at the seeming message of these last two stanzas. A fat lot of good it would be to try to get into the holy place in the Temple. Even if he were not a leper, they would still have him stoned for blasphemy for going where only the high priest was allowed to go and that only on one day in the year, the Day of Atonement, the "Yom Kippur."

But then he recollected the words of Solomon at the dedication of the Temple: "But will God in very deed dwell with men on earth? Behold, heaven and the heaven of heavens cannot contain Thee; how much less this house which I have built."

He smiled a rueful smile at the even more improbable idea of men going up to heaven into the third heaven where the throne of God was situated. He shook his head and muttered, "impossible!" so that a couple of passing women whispered to each other furtively and shook their heads, giggling.

"Surely though, God is everywhere?" The thought seemed to bring a little light. So everywhere must be the sanctuary of God. Maybe, but it was not much of a sanctuary if God's ears were continually assailed by the noise of swearing and fighting and of the clash of armies.

All the various bits of knowledge he had either learned from his reading, from his schooling, or from his

לִהֲבֹשׁ לְנִשְׁבְּרֵי־לֵב זָרָא לִשְׁבֻיִם דְּרֹור וְלַאֲסֹורִים־ פְּקַח־קֹוחַ׃

time with the rabbis, and which he had meditated on so
often over the years, began to swirl about in a confusing
jumble in his head. As they did so, he found some of
them began to fall into place and to fit in with other,
hitherto isolated, bits of knowledge.

Did not the rabbis say that Messiah was "the Leprous
One"? How could that be? Yet Isaiah spoke of a suffering
Messiah. He was a Messiah who was "despised and
rejected of men, a man of sorrows and acquainted with
grief." He was a Messiah who was wounded, bruised and
chastised. In another of the psalms it spoke of a Messiah
who was forsaken by God. One who seemed to be alone
in an extremity of suffering. If this was Messiah then He
was to go through far more than he had yet gone
through. Far, far more; far, far worse.

A Messiah who was like he was. A Messiah who knew
about leprosy, who experienced suffering and who was
treated with extreme violence. That would indeed be a
man to follow. But as soon as the thought had been
framed he saw that it too was ridiculous. Even if Messiah
did want him for a follower, and he did not know that He
did, what use was a Messiah like that? If He was leprous,
then how could He help the leper? If Messiah was
exposed to violence and suffering then how could He
stop the violence and the suffering?

The words of Daniel slowly formed themselves in his
mind: "To finish the transgression, and to make an end of
sins, and to make reconciliation for iniquity, and to bring
in everlasting righteousness ... "

It was all too complicated to understand. One day,
the rabbis insisted, Messiah would make everything clear
and all would be fulfilled. He had a horrible feeling that
it would be too late for him by the time that happened. If
the rabbis did not really know then how could a poor

לְהָבֵשׁ לְנִשְׁבָּרֵי־לֵב זָרָא לַשְּׁבוּיֵם דְּרוֹר וְלַאֲסוּרִים־ פְּקַח־קוֹחַ׃

semi-ignorant peasant, who was now an outcast with leprosy, ever hope to understand?

The sky was lightening somewhat. He gathered up his few possessions and rolled them up in the threadbare blanket and then that in the tattered cloak, someone's cast off which some person, loath to throw it away, had donated to a leper. The cloak served to keep out some of the weather during the day, and, with the blanket, kept out some of the cold at night. If it was hot they could be spread as a covering from a branch to give him some shade. He would go down to the lake to wash his clothes, then he would wrap himself in the cloak while the rags which served him as clothing dried in the sun. With his bowl for food and a knife to cut it up and to serve as a weapon against predators, animal or human, he had all he needed.

He lived from day to day. Sometimes he went hungry; at other times he did well. The lakeside was a good place to beg, then afterwards he would go back and sit by a road leading to Capernaum where people would be returning from the fields, some with bags of grain or vegetables for the evening meal. These would often donate a handful or two of their produce, or if not burdened, they might spare a small copper coin.

He hated begging, but he had to beg. It was a matter of survival. He had to eat and he tried to keep himself clean, though this got increasingly difficult with the progress of the disease. Some people, moved by the injunctions in the Law to care for the poor and the fatherless, brought gifts of food. He wondered if they did this out of genuine compassion, or whether it was done to show God how well they obeyed His laws. At least the donors were Jews; he did not have to accept gifts from idolatrous Romans, Greeks or Syrians, though he would

לְהַבֵשׁ לְנִשְׁבָּרֵי־לֵב זָרָא לִשְׁבוּיִם דְּרוֹר וְלַאֲסוּרִים־ פְּקַח־קוֹחַ׃

have taken these had they been offered.

His thoughts went back to Naaman, a Syrian. Then to the little Hebrew slave girl, serving a hated Syrian woman and yet not hating her, caring enough to wish for the health of her husband. The King, Naaman's master, had sent him to the King of Israel. That just showed how mixed up people got. No king, not even Caesar, could cure anyone of leprosy. Only God could do that and the little girl had expressly told her mistress that the man of God would cure him. The King of Israel had flown into a temper thinking that this was simply to create a diplomatic incident as an excuse to start a war.

Elisha, the man of God, had not greeted the king with any of this, "O King live for ever," nonsense. No! He had simply, in effect, demanded, "Do you think there is no God in Israel? Send Naaman to me." Then what had he done when the great Syrian general had come to his door? He had not even bothered to come out to him but had simply sent a messenger to tell the Syrian to bathe in the Jordan. No fuss, no shouting and arm waving like the gentile priests in their idolatrous ceremonies, just, "go and bathe."

That was all a long time ago. Even if it was only a story it raised the question as to who was the most powerful. Clearly it was Israel's God and He seemed to have worked through Elisha, the Man of God, whose name meant, 'My God is salvation', and who was clearly not impressed by human pretensions of power, but who treated kings and generals of armies with almost cavalier and off-hand patronising discourtesy. In which case he had humbled himself even to recognise their presence let alone answer their request. Again the complications multiplied, and yet, somehow in his soul there was a glimmer of hope.

לְחָבֵשׁ לְנִשְׁבְּרֵי-לֵב ׀ רָא לִשְׁבוּיִם דְּרוֹר וְלַאֲסוּרִים- פְּקַח-קוֹחַ׃

Crouched inconspicuously against a wall, in the shade of a fig tree, drying his clothes and watching the fishermen landing their catches a hundred yards or so away at the jetty, he overheard snatches of conversation.

"You Galileans don't know the Law; has any good thing ever come out of Nazareth?"

Clearly the other person in the conversation had expressed a negative, possibly by a shake of the head, for the speaker, obviously a visitor who viewed Galileans as uncouth, uneducated country bumpkins, went on: "So why then do you think that anything good comes out of Nazareth now?"

This time the silent, unnoticed listener heard a reply, mumbled as if ashamed to concede to the reasoning of the other. "I suppose not," he said.

"Anyway," continued the other, "just look at his followers: fishermen, even a tax collector and certainly one very questionable character, a zealot – bandit more like." He had added the last vehemently as if to spit out with contempt. "Think about it," he went on, "have any of the lawyers or the scribes, have any of the priests, followed him?"

The reply was a similar one, once more in the negative, then the two moved away and their voices were lost in the chatter and repartee of the fishermen, most of whom seemed to have had a good day at the fishing.

Painfully he got up and gathered his things together once more. One or two people stared at him indignantly but most ignored him as if he was not there. He made his way slowly, carefully avoiding any crowds, even having to warn a throng of gossips with the detested word, "unclean," before he could move on.

The people were moving back to their homes and the sun was dipping down towards the western horizon. The

155

לְהַבֵּשׁ לְנִשְׁבְּרֵי־לֵב זְרָא לִשְׁבוּיִם דְּרֹור וְלַאֲסוּרִים־פְּקַח־קֹוחַ׃

heat still lingered but the rising air began to draw in cooler air from the sea and from the higher slopes of the mountains. He bent to retie the cord that held his sandal and had to shuffle quickly to the border of the road to avoid a chattering crowd of men and boys who were hurrying back to the city.

"Unclean!" At the dread word the men and boys scurried to the other side giving him angry looks as they did so. He longed for human contact. He hated begging. But he hated even more this having to announce himself as an object of horror, carrying defilement and death on his person. He wanted to hate these people who shrank away from him. But it was no use hating people. He knew he would have done the same had the roles been reversed and if he were hurrying home from the fields to his wife and family and his way were impeded by such an object of loathing and fear as he now was.

"Lepers," said one, "why can't they keep out of the way somewhere? They're not wanted."

Another answered more compassionately and with some understanding of the case. "It may not be their fault, it could just happen."

There then began a debate about what various rabbis had to say about what the Torah had to say about leprosy. He had heard it all before. He had decided to find a sleeping place somewhere near the city where he could spend the rest of the evening, before sunset, begging. Hopefully he could then continue the next day as men went out to the fields and as the women went to fetch water, make household purchases or to go gossiping with friends. He followed at a discreet distance the group who were still talking about the differing opinions of the teachers. He caught a word here and there, but then one phrase made him listen intently.

לְהַבָּשׁ לְנִשְׁבְּרֵי־לֵב זָרָא לִשְׁבֻיִים דְּרוֹר וְלַאֲסוּרִים פְּקַח־קוֹחַ:

"Do you reckon that Yeshua from Nazareth could heal a leper, make one clean? What do you think?"

The questioner was obviously one of the younger ones. One or two of the older men laughed.

"No one can cure leprosy," said one older man.

"What about Naaman and Elisha?" challenged another. The debate went on, interrupted with casual remarks about the road, the weather and the prospects for tomorrow's fishing. He heard the name Yeshua mentioned again and again.

As he neared the city he found some people coming out of it, almost as many as were trying to make their way in. Groups waited at the sides of the road, clustered under trees or sat waiting expectantly on the grass at the edge of fields. A lot of the people were dismissive but many told how this new teacher taught differently from the scribes of the Torah or the Pharisees. Some even said that he was, without a doubt, that prophet like Moses who the great leader had promised should come.

"He's coming!" a boy's voice cried excitedly. He craned his neck from his spot clinging to the rough stones of a wall. Along the road from the city a group of men were following another man. It was a man of average height, of average build; even of average looks.

He raised his clawed hand in hope, then quickly put it down again. He was yet too far away to be seen by the teacher, and it also occurred to him that the teacher would hardly have time for him. People had said that he had cast out a demon from a man in the synagogue, then that he had healed all manner of afflictions at the fisherman's house. But a leper? No! He did not think anyone would bother with a leper. The prophet Elisha had not even bothered to open the door to the great Syrian General Naaman but had merely sent a young

לְהָבִשׁ לְנִשְׁבְּרֵי־לֵב זָרָא לִשְׁבֻיִם דְּרוֹר וְלַאֲסוּרִים־ פְּקַח־קֽוֹחַ׃

man with a message to wash in the Jordan. If the prophet did not go to the trouble to even talk to such a man then the prophet of Nazareth would hardly give him the time of day.

His head dropped onto his chest, weary and despondent. Anyway, he thought to himself, there are lots of other sick, suffering and crippled. The teacher cannot heal all of them. Even if he did, where would it stop? No, he decided, suffering, disease and death have always been the main features of this world. Even Herod, even Caesar, get toothache, and worse if the accounts were true. Why bother to hope to avoid the inevitable?

The group of men were abreast of him now and he raised his eyes to look at them. The shock was like a blow in the stomach. The teacher was looking at him! Emotions raged and churned inside him and he felt the skin of his face, beneath the suntan and the dirt, burn with shame and fear. Dare he? Dare he not! The teacher was turning away. His expression had been one of deepest kindness and compassion. As He turned it seemed to change; there was a look of sorrow as well. As if He were sad that he was not asked. It was as if He too were devastated by the ravages of the disease and shared the suffering and shame.

"Yeshua!" Then he could not hold himself. He did the unthinkable. In one bound he threw himself before the teacher and knelt, then he fell before Him on the ground at His feet.

"Lord! If you want to you can make me clean!" He knew it. He knew the power and the compassion, but he knew too that this was The Lord. He did not think about the theology of it all. He just knew and he had to throw himself entirely on this Man's mercy.

The reply was as stunning as the action of the leper

לְהַבֵּשׁ לְנִשְׁבָּרֵי־לֵב זָרָא לַשְּׁבֻיִם דְּרֹֽור וְלַאֲסֽוּרִים־ פְּקַח־קֽוֹחַ׃

had been: "I will! I do want to! Be clean!" The words were not shouted. They were not even spoken loudly. It is doubtful whether any but the nearest of the disciples could have heard them. Certainly the crowd did not hear. But all could see the result.

It was not a gradual transformation, not a slow change where the marks of leprosy began to turn to a normal skin colour and the scars heal themselves in minutes or even seconds. It was immediate and complete. One moment he was a leper, his crippled feet and his clawed hands dragging him about, covered in scars and putrefying sores, the next he was completely whole. His skin was like that of a baby. His previously clawed hands could move naturally and his fingers reach and stretch out normally to grasp and to manipulate.

"Tell no one!" The instruction was given in that same gentle voice. "Go and show yourself to the priest and offer the sacrifice Moses instructed."

The voice seemed to come from somewhere else. Tears were flowing in a great flood down his cheeks, he could taste their saltiness on his lips. Time ceased to be and he could only stare at the transformation. His clawed hands no longer clawed. Where a thumb had gone and a stump was all that remained, there was now wholeness as if the leprosy had never been. It was the same with his feet. The stumps where toes had rotted away from the disease were now healthy toes with toenails as if they had been pedicured by the trained slaves of some spoiled rich Roman lady.

He heard no sounds of the voices of the people, nor the wind in the trees, nor of the words of the disciples. There was a vast silence and joy grew and grew, filling the silence which was his own being. Joy, unspeakable joy, bliss such as he had never known, had never expected to

לַחֲבֹשׁ לְנִשְׁבְּרֵי־לֵב לִקְרֹא לִשְׁבוּיִם דְּרוֹר וְלַאֲסוּרִים־פְּקַח־קוֹחַ׃

know, had never even conceived of. Not the bliss of this world but of an entirely other world. It was the joy of heaven flooding his soul, as the tears rolled down his face, washing away the dirt and the dust of trouble and hurt and self-loathing.

The Teacher moved on with His disciples following or crowding close to Him as if to catch His every word. The man who had been dead while still alive stood, his eyes brimming with tears, looking after the person who had done so much. Yet the wonder was that only the disciples had noticed. One minute he had been a leper and now he was clean, free from the stink and the loathsomeness of his rotting flesh. All the people had seen was a man in rags prostrate himself before the Teacher. They did it all the time. Then the Teacher had moved on and the man had got up and stood gawping in surprise, in deepest gratitude and wonder; his face suffused with happiness and love.

Some of the bystanders said they had seen it all before, so what was new. Others said that these common folk were too superstitious and too emotional. They lacked any sense of decorum. Others wondered, and a few became followers. The man who had been dead went off to find a priest to be declared officially free of leprosy. Then he would find work, to earn the money to present the sacrifices in the Temple at Jerusalem. After that, he thought, he would also become a follower of Yeshua whom he had called "Lord." Of Yeshua who was now his Lord and would be forever.

(This can be found in Mark 1, Luke 5, and Matthew 8.)

9

birthday in machaerus

(Concluding part of John the Baptist's story.)

He was feeling better than he had felt for months. The hot air on the east of the Dead Sea seemed to stimulate him and cheer him up. His forebears had, after all, been Idumeans and this was very near their homeland. Their mountain fastnesses had once been thought to be impregnable, though the Romans had penetrated there and brought them under their yoke as they had everyone else. His father had got on with the Romans and had done well out of his friendship with them and with their emperor Augustus whose cause he had espoused.

Herod smiled; tetrarch he might be but he knew how to manipulate men and the Romans were but men. One day he would persuade them of his value to them and they would make him king. He paused to savour the delights of the title, "King" – wonderful. "King Herod"; how well it had suited his father and how well it would suit him.

On the other hand he had to be careful. There was the sad example of his brother Archelaus. The Romans had not been slow to get rid of him when his irresponsible acts threatened the peace and security of Judea. He would not forget Archelaus. But then, he thought, he enjoyed the good life, and life at present was good. The period of doubt and indecision had left him. All his fears had fled. Above all, he had his brother's wife, and fortune, whom the Romans called Tyche, seemed to be smiling upon him.

לַחֲבֹשׁ לְנִשְׁבְּרֵי־לֵב זְרָא לִשְׁבוּיִם דְּרוֹר וְלַאֲסוּרָים־ פְּקַח־קְוֹחַ:

He could have confidence, absolute confidence in the safety of his border fortresses. It would be no ordeal to sit out a siege in one of his fortresses such as Masada, or Machaerus where he resided with his court now and waited for his once father-in-law to make a mistake. Any disturbance of the peace would be a mistake in the eyes of the Romans, and the governor of Syria would be down on him sooner than he could extricate himself. As for himself, he was safe with the fortresses built and supplied by his father. As for his father-in-law, let him make the first move. If he invaded then Herod could sit it out in Masada or, better still in Machaerus, in perfect comfort; then the Romans would deal with him for disturbing the peace of their empire. And he, Herod, would, of course, emerge smelling of all the perfumes of Arabia.

He smiled again to himself. It was a smug, cunning smile, triumphant and savouring the impregnability of his position. His palace was impregnable, and so it seemed was his social and political position. He did not like the Roman governor, nor did he trust him. You could not trust the Romans; one minute you were making a treaty of friendship with them, the next they were taking your realm out from under your feet. Then, on the other hand, you could not trust a Herod and he reckoned he was a match for any Roman, or anyone else living, in cunning that is. The field of battle was another matter of course, no one in his right mind challenged the Roman military superiority. Thanks to that ancient general, Marius, Julius Caesar's mentor and founder of the Roman soldiers' training and all-round toughness, the Romans had the best army the world had seen since Alexander.

His thoughts wandered on. He often let them do that, imagining possibilities and probabilities, weighing one thing up against another. This time he wondered about the Jews. They were fanatical. Hundreds of scholars and religionists had made Pilate climb down when he had

לְהָבֵשׁ לְנִשְׁבָּרֵי־לֵב ןָרֹא לִשְׁבוּיִם֙ דְּרֹור וְלַאֲסוּרִים־ פְּקַח־קֹוחַ׃

tried to bring the legions' standards into Jerusalem. They had, in effect, said to the Procurator, "Go on then, kill us; we shall be pleased to die, only we will not live to see idols brought into the sacred city."

"Sacred," he mused, following on another train. That dirty, smelly conglomeration of narrow alleys and that shining temple which was his father's masterpiece. His thoughts returned to the original theme. What if there had been a Jewish rebellion, in those dirty smelly alleys which he so despised? The Roman soldiers would have been at a disadvantage. With no room to manoeuvre and the Jews raining missiles down on them from the housetops, and them disappearing over more roofs to appear in the rear of the troops and to throw more spears and stones. Volatile, bigoted and furious in argument the Jews might be, but they could fight when they had to.

The Maccabees showed that; Greek-ruled Syria had to give way to them and Antiochus had had to retreat with his tail between his legs. Would the Romans ever follow him? He doubted it, but the outcome of a Jewish rebellion would hang in the balance for a long time. The only immediate loser would be the Procurator, Pontius Pilate. Tiberiuis would have his head off his shoulders faster than that. He grinned again at the vision conjured up in his mind of the haughty social climbing governor being dragged off to execution.

Not unnaturally he started to wonder about his own troops. They were Jews, of a sort, though mixed race ones like himself, and he did not think they would have the same enthusiasm for a fight if he decided to confront Aretas. All the same it was a possibility; a swift victory over Aretas would be a boost to his ego, but then what about the Romans? Perhaps it would be best to sit it out in Machaerus. His father had equipped the place with all weapons of offence and defence. There were supplies of food and water to last a garrison and the civilian population three years if need be. He smiled contentedly.

לַחֲבֹשׁ לְנִשְׁבְּרֵי־לֵב זָרֵא לִשְׁבוּיִם דְּרוֹר וְלַאֲסוּרֵיִם־ פְּקַח־קוֹחַ׃

Yes, that was the answer. Sit it out, then only Aretas would be the aggressor and the Romans would forget to look down their arrogant long noses at a would-be king who had seduced his brother's wife and who, in so doing had upset his former father-in-law. Anyway, who were the Romans to condemn his morals. He scowled; Augustus had not minded making Livia's husband divorce her when she was pregnant with Tiberius, so he could marry her.

The scowl quickly disappeared as he thought about poor old hen-pecked Augustus, who made out that he ruled the roost when common gossip had it that it was Livia who really wore the toga. As for Tiberius! If again the gossip were true, and the gossip from Rome, even if it were not true, was at least highly entertaining, it was Livia again who had intervened. His wished-for marriage with the skinny Vipsania had been cancelled and for his amusement he had turned to catamites and all sorts of perversions. At least he, Herod, was a red-blooded male. He liked women and they liked him. He liked them on the mature side, voluptuous and bosomy. He licked his lips at the picture of Herodias which immediately leapt into his imagination.

Sitting out a siege would be no bad thing if Herodias was here with him, and she had nowhere else to go. On the other hand, he thought, she really had got into his mind and his affections. That could be dangerous; he would have to be careful. It did not do to become too besotted with a woman. Women gossiped and they manipulated. It would not do to let her have too much of a hold over him. Let her think she had, give in to her over trivialities but when it came to the big things in life let her see that it was he, Herod, who was the boss.

His mind returned to his father-in-law sitting out there in the broiling sun short of water, with only preserved and dried provisions. His soldiers would soon get bored, and bored soldiers made trouble. He would

לְהַבֵּשׁ לְנִשְׁבְּרֵי־לֵב זְרָא לִשְׁבוּיִם דְּרוֹר וְלַאֲסוּרִים־פְּקַח־קוֹחַ׃

find it difficult to keep them amused, and any attempt at an assault would be impossible. Even if they could climb a vertical cliff, over three hundred feet high, they would then have to scale the walls which surmounted the mesa on which the palace and fortress was built. It would be suicide for those who did not kill or injure themselves trying to find a path up the mountain where even the wild goats gave up. Yes! Life was good, and it would be his birthday soon; he looked forward to that with relish.

The Romans thought they knew a thing or two about banquets, but they merely gorged themselves silly. He, on the other hand, was a discerning eater; he had the finest cooks this side of Rome and he was anticipating the enjoyment which their art would provide for him. As for entertainment, again the Romans were, at best crude buffoons, at worst utterly depraved. When you had seen one criminal eaten by trained man-eating lions, tigers or leopards, you had seen it all. When you had seen one lot of gladiators hacking at another lot, you soon got tired of the repeat performances. Even the combats of successful and skilled swordsmen grew intolerably tedious. And still the Roman mob screamed for more blood, guts and mayhem. To a civilised man, and Herod considered that he was a civilised man, it was all too juvenile in its cruelty and its total lack of sophistication.

As for the rest of the entertainments on offer by the Romans, most of it was depraved and all of it was in the very worst of bad taste. At least he had with him in Machaerus some of the best acrobats, dancers and musicians to be found anywhere in the province of Syria. Anyway he was utterly entranced and bewitched with the alluring Herodias. Every moment with her was a moment of paradise. Her company, he decided, was better by far for pleasure than anything the rabbis could come up with about the hereafter.

All the most learned of the rabbis assured him that the pleasures of this world and of the flesh were not even

לְחֲבֹשׁ לְנִשְׁבְּרֵי־לֵב זָרָא לִשְׁבֻיִם דְּרֹור וְלַאֲסוּרָים־ פְּקַח־קֹוחַ׃

to be compared to that paradise they referred to as "the Bosom of Abraham". Where it was and what it was they did not seem to be too certain about. Nor could they define the pleasures that were there. It was all rather shadowy and vague and Herod had long ago decided that the very real pleasures of the flesh in this immediate world he inhabited at the present were of far greater gratification than anything on offer in the next world. This was especially so since the theological experts, who made out they knew so much about it, had to try to explain it in stories and with metaphors. They were the experts, he thought, so if that was all that they could come up with he preferred his entertainers, his food, and, above all his Herodias. He savoured that: his Herodias. It sounded good and gave him the satisfaction that he could possess just about anything he set his heart on.

Indeed, he thought, as his mind went back to the question of an after-life, the Pharisees and the Sadducees disagreed about it and some were not even certain that there was one. Maybe when that Messiah the rabbis were always on about had appeared they would be told. He paused and looked out over the landscape. Much of what he could see was his, but only by the gift of the Romans. When it came down to it he really did resent the Romans. He could understand how the Jews felt. He could understand their longing for a Messiah to put things right for them. If the stories were correct, and Herod had an open mind on that, then Messiah would make the Jews top dogs in the world.

He shook his head; he could not see that happening. Maybe in some dim and distant future, but not in the present circumstances. There was no chance of that at all. He tried to dismiss these more serious thoughts from his mind. After all, the immediate future was what really mattered; he would be long gone somewhere in that murky and dismal Sheol the rabbis taught was the end of it all. Some had said that John might be the Messiah. Or

לְהַבֵּשׁ לְנִשְׁבְּרֵי-לֵב זָרָא לִשְׁבּוּיִם דְּרוֹר וְלַאֲסוּרִים- פְּקַח-קוֹחַ׃

'a Messiah', if again Jewish fables had anything to do with it. There was to be a priestly Messiah then a kingly Messiah. Perhaps John had been the priestly one. But, he thought again, that could hardly be true; even a priestly Messiah would hardly allow himself to be shut up in a dungeon at the mercy of the Tetrarch of Galilee and Perea.

Why did his thoughts always turn back to John? He would set his mind on his pleasures and the riotous celebrations to come, a much more pleasant subject for thought. Here he was thinking, yet again, about John. Why was it that the man exercised so much power over him when he could have no power at all? A chillingly cold hand seemed to take hold of his entrails and a bitter wind blow through the caverns of his thoughts; he felt afraid.

Angrily he stalked back to his private quarters, a grim determination set on his face. He would yet find some way to break John; there had to be a way, every man had his breaking point; there was none who had not got some weakness or other which could be exploited by skilful exponents of the art of torture. And yet he hesitated at putting John to the torture. He was still known about and respected, held in awe even. His disciples were still active, and there were rumours of another one, whether a disciple of John or making waves on his own account, he did not know. Not yet!

Perhaps more months in prison with clearly no chance of escape and with very little freedom to move or to have visitors? But then he had tried that. There had been a time when John had seemed to waver. Perhaps the tedium and the restriction of the dungeon would have its required effect and John would break down and show himself to be but a man. But then, he doubted it. John had some inner strength which he could call on. He guessed that John would say that it came from God whose servant he was. What if the God of the Jews really

לַחֲבֹשׁ לְנִשְׁבְּרֵי־לֵב ׀ רָא לִשְׁבֹּיִם דְּרֹוֹר וְלַאֲסוּרִים־ פְּקַח־קֹוֹחַ׃

was with him? What if there was a God in the massive and splendid temple which his father had built? What if John did have higher powers on his side?

Again he shook his head, this time with violence, angrily, with frustration. He could not understand it. If the Jews' God really did exist then why was it that the Jews were a subject nation? Why did they need to cling so desperately to their customs and their land, their temple and their God? Then, on the other hand, the gods of the Romans, Zeus and all the others, they were worshipped but the Romans did it as a civic ritual, not because they believed in them. No Roman with more than a couple of drachmas to rub together believed in the gods.

Yet for all that they were the most superstitious of nations and had fortune tellers, astrologers and wizards on the corner of every street. There were the gods and goddesses of every nation in temples large and small all over Rome and no one argued about it. The Jews, on the other hand, had only one God and they made more fuss about that fact than all the nations the Romans had conquered made over their gods. Why could not the Jews live at peace like everyone else and just accept the Roman gods like the Romans who simply put any new god into their already overcrowded pantheon? It was all very confusing.

What was it that had caused John to take heart and summon up reserves of courage when he seemed on the point of giving up hope? The guards had reported to him that two disciples had a very serious conference with him and then they disappeared for a couple of weeks or so. After that, with John getting more and more anxious they had returned and John had been found smiling. That look of contentment now seldom left him. Even suffering severe privations John was content. Herod almost ground his teeth in frustration. How could a man be content in such a situation? John was a fighter. Yes, he

לְהַכֵּשׁ לְנִשְׁבָּרֵי־לֵב יְ֗רָא לִשְׁבֻיִם יְּדָ֑רוֹר וְלַאֲסוּרִים־ פְּקַח־קֽוֹחַ׃

could fight, not with weapons but with determination, with argumentative skill, and with the confidence that comes from knowing one is right and on the side of righteousness. How could he change a mind like that? He wished he knew. He feared that he had in his dungeon a man stronger than he was. He would not admit the man's strength, could not concede him the victory, and dared not, for to do so would be to admit his own inferiority.

He knew, in his heart of hearts, that he could not have lasted a fraction of the time that John had endured. The knowledge, even if only admitted to the extremities of his mind, was a bitter blow to his pride. He could not kill John because of what people might think, and worse, what they might do. Worse still, he could not kill John because he had to prove something. He had to conquer, make John give up hope, bend him to his, Herod's, will.

He had to break that superhumanly strong, austere and forthright man and so prove that he was the better, the stronger and the one who always won. But he knew he could not and was not. Would not be able to break John and could never prove himself better than the Baptist because he was not.

He had underrated the threat from his father-in-law. That was true. But on the other hand he had been wise to go off in good time to Machaerus. Everyone knew it was one of his favourite places and where better to celebrate his birthday. Poor Pilate the Procurator must be wracking his brains in frustration to know what he was up to. Let him, he thought. Let him worry himself, if not quite to death, at least into an early grave. Pilate was bad enough but 'better the devil you knew'.

Herod considered himself more than a match for Pilate when it came to cunning and deception. He wondered what messages Pilate was sending out to his spies. Well, they would do no spying here in Machaerus. It was a wise choice; he could call all his senior ministers

לְחַבֵּשׁ לְנִשְׁבְּרֵי־לֵב ;קְרָא לִשְׁבוּיִם דְּרֹור וְלַאֲסוּרִים־ פְּקַח־קֹוחַ׃

and all his military commanders, and not be suspected of anything. Who else should he invite to a birthday party? Certainly not the High Priest, who would look down his aristocratic nose, suspecting he was being invited to some sort of Roman banquet where there would be pork and fried eels and all sorts of other suspect foods. Certainly not Pilate; their dislike of one another was palpable and they avoided contact unless on the most urgent government or diplomatic business. No, not Pilate, not the High Priest, nor his family. Who else then but the men who owed him their position and who would advise him or keep quiet at his bidding.

With all his government ministers present he could plan what measures to take if Aretas was foolish enough to invade. With his military commanders he could also plan what military moves to make, if any. An afterthought occurred to him. It might be wise, he thought, to call on his astrologers to advise him. Their forecasts were all too often ambiguous, but no one would be able to say he had left any stones unturned.

A birthday was as good a time as any and a better time than most to consult the astrologers, especially with his father-in-law on the warpath. After all, Tiberius had astrologers in plenty, especially wily old Thrasyllus who always seemed to tell the Emperor exactly what he wanted to hear. You would think he really did have 'the sight', thought the tetrarch. He was another example of a man in his own field who was totally and completely successful. Well! So would he be! And the Romans could not call him an atheistic Jew because he did not take the precautions any sensible ruler would have done, and that included divination and the astrologers.

Antipas, in fact, had more than his fair share of superstition. Like the Emperor, he professed to despise religion and yet he was deeply superstitious, and an unfavourable omen could send him into paroxysms of fear and even trembling. The awe he felt for John the

לְהַבֵּשׁ לְנִשְׁבָּרֵי־לֵב זְרָא לִשְׁבֻּים דְּרוֹר וְלַאֲסוּרִים פְּקַח־קוֹחַ:

Baptist was largely made up of superstitious fear coupled with admiration for his hard-hitting truthfulness and for his toughness and courage in enduring adversity. John was an enigma who grew more puzzling the more Herod learned about him. He was also deeply disturbing.

The celebrations were still some days away but already guests were arriving. Machaerus was much more than a fortress with a palace attached. Nearby, at the far extent of the mesa there was a small town. Here lived the servants and the entertainers, the cooks and the flunkies who served in the palace. The guards and other soldiers were quartered in the barracks attached to the castle itself while the guests were either accommodated in the palace, or, if they were of lower status, quartered in the town in houses set aside for guests. When all who were expected had settled in, there began a round of conferences followed by banquets and then by more conferences, often far into the night.

When he put his mind to it Herod Antipas could show a lot of the energy which characterised his father. He had needed it, for without it, and more than his fair share of cunning, he would not have survived Cleopatra and her paramour, Antony. He had made a convenient and fortunate friendship with Octavian, later to be called Augustus Caesar. He wished he could have such a profitable friendship with the present emperor, Augustus' successor. However, with his suspicious nature and with his contempt for religion in general, and for that of the Jews in particular, there was no chance of that. So he had to do the best he could with what he had. Hence the meetings at Machaerus and the lengthy conferences.

Sometimes Antipas was closeted with just one of his ministers alone. Sometimes he conferred with several at a time. No one, apart from the participants themselves, knew what went on at these meetings. At other times he had his military officers with him and, at others, the civil

לְחָבָשׁ לְנִשְׁבְּרֵי־לֵב זְרָא לִשְׁבוּיִם דְּרוֹר וְלַאֲסוּרֵים־ פְּקַח־קָוֹחַ:

administrators. He intended that all business be completed before the commencement of his birthday celebrations. He was childishly anxious that nothing should spoil the happiness of those days of feasting and entertainment. He was determined too that Herodias should enjoy herself. It was not often a Herod felt genuine affection, he thought to himself, and smiled. It was maybe the first time he had ever really wanted to please another human being other than himself. It was a surprise, and a not unpleasant one either.

What Herod's great ones did not know and what Herod would never tell even his new wife was that from time to time he visited his captive and attempted to dominate him in argument. To his regret and his frustration, this had never even looked like succeeding. Indeed, as the visits continued, Herod became more and more fearful. John was uncompromising in his stand concerning the tetrarch's adultery with Herodias and concerning God's kingdom. In spite of himself Antipas often found himself asking John questions he did not want to ask, with answers he dreaded. He would leave his prisoner's presence inwardly cursing himself, angry and humiliated.

John was completely in Herod's power and yet John did not fear him. Though the Baptist spoke respectfully to him Herod sensed that this was courtesy rather than the grovelling respect with which even his senior servants treated him. As months went by Herod realised that it was he and not John who was fearful. Even a tetrarch was human and, worse still, mortal. John behaved as if all this was but a prelude to something infinitely greater. It was as if imprisonment for John were almost a privilege.

It was something of that spirit, which he could never understand, which had led the Jewish leaders to throw themselves down before the Procurator's soldiers and offer them their throats. Power, riches, titles and recognition in this world were the things which mattered

לְהָבֵשׁ לְנִשְׁבְּרֵי־לֵב זְרָא לִשְׁבוּיִם דְּרוֹר וְלַאֲסוּרִים· פְּקַח־קוֹחַ׃

to Herod. None of these things seemed to matter a jot to John. It was as if he lived in another world entirely. Herod tried to understand; he tried and failed utterly.

Why was it, since the Romans controlled the world, that Jupiter their god of heaven and father of the gods was not universally worshipped? Why was it that the Jews held so tenaciously to their God when he was either powerless to prevent the Romans and before them the Greeks, the Syrians and the Persians from ruling them or he had abandoned them? Here was John, he had preached about One who was to come, about a kingdom of righteousness and peace, and about justice, yet it had all come to nothing. Surely common sense argued that Jupiter must be stronger than the God the Jews worshipped? Why was that not so? Why did he still have doubts and fears? Why did he feel a lurking awe for John and for the invisible God whom he served?

Herod was desperate for the title 'King' to be conferred upon him. John lived with sweat, dirt and his own filth in a stinking cell beneath the floors of the castle. Yet it was as if he lived up there among the stars and heard their songs, joining in that eternal choir of supernatural angelic music. Herod confined his body but he could not chain the spirit of the man, which soared to worlds brighter and more blessed than ever the tetrarch could dream of.

"You only have the power God allows you to have," John told him. "It is delegated and not yours. Indeed it is twofold delegated; first from God to the Romans, to whom God has allowed the rule over the whole world and then from the Romans to you over Galilee and Perea."

Herod's anger had been kindled and he had barked: "You are my prisoner and I can have you executed at any time I choose." His carefully constructed psychological defences were crumbling before the plain reasonableness of John's words: "You only think you have power."

173

לָהֲבֹשׁ לְנִשְׁבְּרֵי־לֵב זְרָא לִשְׁבֻּיִם דְּרֹור וְלַאֲסוּרִים־ פְּקַח־קֹוחֲ׃

Did Herod detect a note of patronage in John's voice? He sounded all too calm and rational, as if he were trying to explain to a spoiled and wilful child.

"The Romans could call you King, but would that really make you a King? The only real King is God! All the rest are empty human titles; men wear them for a season and they die." He went on to explain the political realities, as if Herod was not fully aware of their implications. "Equally they could send their legions who would crush you and your soldiers as you would a cockroach. That is how much you matter to the Romans. And I tell you truly God could, and will crush both you and the Romans in His own good time."

It was as if the Baptist could see into his very soul and was not impressed with what he found there. Moreover, he did not like being talked down to as one would to a cretin. The frustrating thing about it was that he knew deep inside himself that what John said was true. He could not deny it. John's plain and simple arguments left him feeling small and defeated. And yet he went back for more. The Baptist's words flayed him, they laid open his very soul and exposed it as something very small and of no great value.

John went on, "You, your emperor, and the whole Roman senate may strut and posture and men may fear you, but when you face the Eternal Throne what will you be then? You will be naked, poor, powerless and laden with sins which will forever shut you out from the light and the bliss of the beauteous presence of God who is light, who is love, and who would even now forgive you if you did but repent."

At that, Herod had burst out: "Repent! You mean change my mind? Do an about turn in my thinking?" He had gasped incredulously and at the same time was aware, perhaps also for the first time, that he was posturing. John's words did that to him. They laid him open and he saw what he did not want to see. He,

לְהַבֵּשׁ לְנִשְׁבָּרֵי־לֵב זֶרָא לִשְׁבֻיִם דְּרוֹר וְלַאֲסוּרִים־ פְּקַח־קוֹחַ:

momentarily, until his mind dismissed the revelation in a mist of self-inflating rationalisations, understood things as they really were. He, for a second or two, partly viewed them from the point of view of eternity.

At that point he stumbled with trembling knees towards the door which the jailer hastily swung open for him. It was as if the air grew thick and hard to breathe. He could feel his heart rate increase and he gasped for air. Why did he concern himself with this criminal, with this Jewish madman who spoke about Israel's unique and unbelievable God as if he were his own personal friend? His friend and yet supreme, almighty and awesome. How was it that this peasant son of a peasant priest could talk like this? How was it with Herod and with the world, if all that John said were true?

It could not be true, thought Herod. If it were then all that Herod was and all that Herod stood for was but mist, the dew upon the grass soon to be evaporated by the sun's heat; or like moonlight before the clouds draw their veil over the source of that light. Moonlight could not be picked up or touched and vapour was almost as insubstantial. So was he, Herod, as insubstantial as all that?

He stepped out into the cool evening air and breathed in deeply. He needed to clear his lungs of the smell of the prison and he needed to clear his mind of the confusion and the frustration which his visits to John tormented him with.

He decided on a glass or two of wine to help him sleep, but he could not rid himself of the disturbing thoughts which the Baptist had fixed indelibly in his mind. It was not a happy tetrarch who went to bed that night. Moreover he went to bed alone. Having decided to send his valet for the wine he perceived that the man looked uneasy and guessed that all was not well. He sensed it had to do with Herodias who was conspicuous by her absence from their private quarters. Nor were any

175

לַחֲבֹשׁ לְנִשְׁבְּרֵי־לֵב זְרֵא לִשְׁבוּיִם דְּרוֹר וְלַאֲסוּרִים־ פְּקַח־קוֹחַ׃

of her maids in evidence in the anterooms to their private apartments.

"The Lady Herodias," he growled, "where is she?"

The slave shook with fear and his mouth went dry. He could see one of his master's notorious rages coming on and knew that if it did then slaves were likely to be beaten, however proficient and however diligent they were and had been, he would take out his anger on those nearest to him.

Stammering in terror the slave managed to explain: "She absented herself, my lord! I ... I ... I think she may have been tired."

Herod's eyes bulged and his features turned red and puffy. "You worm, tell me the truth, tell me what she said!"

The growl had turned to an angry roar. The valet cringed and blurted out: "She said you preferred the Baptist man's company to hers; she was angry and beat one of her maids. She's gone to her own apartments my lord, that is what she said. It is true, please ... "

Herod held up his hand to stop the man's frightened blathering. "Get out!" he snapped. "Get out and send in a cup bearer with a jug of wine, the best! Send a messenger to one of my wife's ladies to tell her that I will see her in the morning."

He turned as the man slunk out of the door and ran down the corridor desperate to be away from the destructive anger he knew could explode at any second. Herod heard the sound of his feet slapping on the stone paving until it died away. He strode up and down his chamber angrily; he kicked over the brazier where on cold nights charcoal gave off a pleasant heat to the room. He realised he was being foolish and he knew the snub would be all over the palace by the next day.

A knock on the door announced the arrival of the wine and a cup. They were carried on an ornate tray by a frightened boy who served with his butler down below in

176

לְהַבָּשׁ לְנִשְׁבְּרֵי־לֵב זָרָא לִשְׁבֻוּים דְּרוֹר וְלַאֲסוּרִים פְּקַח־קוֹחַ:

the servants' quarters among the storerooms. Not trusting himself to speak he pointed to a table made from ebony wood and inlaid with patterns made of pearl shell. The boy put down the tray and Herod dismissed him with a wave of his hand. All company had become distasteful to him – even his own company with its worries, its doubts and its fears was to be dreaded. Here he was, surrounded by luxuries, with servants and slaves who cringed if he spoke roughly to them and who ran to do his bidding. Here he was, where his slightest whim was catered for, yet he could not bear to be alone, nor could he stand the experience of his own turbulent thoughts. By contrast there was John, locked up, guarded by cynical and brutal men, confined to a space little more than six feet by six, and yet who seemed content. How could he be content? He wanted to kick out at more things, but restrained himself and poured wine into the cup and took it out onto the roof to enjoy the stars and the vast panorama to the Dead Sea and the wilderness to the south.

As his birthday approached, Herod's mood became more complacent. Life was not so bad after all. His wife had returned to him in the early hours all repentant and compliant and anxious to make it all up with him. He was surprised and pleased with what seemed to be her genuine affection for him and her anxiety to please him after the previous evening's spat.

They enjoyed a private breakfast together and then strolled upon the roof of the palace. He suggested they visit the kitchens to view the preparation for the banquet, but she laughed and told him:

"Certainly not, that chef of yours is an artist and if you disturb him he will have a fit of the vapours and spoil everything."

"Let him!" replied the tetrarch. "I shall have him beaten if he does and set him back to work."

"Then he will sulk and the very moment he gets a

לָחָבֵשׁ לְנִשְׁבְּרֵי־לֵב זְרָא לִשְׁבֻיִם דְּרוֹר וְלַאֲסוּרִים־ פְּקַח־קוֹחַ׃

better offer of employment he will be away to Syria, or even to Rome. I am sure his skills will be better appreciated by Pilate, or he could even cook for Caesar. You know he is a treasure. You have to indulge great culinary artists like he is if you want the best from them and you want to keep them."

Her protest made sound sense and Herod laughed delightedly. "You're quite right my dear, I shall reward him suitably when the celebrations are over. What do you suggest for a gift to the best chef in the Empire?"

Herodias promised to think about it but suggested it would mean a lot to the man if after the morrow's banquet he be called in to receive the congratulations of Herod himself and of all his guests. Herod nodded his agreement, thinking how the chef, already red and perspiring from his exertions in the kitchens, would go a deeper red with pleasure when his artistry was acknowledged by all the great ones of what he thought of as his kingdom.

They spent the day relaxed and happy. He was not allowed anywhere near where preparations were being made for the partying, and he strongly suspected that Herodias was having her obnoxious daughter coached by professional dancers so that she could put on a performance for him. Well, he would pretend delight and give the girl some trinket for a reward. He had watched her eyeing some of his treasures and noted how her eyes had glistened with covetousness over a ruby and diamond necklace with a matching bracelet. He would give her those, though it might be fun after the performance to ask her what she would like. He would note her indecision and suspected that she would have to consult her mother and ask her to intercede on her behalf.

The girl was not really mature enough to wear the bracelet and the necklace but she was welcome to them if it made the mother happy, and Herodias seemed

לְהָבֵשׁ לְנִשְׁבְּרֵי־לֵב קְרָא לִשְׁבוּיִם דְּרוֹר וְלַאֲסוּרִים־פְּקַח־קוֹחַ:

unable to deny her daughter anything she wanted.
The banquet when it came was all he could have
wished for and more. After the guests had finished
eating, when even old Phineas, his secretary and
accountant, was unable to have yet another helping, they
called in the chef and his team of kitchen slaves and
servants. Herod got up and made a brief speech about
how they were the finest cooks in the world and how
they all owed it to Apollos the head Chef. The assistants
and the slaves were given gifts of money but Apollos was
sent round to each guest to receive his or her thanks and
to be given a small gift.

When last of all he came to Herod, the tetrarch
presented him with a miniature set of gold ladles and
kitchen knives. He told the man that Herodias was
thinking of a suitable inscription but wanted them to be
hung where everyone who came to the kitchens could
see them.

"I want everyone to see how a supreme master chef is
appreciated in my realm," he said, and went on: "I want
you to know that you are lord of all chefs and chief of all
cooks, without a peer."

The close of the speech was signalled by Herod
clapping, which led to a loud burst of applause. After
bowing to the tetrarch and to the company, the chef, his
face alight with pleasure, bowed himself out to produce
more fancy creations for the guests before they left.

Hardly had the artist of the kitchen left the hall than
music signalled the turn of the acrobats, the jugglers and
the dancers. Servants circulated with jugs of finest wines
making sure that no guest's glass was empty for very long.
A clown came on next and then a puppet theatre
performing a comic play. Herod was happy. Never had
he felt so at peace with the world and never had he been
surrounded by such a pleasant gathering of courtiers and
friends. He relaxed on his couch as music again from the
orchestra up in the gallery signalled yet another form of

179

לְהַבֵּשׁ לְנִשְׁבְּרֵי־לֵב זְרָא לִשְׁבוּיִם דְּרוֹר וְלַאֲסוּרִים־ פְּקַח־קוֹחַ׃

amusement.

A dancer appeared from behind a curtain. She seemed to float over the floor, buoyed up as it were, by the rapturous music. Slowly she wafted round the hall, always keeping Herod himself as the main focus of her gyrating, sinuous movements. Her arms described pleasure palaces in the air and her veil slipped, by design Herod guessed, to reveal the daughter of Herodias.

He smiled and nodded his head delightedly in time with the music. His fascinated gaze fixed on the young girl who so skilfully interpreted the music and the contentment of his mood. Her dress was red with a touch, here and there, of yellow. Like a flame she danced, a cool flame yet warm with pleasure. The music was a song of pure joy, of happiness and of pleasure, and she, as she danced, was its spirit. She was the wind, she was the flame all ethereal, light as gossamer. All the pleasure of the banquet and the succeeding entertainments were expressed by that lithe young body as it moved, now gently, now faster, with the lilt of the melody of the music.

The girl was a smaller, slimmer version of her mother, but at that moment she seemed a grown woman though scarce fourteen years. At that moment he really liked her. Warmth and happiness filled his being and he rocked his body with the dance and the melody played by the flutes and the strings. At the end, as the last notes drifted and died in the stillness, the dancer, like a falling autumn leaf, settled, head down, to the floor before his couch, her head bowed to the ground in submission before him and arms outstretched in supplication.

He had never seen anything like it and had no idea that the girl, whom he had regarded as nothing more than a spoiled brat, had such talent and could be coached to such a level of skill. He realised that she had far more self-discipline than he had credited her with. Such a performance did not come about without hours

לְהַבְשׁ לְנִשְׁבָּרֵי־לֵב קְרָא לִשְׁבוּיִם דְּרוֹר וְלַאֲסוּרִים־פְּקַח־קוֹחַ:

and hours of arduous practice and grindingly painful repetition. He got to his feet, clapping his hands and applauding. The company rose with him and added their plaudits. They were not cheering to please Herod, the response they made was a genuine reflection of their admiration for the girl's performance.

As the applause died away the girl lifted her head. Her stepfather smiled at her proudly and admiringly.

"That was magnificent," he congratulated her, "that was without a doubt the best dance performance I have ever witnessed."

He held out his hand and raised her to her feet. "Now!" he said, benignly, "You shall have a reward. Ask whatever you want ... " A small voice was trying somewhere to warn him but he pushed it to the back of his mind. At that moment he was Herod, giver of rich gifts, generous and noble. "And not a little drunk too," he thought to himself, giggling inwardly.

"Whatever you want," he continued in his expansive mood, his generosity and his recklessness running away with him. "Just name it; you can have anything, up to half my kingdom."

Some of the guests gasped at this but then, they reasoned, such language was hyperbolic, expressing his delight and not really meaning what it said it did. The girl got to her feet awkwardly; a look of fear flitted across her face and was quickly changed to a nervous confusion. She blurted out, hurriedly: "I've got to ask my mother, please, my lord, may I ask her?"

Herod smiled indulgently and gestured to the woman on his right hand who could hardly hide the look of triumph on her face. There was a cruelty there too, though most of the guests missed it, thinking that she was just pleased with her daughter's performance and that they should hasten to add their congratulations as soon as it was feasible.

The girl trotted to her mother and whispered in her

לַהֲבֹשׁ לְנִשְׁבְּרֵי־לֵב זְרָא לִשְׁבוּיִם דְּרוֹר וְלַאֲסוּרִים־ פְּקַח־קוֹחַ׃

ear on the other side from the tetrarch. The mother smiled at her daughter and whispered something back. Again a look, fearful and unbelieving, crossed the daughter's made-up features and she turned hesitantly back to Herod. Slowly she approached and looked up at him still on his feet.

"I would ... " She stopped, confusion and dismay clearly written on her face. Herod nodded for her to go on, to reassure her of his generosity, thinking now of the necklace and the bracelet which he had given to the slave who stood behind him to mind for him.

"I would ... " She looked again for encouragement at her mother, who scowled at her and nodded fiercely. With an effort she summoned up courage and blurted out: "I would that you gave me John the Baptist's head on a dish."

Herod sank down onto his couch and summoned the slave. He shook his head angrily when the slave thought he meant him to give the jewellery which he had in a leather bag hanging round his neck. Herod shook his head again and gave him his instructions. Immediately the man ran off in the direction of the stairs leading down to the dungeons.

The silence in the hall had been that of Hades, where Pluto, god of the underworld, presided over his grisly banquet. Herod's face was colourless with shock and his hands shook so that he grasped the sides of the couch in an effort to steady them. He looked round with horror on his wife whose own expression was one of malignant glee.

No one moved; the girl crouched on the ground and Herod looked down at her with distaste. He had given his word before his high captains and ministers of state. He could not go back, but this moment which stretched out to an eternity was to haunt him for the rest of his life. The executioner was preceded by the slave messenger who quickly scuttled behind Herod's couch as if to

לְהַבֵּשׁ לְנִשְׁבְּרֵי־לֵב ;רָא לַשְׁבוּיִם דְּרוֹר וְלַאֲסוּרִים־ פְּקַח־קוֹחַ׃

dissociate himself from the ghastly spectacle of the executioner carrying a large dish with, in its centre, the bleeding head of a man. The hair of the apparition had turned grey because of the rigours of incarceration but there was still a nobility there. The eyes were still open, and instead of the blank look Herod had seen on most corpses, there appeared to him to be one of accusation and of triumph. John had come to say his 'goodbye' and had quitted this world to that better place he had represented during all those years of preaching in the desert places. His look also dared Herod to think about his own journey now. Herod knew, downward, it could only be downward, in every sense of the word.

Cold fingers gripped his entrails and he grimaced with pain and with dread. He could already hear the dismal shouts and anguished screams of the damned mixed with the howls of fiendish delight as dread Hades began to open its doors before him while skeletal fingers beckon to everlasting regret and permanent pain.

(This incident can be found in Mark chapter 6 and Matthew 14.)

10

Look to the Earth

Did doctors really know anything? Why did human
suffering and pain come about? What had God got to do
with it? Surely He was omnipotent and benevolent, so it
ought to follow that He would alleviate suffering. It was
all very complicated and worrying too. There was the fall;
Eve, the mother of all living, who had tasted the
forbidden fruit and had persuaded her husband, Adam,
to eat of it also. So the sin of the first humans, the parents
of the rest of humanity, meant that everyone had to
suffer. They had lost the glory that had surrounded them
and had been driven out of the garden. But then, God
had clothed them in the skins of domestic animals and
had promised a Seed who would "bruise the serpent's
head," that is, would defeat and kill him. The Seed
Himself was to be bruised in the heel and those animals
themselves who provided Adam and Eve with covering
had also to die.

She shook her head sorrowfully. She did not
understand it and she did not understand the rabbis who
said that Messiah would reveal all and that if Israel were
righteous for only one day then Messiah would come and
restore the nation.

"What about the gentiles?" she had asked once and
had received a pitying glare from the rabbi as a reply.
She still wanted to ask the question though she knew she
would be answered angrily. The Greeks were corrupt and
effeminate, the Syrians and the Babylonians were worse,

לַחֲבֹשׁ לְנִשְׁבְּרֵי־לֵב זְרָא לִשְׁבוּיִם דְּרוֹר וְלַאֲסוּרִים־פְּקַח־קֽוֹחַ:

they were even more depraved, for they sacrificed babies to Baal.

As for the Romans, well, in spite of their boasted morality, their gravitas and their ideals of honour and service, they were cruel, greedy, and thoroughly untrustworthy. At least you knew that a Greek, a Syrian, or a Phoenician was going to try and cheat you, but a Roman boasted of his honesty while he took your country away from under you and then made you pay taxes for protection. Who else did you have to be protected from if not from the Romans themselves?

Life seemed to be very hard, unfair, and determined to put the underdog even further under the heel of whoever made himself its master. If God was God, she argued with herself, then really He ought to have done something about it long ago. Some of the rabbis said that this life was a preparation for something better. Some clearly did not know, though they pretended they did; others told her that she had to endure what God sent her and not complain.

Most of them also added that she should search her conscience for sins she had committed so that she could offer the prescribed sacrifices in the Temple. Inevitably all the rabbis she talked to were well dressed, well fed and comfortably off. Reading once in the book of Job she thought they reminded her of Job's comforters and felt like spitting out Job's complaint, "miserable comforters are ye all."

"If we must have pain," she thought, "then why have doctors who do nothing about it and charge us for what they do?" She shook her head dismally. She was not one of those people who give in easily to misfortune, though misfortune had been pretty tough on her. She fought back as best she could, speaking up about the world's

לַחֲבשׁ לְנִשְׁבְּרֵי־לֵב ۚ קְרָא לִשְׁבׂים דְּרׂור וְלַאֲסוּרֵים ־ פְּקַח־קׂוחַ ׃

injustices, though invariably cheerful with those who were close to her. The rabbis, like Job's censorious friends, were bad enough but the doctors, she was sure, were mostly humbugs of the worst sort. She had gone to one for a remedy which he had assured her would do her good – only to find later that he had prescribed the same draught for an entirely different ailment in another person.

She had become cynical as a succession of healers had drained her resources of cash and of patience. It was maybe good for her that she had no great store of wealth, for her husband was not a rich man; for if that had been the case it must surely have all been wasted. Worrying at these problems had given her a certain cynicism but also a mental toughness and a very sharp tongue. People were careful what they said in her presence, for they knew what it was to feel the edge of it.

Sometimes she compared herself with those she imagined to be worse off. "At least you can see where you are going," she said to herself. She added, in her mind, "You are not deaf so you can hear what people are saying and you are not dumb so you can answer back and put people in their place, for you do not like being pitied, nor do you like being patronised."

She smiled to herself, knowing full well how scathing her remarks could be, and how deflating to those who tried to be sympathetic. Sympathy she did not want. Understanding she did appreciate and her husband appreciated her. For that she was grateful and she loved him.

"They might pity you, but your skill with words more than makes up for any disadvantages you may have," he would say to her. Always tactful and considerate, that was how he put it. "Skill with words" indeed! She could

לְהָבֵשׁ לְנִשְׁבְּרֵי־לֵב קְרָא לִשְׁבוּיִם דְּרוֹר וְלָאֲסוּרִים־פְּקַח־קוֹחַ:

out-argue the Pharisees if she put her mind to it.

Though he always spoke gently to her, he was aware that her sharpness of tongue tended to make others a little fearful of her and that, in its turn, tended to make her react to them with suspicion and sometimes hostility. He worried that there might be a serious deterioration in her character. He loved her, seeing the eager, exuberant girl he had married and enjoying with gratitude the life of deep tenderness they shared together. People did not understand; they often saw someone who had been smitten by God for some real or imagined sin.

The failure of doctors to find a cure had further embittered her. It was her sense of humour which saved her from becoming totally alienated and angry. When people saw a woman bent and old before her time through suffering, they often thought her stupid as well. With a twinkle in her eye that only he could see he would watch and listen as she led them on in their delusion, only to make some remark which embarrassed and utterly confused them with its intelligence and its sense of the ridiculous. Her spine might be bowed but there was no weakening of her intellect. A crippled body did not make for a feeble mind.

There were times when her impatience, especially when her back pained her more than usual, made her abrupt and impatient even with him. He was often wary, and took care how he spoke, so as not to upset her. Being so circumspect destroyed the spontaneity they had enjoyed together and put a strain on their relationship.

"Alright!" He would burst out, "so your back is bent. So you can only look to the ground and find it difficult to look up. Devorah! I am truly sorry and I would make it better if I could, but I can't. We must endure it and not let it spoil the things which we have."

לַחֲבֹשׁ לְנִשְׁבְּרֵי־לֵב ‏ זְרָא לִשְׁבֹוִּים‏ דְּרֹור וְלַאֲסֹוּרִים‏ פְּקַח־קֹוֹחַ׃

"It's alright for you," she would retort, "you do not have to look down and see only dust and other people's shoes."

With a smile he would reply, "Hm! Maybe a woman as clear-sighted as you could learn a lot from the state of other people's shoes. Now what about Rabbi David? If I am right, he has had his shoes repaired. There was a time when he would just have bought new ones. Is his money running out, do you think? The other Pharisees will not think much of him; shoes are very important to the Pharisees. He has probably lost all standing among them. And," he added, "that ought to do him a world of good, make him more human, more common."

She would gently slap his arm at these remarks. How his carefree attitude to life lifted her spirits and how the way he would pull a face or look at her with mock seriousness took her out of her dark moods. She could never be angry or bitter for too long while he was there to make her laugh and to encourage her.

"Devorah!" he would say, serious again and now reasoning her out of her depression: "Devorah! You might look down but you also look down on people. And," he hastened to add, "you have a right to, for you see things which they do not. You see it dusty or muddy but that is how life really is. You see the reality while most people escape into fantasies or into the minute details of living. They fail to see the vast landscape in looking at the bricks and the trees and the cooking and the sweeping."

She would look at him questioningly but with a smile returning to her lips. "Is that it then?" she would ask, and go on to challenge. "So I look on the ground but my mind is up in the clouds looking down. I think someone has his head in the clouds and it is someone I love

לַהֲבֹשׁ לְנִשְׁבָּרֵי־לֵב ۚרָא לְשְׁבֻוִם דְּרֹור וְלַאֲסוּרֵים־פְּקַח־קֹוחַ׃

dearly." She would laugh and shake her head at his flight of fancy, as she saw it.

He was right, she supposed, but how dull it often was. And how much duller and depressing it would be without her Abner. For all she had the dearest and best of men she still wanted somewhere else to look than the dirty road and at other people's footwear. She wanted to lift her eyes to the treetops, to see the birds that perched in the branches. She wanted her gaze to roam the skies, to really have her head in the clouds instead of her imagination.

Seeing reality in the dirt was all very well, but it meant she missed out on the beauty which she could only imagine or strain to reach out to.

"I'm sick of reality," she complained. "I want to see the stars. I want to sail among them in my thoughts while I gaze up at them and I want to visit God in the Third Heaven above and beyond the stars."

Abner shook his head. "You had better ask Rabbi Eleazer about that," he said.

She looked at him despairingly. "Him!" She hooted the word derisively. "He knows as much about it as a Roman would or a Syrian soothsayer." She laughed. "If anyone has his face in the mud it is him. And he thinks the mud is the only real heaven. It's a good thing all the rabbis are not like him."

"I think you see the stars and the heavens better than most people," answered Abner loyally.

She squeezed his arm. "Yes my dear, you always say the right thing. But I really would like to be able to look up and to see the stars. I want to see the eagles and the vultures too, soaring and swooping on their mighty wings. I want to be able to watch them and to imagine what it must be like to ride the wind, noble and free."

לָחֹרֵשׁ לְנִשְׁבְּרֵי-לֵב יִרָא לִשְׁבוֹים דְּרוֹר וְלַאֲסוּרִים- פְּקַח-קוֹחַ׃

He thought that such birds were only looking for the next meal, but decided he ought not to say so because of the mood she was in. She went on: "I want to see the tops of the trees swaying in the wind and the storm clouds loaded and dark with rain. I want to see the lightning and the blue sky after a storm with the white fluffy clouds floating free." She sighed longingly.

Her husband looked down at her and started to say something but then changed his mind.

"What is it then?" she demanded. "You've got something on your mind, I know you; you start to stutter and stammer then ages later it all comes out. So!" she ordered, with mock strictness in her voice. "Out with it. I won't give up until you tell me, so you may as well get it off your chest now."

She looked at him, her head a little to her right so she could see eye to eye with him. "If you make excuses and prevaricate, it will be too late when I finally nag it out of you."

He knew perfectly well that this was so very true. She would keep on and on until he had said what was on his mind. Indeed he thought it ought to be said, but how to say it was the problem. She was thin skinned and he spent most of his waking moments thinking how to make life easier for her, or at least, less difficult.

"It's just that ... Well ... er ... I was thinking."

She laughed. "You're always thinking and a lot of it concerns me. I won't snap at you, dear, I promise. I know you always mean well and I know you are usually right."

"But will you listen? You know, do something as I advise you. You won't get cross and dismissive, will you?"

She thought, "Anyone would think he was afraid of me, but it isn't me he's afraid of but of hurting me." She

לְהַלְבֵּשׁ לְנִשְׁבָּרֵי־לֵב ׀ רָא לִשְׁבוּיִם דְּרוֹר וְלַאֲסוּרִים־ פְּקַח־קוֹחַ׃

hugged his arm with both hers. Clinging to him, knowing him to be her lifeline. He always meant well, she knew. She also knew she ought to be patient with him, and from that moment she resolved to be a lot more patient than she had shown herself in the past.

"Please go on," she pleaded. "I won't snap, I will listen and I will try, I will really try to take your advice. I promise."

He looked at her, puzzled. His Devorah was making an effort, so ought he – but how to begin?

"He made water into wine at a wedding in Galilee," he started, by plunging into the middle of his subject which did not really have a beginning.

She bit her lip to keep her mouth closed and not interrupt. "Who did, dear?" she asked sweetly.

"Yeshua the carpenter," came his answer, and he continued: "He fed thousands of people with just five loaves and two fishes," he paused and added, "or was it five fishes and two loaves?" He was unclear on that point but it did not deter him, whatever it was it was a miracle.

"There was a demon-possessed man at Gadara and he drove out the demons, a legion. Well, that's what people said it was; his name was 'Legion', there were lots of them. Kephas, one of his followers, said so." He went on, the words coming out without any order or logical sequence. The matter had been mulling over in his mind for some time and he wanted to get it all out before she stopped him.

"Jairus, the ruler of the Synagogue, had a daughter; some said she was at the point of death, others that she was dead already. He just spoke to her and she was completely better. She got up and got out of bed as if she had never been ill. The Centurion, the one in Capernaum, had a servant who was ill and Yeshua just

לְחַבֵּשׁ לְנִשְׁבְּרֵי־לֵב ‏ זְרָא לִשְׁבֻיִם דְּרוֹר וְלַאֲסוּרִים־ פְּקַח־קוֹחַ׃

said the word and he was cured. Then one of Herod's officials, high up, a rich man, his son was dying and Yeshua simply told him to go home and the boy would live."

He paused for breath and continued: "He has done so many wonderful things. A widow was burying her son and He stopped the funeral procession to the burying place and lifted the young man up. Right out of the bier, and restored him to his mother. Oh yes! There was a woman who had been haemorrhaging for years. She was dying. She just reached out and touched Him and she was completely and immediately cured."

He looked at her, almost out of breath with the recital of all the incidents which poured from his lips. Would she listen and go on listening, he wondered. Would she fly into a temper and say that she had heard it all before?

Covertly he stole a sideways glance at her, this woman he loved. However many times he did it he felt the same surge of emotion mount up from the pit of his stomach. His heartbeat and his breathing increased their pace and his throat felt dry. There was an excitement in knowing and loving her. If he had spoken at that moment his voice would have been hoarse with love and with the wonder of it.

Love, with yearning affection, welled up in him and the tears began to form in their ducts under his eyes. When he looked at her like this it was to see a composite woman. When they lay together at night it was the warmth of that same woman he felt beside him as he closed his arm over her protectively. She was the joyful girl he had married, but he saw beyond that to the mature woman whose wisdom he respected and whose conversation he so much enjoyed. He saw also the bent, hurting woman who so bravely battled her affliction and

לַחְבֹּשׁ לְנִשְׁבְּרֵי־לֵב לִקְרֹא לִשְׁבוּיִם דְּרוֹר וְלַאֲסוּרִים־פְּקַח־קוֹחַ׃

who gained strength in that battle. Even as she seemed to be losing it her character rose above it all and he loved her too for that, admiring her, admiring the courage she showed, recognising that he might not have achieved so much if he had been so troubled.

Day by day and moment by moment she fought relentlessly her pain and her disability, refusing to let it conquer her will and her spirit. To the end, he knew she would go on fighting her losing battle, losing but never defeated. Day by day and moment by moment she also fought the ignorance and the prejudices of those around her who assumed, without any evidence for the assumption, that her suffering was a punishment for some terrible sin committed secretly and known only to herself.

She remembered with thankfulness the passage written long ago by Solomon: "Two are better than one; because they have a good reward for their labour. For if they fall the one will lift up his fellow. But woe to him that is alone when he falleth." Woe indeed! She shuddered and grasped his arm more tightly.

Abner pressed her hands as they gripped his own arm. Her grasp was dependent, clinging to him, yet it gave him the strength of knowing that he shared her suffering, shared her battle with misfortune, and had some little part in giving back to her something of what she gave to him. So they responded to one another's need and to one another's love, in mutual comfort and mutual hope against hope.

He had long wondered how and why it was that there was no physical remedy. He had begun to think of it as chains which bound her shoulders, dragging them down, forcing her gaze to the earth. He thought of all the people

לַחֲבֹשׁ לְנִשְׁבְּרֵי־לֵב זְרָא לִשְׁבֿוּּים דְּרֹוֹר וְלַאֲסֿוּרִים־ פְּקַח־קֹוֹחַ׃

he knew who could look up but who saw nothing and whose minds were filled with the dirt, the dust and the worn pavements and roads of the town or the muddy byways of the countryside. It had long since dawned on him, as he tried to explain to her, that she usually saw things more beautifully and more clearly than those folk who thought themselves better and more privileged than her.

It had been slowly forming in his mind that perhaps this was not a physical affliction at all. It was, he thought, spiritual rather than physical; something to do with the unseen heavenly conflict which went on remorselessly day and night between the forces of darkness and those of light. Not, of course, as the foolish ones whispered behind Devorah's crippled back that she was being punished, but rather that she was a victim, a casualty in that implacable warfare being waged in the heavenlies and whose malign effects were sometimes felt on the earth among the sons and daughters of men.

There had been times when she had gathered all her puny strength and fought back so that whatever it was that was binding her had relinquished its hold for a little while, only to return and to sink its claws more firmly into her. It returned and it would go on returning and it would not let her go until it had destroyed her.

But then, he puzzled, cudgelling his mind with unanswered questions. If she were somehow involved in a heavenly conflict, and, if she was a casualty, perhaps she would be taken up to the throne of the Lord. Or! And he hardly dared frame the thought, for it gave him hope. Though not yet ready to give way to despair, he dared not hope too much lest those hopes be cruelly dashed in tragedy to the earth and into the dust of death. Or, just maybe, perhaps, God would be merciful to her and heal

לְהִבָּשׁ לְנִשְׁבְּרֵי־לֵב זָרָא לִשְׁבוּיִם דְּרוֹר וְלַאֲסוּרִים־ פְּקַח־קֽוֹחַ:

her. He dared not hope. Dared not mention it to raise her hopes lest they be dashed. Yet dare he not? So he had brought up the subject that was on his mind and was troubling him. He had brought up the subject of Yeshua of Nazareth, Yeshua the carpenter's son.

He dared not voice any of these thoughts to her for fear of upsetting her. He had wondered if perhaps it might cheer her but he realised there were aspects of her character which he did not fully know and about which he could not speculate. She was a complex person, and he looked on her with wonder, this woman he had known for many years.

He had to keep these matters to himself and to pray, so that he too entered into that heavenly battle that somehow involved his dear one. Maybe the solution did lie with Yeshua, but again he dared not get up his hopes. If He were a prophet would He want to visit an obscure town, little more than a village in Perea? He thought not and he wondered what she was thinking at that moment and whether, if Yeshua were to visit their town, or if they dared to travel to find Him, she would consent to ask for His intercession and His help.

For her part, she had to be sure. Abner seemed convinced, but she could not forget that there were always rabbis who claimed to have healing gifts or efficacious prayers. She wondered how this rabbi could be different from them. She wondered too what the rabbi, or carpenter, or whatever he was, would get out of it for himself. There was no one who did things like that for nothing. Indeed, to be well again was the one thing the sick or the infirm wanted most of all, above everything else. And often, she thought, they were willing to pay for it with money or with favours. An ambitious man could do well with a few apparently efficacious

לְהַבֵּשׁ לְנִשְׁבְּרֵי־לֵב ;רָא לִשְׁבֿוּיִם ֿדְרֹור וְלַאֲסֿוּרִים־ פְּקַח־קֹוֹחַ ׃

prayers if he wanted to get on as a rabbi and have people follow him and hang on his words as if he were Solomon himself.

She turned again to look at him, this husband of hers. This man who loved her come what may and whatever her infirmities. She suddenly realised that, however sceptical she might be about the prophet from Galilee, the Carpenter, she ought to see him if she could. Maybe he would be able to heal her. Even some temporary relief from her suffering would be a great boon. But most of all she needed to see him for the sake of this man who had loved her through thick and thin. She always turned down his suggestions because she was convinced they were born from his desperate need to give her hope. She realised how as, over the long years, she had been disappointed, so she was hurting him by not listening to him, by not taking him seriously. That moment she made a resolve to consider her dear man in all things, as much as she could anyway.

They were walking together back to the town. It was not unusual as towns go. It had no distinguished citizens, nor had any famous events like great battles happened near it. It had a market; it had its magistrates who administered justice and it had a synagogue. So had lots of other small and larger towns all over the territory of Herod the Tetrarch. So were there in the area ruled by his brother and so were there in Judea where the Roman governor divided his time between Caesarea and Jerusalem. But it was home and they looked on it with the knowing affection of long familiarity. It had been dry and the dust was somehow pleasant to their feet. They looked forward to getting home and putting their feet in a bowl of cool water to wash away the tiredness with the dust.

לְהַבֵּשׁ לְנִשְׁבְּרֵי־לֵב ۪ קְרֹא לִשְׁבוּיִם ۪ דְּרוֹר ۪ וְלַאֲסוּרִים ۪ פְּקַח־קוֹחַ ۪

Abner was pointing out the olives, the corn and the vines, making the sort of comments only a countryman would make who had a daily experience of such things and who found, in the changing seasons, the flight of the birds and the doings of the wild beasts, a wealth of interest which would be inconceivable and tedious to a townsman. His work was with such things and from where they lived on the edge of the town they shared both the life of the country and that of the town.

She listened, but with only half an ear. A new light was dawning in her soul and she gave wondering attention to the things that light was revealing to her. All these years she had known that Abner loved her. He had proved his love a thousand times over and more. He had proved it by his patience, by his gentleness and by his care of her. Her affliction had brought out that love, showing it to have facets it could never have revealed had she not been so tormented. Like something valuable and precious, his love, like a beautiful stone hung on a gold chain around a woman's neck, it glowed with virtue and added lustre to their ordinary daily existence.

Fresh understanding was opening up to her and the wonder of it gave her that fluttery feeling of butterflies in the stomach. Abner loved her, however miserable she got, however sharply she spoke to her neighbours, he loved her all the more. Considering the wonder of this a fresh wonder began to dawn on her. It was as if one thought entered her mind but it left the door ajar for others to crowd in after it. Larger, more wondrous thoughts which almost made her gasp.

If Abner loved her then what about God? "God might love us like that," the thought insisted, "but more so. Why not? God loved Israel, did He not? So!" the thought went on remorselessly, "In spite of ourselves, in spite of

לְהַבְּשׁ לְנִשְׁבְּרֵי־לֵב יָרָא לִשְׁבוּיִם דְּרוֹר וְלַאֲסוּרִים־ פְּקַח־קוֹחַ׃

our sinful, sordid and shoddy lives, God still loves us –
He must." But then there came up from the depths of
her mind a favourite saying of her father's, that stern old
man who could not believe anything good of anyone.

"God only loves the good, the just, and the pure." He
had said it as if it were just possible that a person could
be all that.

She did not think so, but it had been said with such
certainty that she had to admit the possibility that it just
might be true. She shook her head. It couldn't be. Could
it? But then the opposite thought slipped in through the
half-open door of her mind. If Abner's love was as real as
she knew it was then must not God's love be more so?
She remembered the prophet Hosea. God was a
husband to Israel and the prophet had been an example.
He had loved his unfaithful wife and he had bought her
back to him out of slavery. So then, just like Hosea, God
was a husband to Israel and God loved Israel. So God
would do all He could to buy back the people He had
saved from out of Egypt. In spite of Israel's adultery with
idols, God would have them back, would even buy them
back. But at what cost, she did not know. She did reason
that if the nation mattered then all the individuals who
made up the nation also mattered. So, therefore, *she*
mattered. She stopped to consider the thought. She
mattered to God; did she? She must, if God was God.

"What are you thinking about?" Her husband
disturbed her reverie.

She pursed her lips, even more determined to pursue
this quest he had suggested to her. "This Yeshua," she
began. He nodded and signalled his assent that he was
listening, with an encouraging grunt. "Hm-hm?"

She looked round at him anxiously. "Does he ask for
money, for favours? The rabbis do; is he a rabbi?"

לְהַבֵּשׁ לְנִשְׁבְּרֵי־לֵב זָא לִשְׁבֻיִּם דְּרוֹר וְלַאֲסוּרִים־ פְּקַח־קוֹחַ׃

"I don't think so," he answered with just a little hesitancy. "Well," he added, "He does not seem to. I have heard nothing about Him asking for money or for anything in return. Somehow He does not seem to be that sort of person. He is poor but He does things for nothing, as if it were all His and He were in control of it all. If you see what I mean."

His reply seemed rather lame and he screwed up his eyes in perplexity and some embarrassment with the effort to his imagination.

Determined to find out all he knew about Yeshua, the rabbi who was a carpenter, she pursued the subject. "How do you know all this?" she demanded with some of the old sharpness. "Where did you hear all these stories?"

She had in fact also heard some, but she would not yet tell him what she knew. She wanted to hear what he knew and what his sources for the knowledge were, and if those sources were reliable or not. There had been excited gossip in the market a year gone by about a prophet from Galilee who had driven out the cattle and sheep from the Temple and who had overturned the tables of the money-changers. She wondered if the stories, as they so often do, had grown in the telling. She looked at him again, willing him to go on.

"People," he started vaguely and she interrupted him: "What people?" she demanded before he began to ramble and get off the subject. He concentrated and listed those he knew who had brought their tales of the rabbi or prophet from Galilee.

"Moishe ben Yisrael, for one, then Levi camel driver. They travel a lot. They hear things. They had been to Galilee and said they had seen Him. Moishe said he had seen a miracle. Well ... " he corrected himself. "He was there and a woman reached out to Yeshua and touched

לְחַבֵּשׁ לְנִשְׁבְּרֵי־לֵב זֶרָא לִשְׁבוּיִם דְּרוֹר וְלַאֲסוּרִים־ פְּקַח־קוֹחַ׃

Him and she claimed, later, she had been haemorrhaging for twelve years and could not be cured though she had spent all her money on doctors and cures.

"Moishe was in the crowd and said that is what she said. Levi said he was travelling south from Capernaum and there was this crowd going along the road. They stopped, were held up by another crowd – a funeral procession; it was evening and they were following a widow taking her only son to the burial ground. He could actually see what happened, for he was on a high point of ground.

"Yeshua stopped them. He had been with the other crowd, and He reached out and touched the bier. Catch one of the Pharisees doing that, or the priests, they ... "

She interrupted impatiently, "Yes! Yes! Go on, what did Yeshua do? Never mind the Pharisees and the priests."

He collected himself. "Oh. Yes! Well ... er ... He sort of lifted the young man up and gave him back to his mother."

"Just like that?" she asked. "No ceremony, no prayers, nothing?"

"No!" he answered, "I don't think so and Levi is usually reliable. Moishe might tell a few tales, or embroider them; you know, make them more interesting, but not Levi, he's a man of few words."

They walked on in silent companionship, he pleased that she was showing an interest but not daring to hope that they could ever find the rabbi from Nazareth who did not ask for money nor for favours.

She felt an uplifting of her spirit. Somehow she knew that if by searching out this prophet or rabbi there was a remote chance of healing for her, then it was something they must do. She decided that she would think

לְהַבֵּשׁ לְנִשְׁבְּרֵי־לֵב זָרֵא לִשְׁבוּיִם דְּרֹוּר וְלַאֲסוּרִים־ פְּקַח־קוֹחַ׃

seriously and plan. Maybe they could afford a journey to Capernaum, for that was where He was heard of most. Maybe they might meet Him on the way, or perhaps they should visit the capital first.

She weighed these possibilities in her mind and decided she would ask trusted friends and her sister to look in on their house while they were away, just to see that all was well. Making plans buoyed up her feelings even more. She felt that, at last, she was taking her destiny into her own hands. Up until then she had been fighting back blindly; now she had a plan of campaign. It involved seeking help, but she had to; in the matter of a cure she was impotent, so she had to look for someone with the power.

Both of them resolved that they would seriously pray and trust in the God of Israel. Both of them marvelled in themselves that they had not thought of it so seriously before. They had prayed, but the prayers had been of the ritual, complaining kind, much like the way one argues the scandal of the price of things in the market or the greed and duplicity of the tax collectors. Having purpose made them determined; being determined gave them direction and this lifted their spirits and gave fresh hope.

The next day was Sabbath. It had dawned bright and sunny and the clear skies promised heat later on. Of course all the essential work that was not lawful to do on the Sabbath, had already been done. She had worked hard all day so that after the sun had set they could relax. The meal was already set out and they would eat it after Abner returned from the synagogue. Everything had to be ready and in order before sunset. She had given a last look round, her eagle eye ready to catch the slightest misalignment in the domestic utensils on their shelves or where they were neatly stacked. She had made a double

לַחֲבֹשׁ לְנִשְׁבְּרֵי־לֵב זְּרָא לִשְׁבֻיִם דְּרוֹר וְלַאֲסוּרִים־ פְּקַח־קָוֹחַ׃

trip to the well, for the water she drew would have to last them for two days.

Abner had gone out as usual to the fields and had returned, washed, put on his good clothes and had gone out to the synagogue. She was ready to recite the blessing over the Sabbath meal and to light the Sabbath lamps. All was well and a peace settled on her soul as she relaxed. Sabbath was a good day, a beautiful day, a day of peace and of rest.

The morning sun shone slantwise through their window in the front wall of their house. As the morning slowly grew to its maturity so the sun would begin to shine with its full strength directly into the window and then it would start its slow crawl across the back wall of their room until it was cut off by the protruding corner of their house and the house would grow cool in the shade while the rest of the world was sweating and panting in the midday heat. The little courtyard at the back was always in the shadow and was a pleasant place for them to sit together in the evenings – she with her sewing and he carving things from odds and ends of wood he picked up. These he could sell in the market place when he had enough of them. Toys they were, mostly, toys for children but there were utensils too.

She smiled, knowing that when he had sold them he would not come home with all the money he had earned but with some present for her, often something they could ill afford but which gave her such joy and made her feel fifteen again as when they had been betrothed and he had been in the habit of carving her little things to adorn their house. She had them now; they lined the walls, or they reposed in her basket of handy things. There were spoons, there were rings of various sizes and of different woods. She liked the olive wood spoons and

לְהַבֵּשׁ לְנִשְׁבְּרֵי־לֵב זְרָא לַשְּׁבוּיִם דְּרֹור וְלַאֲסוּרִים־ פְּקַח־קָוחַ׃

slices best, for there was a rich variety of colours in the grain of the wood and Abner knew how to show these things off at their best. She treasured a little box with a lid and her name carved on it. He had given it to her, with other things, on their wedding day. She treasured it above the other, more expensive gifts because he had put so much of himself into it.

She gave a last look round. She knew everything was as it should be, but this Sabbath morning was somehow special. Everything was, of course, spick and span as it should be. Everything was in its place. Everything was clean, washed and polished. The things of metal were scoured and they shone and glistened in the morning sun as if they too were putting on their best to greet the Sabbath morning and God who had given to men and to creatures the Sabbath, the gift of rest and peace. The clay jars, jugs and platters were all washed, dried and wiped to a brilliance that turned common pottery to pure gold. They reflected a warm glow as the sun's clear white light lit their surface.

There were baskets too. They were for storing vegetables and grains. They were stacked neatly, row upon row on their shelves. Their ample supply promised the stranger and the friend a welcome with a meal or with the refreshment of the watered wine of the country. As she looked round she smiled an inner smile of satisfaction. No one could accuse her of neglecting her household duties. Bent she might be but her house was straight; everything was in its place and there was not a speck of dirt to be seen. She might be afflicted, but no one could criticise her of anything unclean or defiling, either in her personal life or in her housekeeping duties.

"So! Let them criticise," she thought to herself. "If I held some guilty secret would God so have blessed me

לַחֲבֹשׁ לְנִשְׁבְּרֵי־לֵב זָרָא לִשְׁבֻוִים דְּרֹור וְלַאֲסוּרִים־פְּקַח־קֹוחַ׃

with a loving husband as good as kind and gentle Abner?
Would I have the strength to be as quick and as energetic
as I am? Would ... "

Then she realised the thought her mind was about to
frame, almost as if it were put into words in some inner
dialogue with herself. She was about to allow the thought
that most of her neighbours admired their beautiful
home and not a few were envious. She felt a guilty glow
of triumph but quickly stifled the feeling and what
remained of the thought not yet relished in her mind.
Ruefully she recognised the sin of pride, but she also saw
that there was a legitimate pride in work well done. This
was different from the arrogance which, in one's own
estimation, put one above one's fellows. She hoped hers
was of the former sort, but she was not quite sure.

Abner too, in his quiet methodical way went about
his work in the fields and the orchards with a similar
diligence. He was conscientious and careful and only
gave of his best. He was a man of skill. He said little,
listened much and was not always impressed by what he
heard. He sometimes felt a little guilty too because he
despised some who talked much but who did little. He
thought of the proverb: "In all labour there is profit. But
the talk of lips tendeth only to penury."

His tools were all cleaned and put away. They had
been wiped over with a greasy rag to prevent rust though
it was but for a day and two nights. Everything had to be
good for Sabbath; everything had to be ready as if for the
Lord of the Sabbath who had Himself rested on the
seventh day. It was a day of completeness as well as of
rest, a day of finality. It might be that Messiah would
come to Israel on Sabbath and usher in a Sabbath and a
Jubilee for the nation and for the world. So, Abner's tools
were as highly polished as his wife's pots and pans, as if

לְחָבֵשׁ לְנִשְׁבְּרֵי־לֵב ۚ זְרָא לִשְׁבֻיִם ۚ דְּרֹוֹר ۚ וְלַאֲסוּרֵים־ פְּקַח־קֹוֹחַ ׃

ready for inspection by Messiah Himself.

He was dressed in his Sabbath best, standing just outside the door in the growing warmth of the morning sun. He lifted his head to watch the sparrows fluttering, quarrelling and busy about nothing on the rooftops and on the tops of the walls of courtyards. The world was bright and clean that morning and the air smelled fresh. What breeze there was wafted a fragrance from the blossom on the fruit trees outside the village.

He glanced back at his Devorah and smiled, a fond indulgent smile. How like a busy little sparrow she was. Her business, however, was always to a purpose; she was never idle. How like the brightness she was with everything shining and sparkling in the rays of the sun. He remembered how she had been saying that she wanted to be able to look up without having to lean so far back, so she could watch the clouds and the birds as he had been doing. It crossed his mind that she would find little difference, since people seemed to be just like the sparrows: chattering, quarrelling and fluttering about on all sorts of business which was seldom their own. He shook his head and turned back to contemplate the sparrows and the pigeons.

His reverie was disturbed by a voice at his side. "Come on then, we can't stand here all day looking at the sky; we'll not let Avram and Rebekah of the wool-washing and fulling business get there before us."

He laughed as she took his arm and urged him forward. With firmness she guided him out of the house and into the road to the synagogue. They walked as quickly as they could, for it was said that you should hurry to the synagogue but go away reluctantly.

At the entrance to the synagogue they parted, Devorah to go to the women's gallery and Abner towards

לְחָבֵשׁ לְנִשְׁבְּרֵי־לֵב זֶרָא לִשְׁבוּיִם דְּרוֹר וְלַאֲסוּרִים־פְּקַח־קוֹחַ׃

the front, though not too near. He hoped to be called up to read but this did not happen as often as he would have liked. His hand lingered on hers for a moment, but it was a moment and a touch that told her much. It told her that even as she made her way to the women's gallery at the back and the side of the synagogue he would still miss her and was already looking forward to the time when they would be reunited to walk home together.

It was not an orthodox way of thinking for one should love the Torah above all else; but Abner knew where his heart lay and he delighted to let Devorah know it by those little shared secrets which all the best and happiest of married couples have to themselves alone. It told her of his devotion, that he wanted her near him and of his need of her every waking moment, and every sleeping one too. Turning her head to the left she gave him an encouraging smile which was also a little anxious and a little maternal as a mother with some venturesome child, afraid it would get into mischief or danger if she was not there to watch over it.

Everyone settled into their places, some with the self-importance of knowing their high standing in that small community. Others did so with a humility which either betrayed them as those rare beings who are truly humble and are able to share something of God's perspective on the human race, or as those who know their place in the society and know that it is not a great one. These often felt that they should not intrude their persons among their neighbours who were persons of worth and of standing and so ought not to be inconvenienced by having to notice the lower orders shuffling and coughing at their elbows.

On nearly all, the outer appearance belied the inner state. The solemnity and the decorum inculcated by the

לְהַלְבֵּשׁ לְנִשְׁבָּרֵי־לֵב זְרֵא לִשְׁבֹּיִם דְּרֹוֹר וְלַאֲסוּרִים־ פְּקַח־קוֹחַ׃

synagogue, its ritual and the reminders of their history in the quotation from the Torah, the Prophets and the Writings enforced the need to put on a front of humble dignity and solemn humility. In many the inner turmoil continued, as it did with Rabbi David. He was now hardly recognised as the young man who had attended the Jerusalem schools and he was shunned by the other rabbis, particularly by those of the Pharisees.

Beneath a stony exterior he boiled with anger and disillusionment at the injustice of life which had brought him to disgrace and to what amounted to poverty for a Pharisee. He no longer took a lead in the services. He was no longer consulted by other rabbis; nor was he held up as an example of piety to the young. His wisdom was discounted and his learning discredited. The elders and the ruler of the synagogue now treated him with a cold politeness which was not politeness. They were correct and their correctness hurt as only unfeeling correctness without sympathy can hurt.

There was remorse as well as anger. He had been overfond, overindulgent some would have said, of a spendthrift son. He had invested money which he should not have done, for even he knew that the son's business ventures were unsound and always ended in ruin. The business partner had disappeared and the remainder of Rabbi David's money with him. The vineyard and the winepress were not all that the vendor claimed for them and the son still owed money on the venture. It had been a disaster and Rabbi David was wearing a patched shoe, which for a rabbi and a Pharisee was worse than disgrace, it was an admission of failure. The vines were diseased, the wine press needed rebuilding and the son was making wild and unrealistic plans to recoup his losses which, as everyone knew,

לַחְבֹּשׁ לְנִשְׁבְּרֵי־לֵב לִקְרֹא לִשְׁבוּיִם דְּרוֹר וְלַאֲסוּרִים־פְּקַח־קוֹחַ׃

would only bring more debt and more disgrace. There was much in the way of juicy gossip and plenty of people who were ready to say, "I told you so," but there were few who would give Rabbi David a word of sympathy, much less a helping hand. So Rabbi David was wearing a patched shoe.

Devorah's neighbours had tut-tutted but had offered nothing constructive except to gossip over the dangers of spoiling one's children. Adah, wife of Ephraim the Smith liked to point out to her circle of acquaintances and friends, fewer of the latter than of the former, the dangers of over-indulgence and of giving in to one's children. She and Ephraim had been outstanding examples of moral rectitude in that respect and no one would have dared to have accused them of over-indulgence of children, their own or anyone else's.

No one ever could accuse them of laxity in that respect. Certainly not those particular children; they were the first to admit how rigidly under-indulging their parents had been. One son, the eldest, was living in Babylon where he made a lot of money with the diligence of the sharpest of sharp dealers in that commodity. Another was a seaman sailing out of the port of Joppa and unlikely to visit his ageing parents. Indeed he had not visited them for over ten years. Their daughters had all married and, living in towns in Judea, were busy imposing their parents' views on their husbands and their children to the great benefit of those husbands and those children, who felt the same loyalty to their parents as their mothers towards Adah and Ephraim.

The solemn exterior in Devorah's case hid a mind actively puzzling over life's mysteries. Was it a fault to love one's son? Was it bad to help that son even if he had

לְהַבֵּשׁ לְנִשְׁבָּרֵי־לֵב קְרָא לִשְׁבוּיִם דְּרֹור וְלַאֲסוּרִים־ פְּקַח־קֹוחַ׃

ideas beyond his means and beyond his talents? She thought it better on the whole to err on the generous side; even to be indulgent. She did not agree with Adah and between the two women there was a sort of hostile truce.

While Adah held forth to her cronies Devorah sat quiet, but the disapproval on her expression was clearly apparent. She acknowledged Adah's moral rectitude but felt that moral rectitude without any warmth and without any forgiveness, even if that forgiveness was seen as indulgence, was too much like self-righteousness. Adah had a readiness to condemn others without seeing her own faults as clearly as she, perhaps, might have done. Devorah remembered the bowed heads and the cowed and over-submissive attitude of Adah's children and considered that there were chains forged other than ones of iron forged in Ephraim's smithy.

Around them other members of the synagogue community lapsed into a somnolent state and a few of the more imaginative among them day-dreamed in various shades of colour depending on their personalities and their own hopes, fears, and emotional make-up.

The opening prayers were soon to begin and expectation built up among the congregation. The 'Shema': "Hear O Israel, The Lord our God is one Lord!" would follow. Abner tried to concentrate but found it difficult. At the last minute before the opening prayer there had been movement at the back and a group of men had entered, making the already crowded main room even more so. They had come in respectfully and with reverence. Indeed, their manner and their bearing could not have been faulted, not even by the strictest rabbi from Jerusalem. The ruler of the synagogue had been casting a benign eye over the crowd assembled and

לַחֲבֹשׁ לְנִשְׁבְּרֵי־לֵב זְרָא לִשְׁבוּיִם דְּרֹור וְלַאֲסוּרִים־ פְּקַח־קֹוחַ׃

was congratulating himself on the good attendance, when the strangers arrived. He was a man who was secretly rather unsure of himself. Though allowing himself to judge his success by external factors such as the size of the attendance, he felt easily threatened by the unusual.

It was the unusual which was happening at that moment with the arrival of a large crowd of strangers. The ruler's father had set high standards and the son felt he had somehow not measured up to them. Where the father had spent some time teaching in the rabbinic schools in Jerusalem, the son had only had a brief stay in the capital, just sufficient to get himself recognised as a proper rabbi, but not one of any distinction. He had used every artifice known to social climbing to reach the pinnacle of the social heap that was the little community he led in Perea. Any stranger, much more a stranger who was followed by a company of a dozen or so men of various ages, might be a threat to his standing. At least, that is how he felt rather than reasoned in his soul; and it was his feelings not his reason that governed his actions.

The entrance of the stranger and His friends not only disturbed the ruler of the synagogue. That innate curiosity, which is part of the character of all who are descended from the first ever couple, made many turn round to see who this was that was entering just in time for the start. Some stared, others cast covert glances, while a few concentrated on the business of the day. Abner was among those who attempted to concentrate their minds on the spiritual nature of their worship and their listening to the Word of the Lord. He liked to echo the Shema with a private prayer of his own that God would truly speak to him and that he would be truly responsive; would truly 'hear' and so obey. This time it was his prayer, not phrased coherently nor even with

210

לְהַבִּשׁ לְנִשְׁבְּרֵי־לֵב זָרֵא לְשְׁבֹּוּיִם דְּרֹוֹר וְלַאֲסוּרִים־ פְּקַח־קֽוֹחַ׃

words, but rather with a longing of the heart, that
something wonderful might happen for his Devorah.
The tears came to his eyes as he regarded the ceiling
where the words, "How goodly are thy tents O Jacob, and
thy tabernacles O Israel!" were inscribed with glowing
colours. "If only that were so!" he thought.

The leader of the group newly arrived, was mature in
His manner though young-looking. He did not stand out
especially in any physical way but there was about Him a
quiet dignity. His manner was mild and gentle, lacking
the overt and sometimes arrogant self-confidence of the
accredited leaders of the community and the aggressive
haughtiness of those who were accounted teachers and
learned among them. People who observed Him more
closely were usually impressed, but some were disturbed
by what they saw.

He seemed to evoke, indeed His very presence
demanded, that one was either for Him or against Him.
The humbler folk were immediately attracted to Him,
while the ruler of the synagogue felt a repulsion that
came not from any blemish in His character, nor from
any overt expression by the stranger, but rather from His
moral ascendancy. The discerning among them became
aware that there were qualities in this young man so
special as to make Him unique among the people. His
leadership was only marked by the clear devotion of His
followers. There was also an indefinable quality that
could only be described as 'being at home'. One realised
that this man would fit in with any group without in any
way lowering Himself to take on the standards of that
group. Rather, one knew that He would, by His moral
superiority and perfection, raise those standards in ways
the members of the group could not dream of.

He did not challenge the social order yet one knew

לְהַלְבֵּשׁ לְנִשְׁבְּרֵי־לֵב זְרָא לִשְׁבֻזִם דְּדִּוֹר וְלַאֲסוּרֵים־ פְּקַח־קָוֹחֵ־׃

that the moral and social order would never be the same again after it had experienced His presence. By the same token no individual, one understood, would ever be the same after having met Him. He smiled with real affection and genuine pleasure at the faces turned in His direction with a smile that somehow encompassed those who had not turned. He was genuinely delighted to be there among them. One might have gone as far as to say that a wonderful warmth and love radiated from Him. He challenged no one's authority yet here, one instinctively knew, was a person who had a presence and an authority not based on human qualification nor upon any art or skill. His authority somehow was of a far higher, nobler order. He was goodness; only good with an authority which could only be used for good.

There was also a clear transparency, an openness and a friendliness about Him which came from a personality of such truthfulness that the light of it would have blinded were it not so gentle, so based in love that it drew folk to Him for healing and rest. The truth and love, however, caused those minds full of their own importance or their own grasping for power and influence to reject Him as repulsive or as a threat. His delight at being there kindled an answering delight in the hearts of those near Him and they gladly made room for the new arrivals; so the crowded room became even more crowded and yet there appeared to be room for all.

The ruler of the synagogue took the entrance of the strangers as an affront to his dignity and to his authority. He felt some resentment that his moment where he took control of the proceedings had somehow been taken from him and appropriated by the stranger. He felt cheated of what was his by right; but seeing the deference and the readiness with which He was received, as he turned to the newcomers, the frown that had begun

לְהַבֵּשׁ לְנִשְׁבְּרֵי־לֵב זְרָא לִשְׁבּוּיִם דְּרֹוֹר וְלַאֲסוּרִים־ פְּקַח־קֹוחַ :

to settle on his face began to change into a bleak smile. It did not quite reach his eyes which clashed with those of the stranger who was clearly the leader of the group. The battle lines were drawn. There was truth in those eyes and the ruler of the synagogue had to look away, not because he was out-stared, as in a childish challenge, but because he was ashamed. The stranger had looked into his soul and had seen the shallowness with disappointment and grief.

Conscious that his fellow elders must not see him discomfited, the ruler of the synagogue gritted his teeth and began the opening prayers. He managed them word perfect as always. But even while going through the well-known rituals, blessings and benedictions, which he shared with the senior members of the community, the disquiet he felt at the presence of the stranger unsettled him. It was even more unsettling to know that courtesy and custom required that a visitor be accorded the opportunity to give the concluding sermon, the Derashah. Again the ruler put on his smile and turned towards the group at the back calling on the young man, hardly into middle age, to come forward if he so desired. "If you have a word for the people, say on," he invited.

The stranger accepted readily but without undue alacrity. He showed perfect decorum as He took His place on the bema before the sacred ark. The perfection of His bearing and His modesty only fired the jealousy of the ruler of the synagogue, though the majority of the folk there present were charmed and felt strangely warmed by the presence of the stranger. Briefly He bowed His head then looked upon them all and spoke:

"Rest," he began and paused, looking about Him. All knew in their hearts that it was something most of all to be desired, that Sabbath rest when God looked with satisfaction upon the beauty of creation and pronounced it, "very good".

The discourse was not long but it was filled with that

לְחָבֵשׁ לְנִשְׁבְּרֵי־לֵב זְרָא לִשְׁבֻיִם דְּרוֹר וְלַאֲסוּרִים־ פְּקַח־קֽוֹחַ׃

longing and with the even greater longing of God for that
time when everlasting righteousness would be brought in
and all the universe sing united an anthem of praise, of
happiness, and of thanksgiving. Sin had broken that rest,
He had explained. There was no satisfaction for God in
such a universe. They should not think that the blood of
beasts slain and burned on the altar in the Temple could
possibly take away sin. There had to be a victim but that
victim had to be perfect, one that all his life delighted
God his Father. He explained how Abraham had been
called upon to sacrifice his only son Isaac, 'Laughter', but
had been reprieved at the last minute as God had
provided the ram caught in the bush. So it would be that
God would provide them the perfect sacrifice and sin
would be conquered, Satan would be conquered and
men would have eternal life.

This was not how the rabbis taught. This was new; it
was unusual and it was a message that deeply moved all
that heard. Full understanding of the implications of that
discourse might not have dawned upon all the listeners,
for not all listeners are hearers. The more aware among
those who attended that synagogue that Sabbath thought
deeply about it and marvelled.   Many were still
marvelling at its wonder and its simplicity a generation
later.
    They thought He had finished, but He seemed to
stand up straighter, to rise to greater height and dignity
and to put forth a fresh, powerful authority. He lifted his
hand and pointed to the women's gallery; His finger
unerringly indicating Devorah. His voice was gentle yet
strongly compelling. It was not raised; He did not shout
but all heard it in its clarity and its commanding love.
"Woman!" He said, as He called her to Him.
    As for Devorah, she knew in her heart whose voice
this was and she dared not disobey. Nor did she dare
obey. She felt transfixed, and unable to move. She knew

לְהָבֵשׁ לְנִשְׁבְּרֵי־לֵב קְרֹא לִשְׁבוּיִם דְּרוֹר וְלַאֲסוּרִים· פְּקַח־קֽוֹחַ׃

He would not insist, would not make her go to Him. But she knew also that she had to go to Him if she wanted her heart's desire and much, much more.

She took a few stumbling paces forward. As her neighbours made room, a way opened up in the crowd for her. Even as she responded to His call, full of gentleness, kindliness and love, He addressed fresh words to her: "Woman, you are set free from your infirmity!" Then He laid His hands on her.

That day they heard the voice that would one day pronounce those very words to the whole of creation.

A warmth and a wonderful sense of well-being stole over her, the forces which had bound her for so long relaxed their grip, and though loath to let go of their prey dare not nor could not resist the power which compelled their obedience. The Satanic force unhooked its claws from her. She could feel its malice, its spite and its indignation at so being forced to relinquish its hold. She stood, straight and upright, rooted to the spot by sheer delight and by the joy of her freedom and her overwhelming sense of well-being. She looked directly into the face of Him who had set her free with just a word of His power. She saw love, a smile of happiness so warm and good, yet all of it tinged with a certain sadness. Only He knew what it would cost Him to so set His people free, to redeem His creation from the bondage of sin, of Satan and of death.

She sensed another presence at her other side and turned again to look into the eyes of Abner, who had followed her as she had stumbled slowly toward the front of the synagogue.

She found her voice as, with tears blurring her vision, she praised God: "Oh wonder! Oh joy! Praise God! Praise God! Praise God who has visited and redeemed His people. Hallelujah!"

The people crowded round the little group which had been the centre of all their attention and echoed that

לְחַבֵּשׁ לְנִשְׁבְּרֵי־לֵב זְרָא לִשְׁבוּיִם דְּרֹור וְלַאֲסוּרִים־ פְּקַח־קֹ֑וחַ ׃

praise, glorifying God with gladness and with joy. "Praise God! Praise God! Praise God! He is worthy of glory, honour and praise. Hallelujah! Hallelujah!"

Shocked by the unseemly outbursts, and seriously upset by the actions of the stranger, the ruler of the synagogue felt he had to do something to reassert his authority. Indignantly he raised his voice to attempt to restore some sort of order and decorum. He dared not attack the man who seemed to have taken over his synagogue and the hearts and minds of his people by means of the healing of the woman with the bent back. He turned his attention rather to the people themselves, who were beginning to break up into groups eagerly discussing the events they had witnessed and their implications for the lives of all present.

In clear ringing tones his voice, with its sharp edge of anger apparent, cut through the hubbub. "There are six days in which men ought to work. In them, therefore, come and be healed and not on the Sabbath Day!"

Rejoicing turned to confusion as the talking ceased and all faces turned again to where the Ruler of the Synagogue stood, drawn up to his full height and glaring angrily at the crowd. They expected to hear more in this vein but any further remarks were forestalled by a direct reply from Yeshua of Nazareth. It was He who had led His disciples into the synagogue and who had called Devorah of the bent back to Him, pronouncing the words to set her free. Now his words took on a different tone entirely.

Whereas the Ruler of the Synagogue had spoken to the crowd and, through them, had attempted to rebuke the prophet of Nazareth, He did no such thing, but spoke directly to the ruler. His word was blistering, His anger real but perfectly under His control:

"Hypocrite!" He exclaimed. The word, like a whip cutting into the minds of all present, especially that of the Ruler of the Synagogue, stung everyone into horrified

לְהַלְבֵּשׁ לְנִשְׁבְּרֵי־לֵב נָרָא לִשְׁבוּיִם דְּרוֹר וְלַאֲסוּרִים־ פְּקַח־קוֹחַ׃

silence. The people stood, stupefied, waiting, holding their breath, for what He had to say next.

"Does not each one of you, on the Sabbath, untie his ox or his ass from the stall and lead him away to watering?" The voice was quieter but still contained righteous indignation with, strangely, some minor tones of grief and disappointment.

It was the custom of the rabbis to teach their students to argue so they could prove from the Law that a certain law did not mean what it said. Here, on the other hand was a man who showed, by the Law, the true meaning of the Law and exposed the hair splitting of the Pharisees and of the lawyers. None could argue with that; everyone knew that the Law allowed, indeed prescribed, the care of domestic animals. Of course the Pharisees hedged it all about with rules, but the main point was clear and could not be argued with. Now the Teacher showed that as Moses had legislated for the well-being of animals, so too were the excessive burdens of humans to be alleviated through the true meaning of the Sabbath.

He went on. "Then should not this woman, being a daughter of Abraham, whom Satan has kept bound for eighteen years, be set free on the Sabbath Day from what bound her?"

It was a statement of what ought to be. It was no question though phrased as one. It made the purpose of the Sabbath perfectly clear and folk there thought to themselves, as light dawned on their understanding and their souls, how slow they had been not to see it all before. It was as if they had known it all along but, unarticulated, it had not entered their understanding. Now that the Teacher had demonstrated and explained it, all was blindingly obvious.

They savoured it in their minds. They said it over to themselves: "Then should not this woman, being a daughter of Abraham, whom Satan has kept bound for eighteen years, be set free on the Sabbath Day from what

לְחַבֵּשׁ לְנִשְׁבְּרֵי-לֵב זְרֵא לִשְׁבוּיִם דְּרוֹר וְלַאֲסוּרִים- פְּקַח-קוֹחַ׃

bound her?"

They remembered how, in the Scripture, Job too had been a victim of Satanic oppression. Some of them remembered with shame that they, like Job's comforters, had not understood the work of the adversary in all this. They had put it down to sin on the part of the woman and had been unable to understand the dark forces at work in the heavenly realms. Satan had challenged God, and Job, by his faithfulness and his endurance under suffering, had vindicated God though not fully understanding why it was all happening.

"A daughter of Abraham" who had been a victim of Satanic malice. They shook their heads. Of course it was all so obvious and they mentally kicked themselves for not seeing it before.

Their thoughts and their gaze turned to the Man who had done such a wonder. He had defeated Satan with just a few words of kindness: "Woman, you are set free." Words of power these were. God had truly visited His people and done great things. So who and what was He? Was He God's agent? Was He the long-awaited Messiah? Was He God?   The Angel of the Lord who had encouraged Joshua and the parents of Samson, had been the Lord in angelic form and appearance. How could it all be; in their obscure synagogue, in their obscure town? What a wonder it all was!

A great concourse of people, like a triumphal procession, accompanied the young Rabbi, who many believed now to be the Messiah, out of the synagogue. Tears of joy streaming down her face she clung to Abner's arm as she walked upright by his side. They walked with the One who had given them rest and healing and looked joyfully into His face. He and His disciples would do them great honour by coming under their roof. It would give them everlasting joy and Devorah would become like the Devorah of old in the Book of Judges who had encouraged Barak and the armies of Israel to be bold and

לְהַכֵּשׁ לְנִשְׁבְּרֵי־לֵב זְרָא לִשְׁבֻוּיִם דְּרֹור וְלַאֲסוּרִים־פְּקַח־קֹוַה׃

to trust the Lord God of Hosts. She too would ever be able to encourage her people to trust in the Lord God of Israel who had visited them and had rescued Devorah from Satanic bondage.

How was it, she thought, that He had known that she had been so oppressed these eighteen years? He must have known. He must have so purposed it that He had come to their part of the country that Sabbath and arrived at the synagogue in time for the service to start.

Then He must truly be Messiah, for how else could He have known and have done such things? She looked up at the sky and there above the hills nearby an eagle circled and, nearer still, the little birds quarrelled and fussed in the branches of the trees and on the rooftops of houses. She smiled with sheer joy through the mist of her tears and looked adoringly at her Saviour and smiled back at her husband who had never doubted her, never given up hope; who had supported her through all the long years of doubt and suffering.

In true humility they had sought the God of Israel and He, in His love and mercy had heard their cries. Feeble and ill-formed those cries might have been but He had heard and had sent His Holy One, His Messiah, the Messiah of Israel, to find them and to answer their prayers. Yeshua, Yeshua the carpenter's son was truly the Messiah of Israel and her Saviour. Surely, she thought, He has put down the mighty from their thrones, He has filled the hungry with good things and the rich He has sent empty away.

(This healing can be found in Luke's Gospel, chapter 13.)

11

Lacking One Thing

He waited there in the dark before the sunrise. The myriads of stars twinkled, cold and remote, a deep sprinkling of lights across the night sky's vast emptiness. He meditated, his lips moving silently as he recited the well-known passage: "Look now toward the heavens, and tell the stars if you are able to number them." So God had told forefather Abraham, and so Abraham had obeyed and found such a task to be impossible. So God had promised and so it was that Abraham's descendants were many as the stars in the heavens and as the sand upon the seashore. He wondered – stars and sand, did this just signify near infinite numbers or was there a deeper meaning, as so often with the Sacred Writings? He shook his head at the wonder of it all; yet the gesture was tinged with sadness since there was a remoteness too, as the stars were remote, which he could not understand.

He remembered how, as a little boy, he had tried counting stars and sand. No one could count so many. He had puzzled long and hard over that. Where was God? Was He somewhere way out beyond the stars? Was that the Third Heaven, where the throne of the architect and King of the universe might be, so remote and at such a distance removed that it was impossible for men to understand?

He thought about what God had said in another

לַהֲבֹשׁ לְנִשְׁבְּרֵי־לֵב יָרָא לִשְׁבוּיִם דְּרוֹר וְלַאֲסוּרִים־פְּקַח־קוֹחַ:

place: "Am I a God at hand, says the Lord, and not a God afar off?" If God had said He was near then He must be. And if that was true then why did he feel that God was remote, far removed from his life in this insignificant corner of Rome's great empire? Indeed, why was it that they were subjugated to Rome? Of course he understood that Israel had sinned. They had forsaken their God who was the fountain of living waters. They had given themselves to idols, so digging out cisterns after their own fashion which had no water of life and which could only produce suffering and death. Yet Israel, since the return from the captivity, had purged itself from idols and the rabbis constantly taught the people and encouraged them to be holier in their observance of the laws given to Moses.

Had he not studied? Had he not qualified as a rabbi, exceeding most of his fellows in the study of the Torah, the Prophets and the Writings? Was he not looked up to as having a reputation for modesty? Did he not do his best to show himself exemplary in his carrying out all the precepts of the Law? So why did he feel ill at ease? Why did God, who had been the friend of Abraham, seem so far away from him?

He waited in the dark street off the market square while the stars lost some of the intensity and the glow in the east grew stronger. The pre-dawn glow cast a blue-green hue across the town and, as the sun ascended the sky it lit the walls of the houses opposite with yellow, and pale rose-coloured tints and a promise of light and warmth to come. The house whose entrance he studied was bathed in the light of the morning sun. But more than that its form carried a promise, as if some presence enlightened it from within with peace, hope and the blessing of joy and truth. The watcher gazed longingly,

11 Lacking One Thing

לַחֲבשׁ לְנִשְׁבְּרֵי־לֵב זֶרָא לשְׁבוּיִם דְּרוֹר וְלַאֲסוּרִים־ פְּקַח־קוֹחַ׃

for there was hope for him here that his troubled mind might be relieved and the dark shadows of his doubts removed by a meeting with one who had rested the night within.

Workmen on their way to the fields and an early start, passed where he waited without a glance, dourly plodding to their toil – a reflection of the toil decreed for Adam those long years ago. Soon the roadways would be filling with men off to the fields, with women too and traders opening shops and setting up stalls, anxious to catch the early trade from housewives looking for fresh produce from the land round about. Soon carts would roll in through the gates of the town and the noise of beasts of burden, the creaking of cart wheels and the cries of traders would fill the square with the noise of the town awakening to a new day of toil, of human joys and sorrows, and of laughter.

It is the people who make of a town a community. Their collective spirits form the emotional and the social climate of that community, and that in turn feeds back into the life of the individuals who make up the community. There is love, some bitterness; there is quarrelling but also much laughter where humans who know and like their neighbours exchange jests and mock the pretences of their social superiors,

As the sun brought promise of rich human activity the birds awoke with song, chirping and twittering and whistling their greeting to the day, readying themselves for the serious business of finding food for themselves and for their fledglings. The avian sounds fit precursors of the human, less musical ones, which would signal that the town was truly awake. After some discreet moments of washing and scrubbing by diligent mothers, the children would emerge, making their way to the

לְהַכִּישׁ לְנִשְׁבְּרֵי־לֵב זָרָא לִשְׁבֻּיִם דְּרוֹר וְלַאֲסוּרֵים־ פְּקַח־קוֹחַ :

synagogue school, not quietly but laughing, shouting, running, teasing, talking, arguing and quarrelling. A lot like their elders really, who would also engage in these activities, but with a more sedate and determined purpose and without the restless high-spirited exuberance of the young ones.

He watched the gate across the wide part of the street, willing it to open and the Teacher to emerge. As he did so his mind went back over his thinking and his difficulties. Sitting large in the forefront of it all was the problem of how to know God so how to have eternal life. What did one have to do that he had not done? What did he have to know that he did not know, or that he could not learn? Where did he have to search so that he might find? Unless, of course, this was to be the end of his anxious quest.

He continued to feel ill at ease. He who had everything, or so it seemed, was not content. It was not greed for more. With his great wealth he was content. The trouble was more profound, deeper. It was a trouble of the soul and of the spirit, and he could not understand what it was nor what it was doing to him. Other young men seemed to be happy. A few of his friends clearly wanted more than they had, though they already had much.

He felt neither happy nor desirous of more wealth. He was not happy though the people whose opinion he respected most, thought he ought to be. Indeed he thought he ought to be. He had everything to live for. Was he not a member of the ruling class, had he not inherited great wealth from both his parents, had he not had an education at the best schools, including those of Athens and of Rome as well as the rabbinic schools of the national capital? He was destined to great things in his

11 Lacking One Thing

לְהָבֵשׁ לְנִשְׁבְּרֵי־לֵב זְרָא לִשְׁבוּיִם דְּרוֹר וְלַאֲסוּרִים־ פְּקַח־קוֹחַ ׃

nation and yet he wondered whether he really wanted them.

He was accounted a clever scholar and might make a great lawyer or rabbi, yet he felt that being a lawyer and a rabbi were somehow missing the point and avoiding the real purpose of life. Already he had been the chazzan, or teacher at the synagogue school, the Beth-hasepher, the House of the Book. Recently he had been elected, by unanimous agreement of the congregation, to the leadership of the synagogue. It was a very unusual thing to happen for one so young. Yet, he asked himself, what was the point? Did life have a purpose? He who said he believed in the God of Israel, the God who had created the heavens and the earth, found himself doubting himself, and the God of Israel seemed aeons, vast distances away from his life in the land of Israel. He was, the young man thought, a God afar off and not near at hand, as people said He was.

He wanted to know God; he wanted to be near to Him who was Life itself. He wanted to be with Him for ever, to have eternal life. But how? He tormented himself with the question time and time again. His young wife, Leah, sensed something wrong and looked on anxiously, not understanding his mood. She, who was also from one of the leading families in the area, was happy married to such a gifted man. She felt at a loss to understand her husband's disquiet and was beginning to worry that it might be some failure on her part. A cloud seemed to hover over their relationship and their home. A cloud which neither of them could lift and, because they did not understand, neither of them could talk about.

How could he doubt when God was so real? If only I could see Him, he thought, and puzzled over the

לְהָבֵשׁ לְנִשְׁבָּרֵי־לֵב זְרָא לִשְׁבוּיִם דְּרוֹר וְלַאֲסוּרִים־ פְּקַח־קֹוחַ׃

problem as to why God did not show Himself to His people as He had in times gone by. "Why does He keep us waiting?" he asked himself on numerous occasions; but no answer came to the question, nor to any of the other questions he asked himself in the silent privacy of his thoughts.

For the Teacher, there was an urgency. His disciples sensed it, yet failed to understand the tension which seemed to surround them. Events in Perea had increased the anxiety they felt. It had been a busy few days, even accustomed as they were to the punishing schedule set by their Master, the pace of events seemed also to quicken. Travelling, always travelling as if there were an agenda, an itinerary to get through, with a crisis, somewhere, looming.

They had arrived at last in this town in Perea. The rabbis of the Pharisees had tried to trap Him as they often did. John the Baptist had pronounced about Herod's divorce of his wife and his adulterous marriage to Herodias. For that he had been imprisoned and had lost his head. It was not so much that Herod himself had cared but Herodias, sensing the precariousness of her position, had persuaded the king to do away with John and had found her chance when Herod had drunkenly promised her daughter anything she asked as a reward for her dancing. So John had died and Herodias, her malice and vindictiveness appeased, looked round her for fresh amusements.

So they thought they would bring up the matter of divorce. "Is it lawful for a man to divorce his wife for just any reason?" If He said "yes" the stricter rabbis would have a field day and if He said "no", Herod would most certainly hear of it and He might well share the fate of the

11 Lacking One Thing

לַהֲבֹשׁ לְנִשְׁבְּרֵי־לֵב זְרָא לִשְׁבוּיִם דְּרֹור וְלַאֲסוּרִים־ פְּקַח־קֹוחַ׃

Baptist. If He agreed that divorce was wrong under any circumstances then only Herod's superstitious mind could prevent a speedy trip to Herod's dungeons. It seemed good to the Pharisees that using Herod to do, unwittingly, their dirty work was a way out of their dilemma with a man who invariably blocked their arguments by His own fresh, even unique, understanding of the Law.

Once again he had answered them from out of the Law and once again they felt cheated of their prey. They vowed that, sooner or later they would trap Him and then He would feel the fury of their wrath.

As the day had worn on, mothers had brought their babies and their little children to Him for Him to bless them. This was something He gladly did, for He delighted in being surrounded with the little ones and their parents. The disciples, ever anxious and worried about His health and His stamina, were less happy to see Him so engaged. They tried to hurry the mothers and their offspring away but He had cautioned them: "Let the little children come to Me and do not forbid them, for of such is the kingdom of God."

The one who waited knew of these skirmishes with the Pharisees. He was himself a Pharisee and his boast was in the Law of God. He was well on his way to becoming a leading rabbi. He had worked at this since his earliest youth as he had learned by heart passages from the Torah at his mother's knee. But even Pharisees could be wrong and he did not have the arrogant self-confidence of many of his fellows and his elders. His trouble was in fact that he was a thoroughly nice young man. Too nice, some people thought, too open, too gentle, not tough minded enough for his own good. He

לְהַבֵּשׁ לְנִשְׁבְּרֵי־לֵב קְרָא לִשְׁבוּיִם דְּרֹוֹר וְלַאֲסוּרִים־ פְּקַח־קֹוֹחַ׃

had long ago resolved to succeed in his studies, not so that he could surpass his fellows, nor so that he could achieve fame and status. Remembering how good King Jehoshaphat had sent out learned men to teach the people from out of the Torah, he too wished to take the wholesome Word of God to the people. He admired men like King Josiah and Ezra the Scribe who also put the Word of the Lord above all things.

He loved to teach, and felt hurt when his students failed to learn through inattention, laziness or foolishness. He did not want to sway others to his opinions with clever arguments, nor to lord it over the poorer people now that he was a junior member of the local Sanhedrin. One day, perhaps, he would be called to join the Great Sanhedrin in Jerusalem as his friends from student days, Abiel and Saul from Tarsus, already had been called. But none of this caused him to think more highly of himself than he ought to think, nor to look down on others who had not had his opportunities of study.

In spite of his diligence and the serious attitude he brought to everything he set his mind and his hand to, he had humility, so no one could feel jealous of his wealth or his success. He had too a sense of humour and, like Jews everywhere, he could laugh at himself and at those who took themselves too seriously. He treated all people the same, with respect and courtesy, so he found himself welcome everywhere he went, and his advice and his ministrations were given a greater credibility than otherwise might have been the case in one so young. He was clever enough to recognise that even the most lowly or the most despised also had their talents and their stories to tell.

Like all Jewish boys he had learned a trade. He found himself drawn to the workshops of the craftsmen for he

לַחֲבֹשׁ לְנִשְׁבְּרֵי־לֵב זְרָא לִשְׁבֻיִם דְּרֹור וְלַאֲסוּרִים־ פְּקַח־קֹוחַ׃

recognised that his skill in the Torah was simply one other craft, one other skill, achieved through long and laborious practice and sheer hard work. He would watch the potter at his wheel and the carpenter at his bench, then he would look in to the smith and feel privileged to give a hand as the master craftsman's striker, or simply to attend the little furnace where the metal was heated. There had been a rabbi who always sat on a barrel of his own making as he taught his students, giving them the additional lesson that a rabbi ought to be master of two trades, the Torah and one requiring skill of hand and eye. He had served under this same smith until he was judged competent to turn out work of a decent and acceptable standard.

It was with sadness, yet with acceptance that humans were flawed, that he viewed the greed and avarice of the tax collectors, the luxury of the men and women of the ruling classes, even of his own people, the priests and the Pharisees. The Herods too, as well as the Romans, indulged a frenzied lust for power and status. There were injustices at all levels of society but he understood, as few understood, that it was not laws, nor governments, nor policing that made a society righteous. Of course these institutions had to be righteous but that did not make the nation righteous. Law-abiding citizens might simply be repressed and in fear of the authorities. Others might be sycophants currying favour with those in power.

For righteousness in society there had to be an inner righteousness within each individual. That could only come from God. He often thought about the words of Ezekiel: "Then will I sprinkle clean water upon you, and you shall be clean. From all your filthiness, and from all your idols, will I cleanse you. A new heart also will I give you, and a new spirit will I put within you. And I will

לְהַבֵּשׁ לְנִשְׁבְּרֵי־לֵב זְרָא לִשְׁבֹּיִם דְּרוֹר וְלַאֲסוּרִים־ פְּקַח־קֹוֹחַ:

take away the stony heart out of your flesh, and I will give you a heart of flesh. And I will put my Spirit within you and cause you to walk in My statutes, and you will keep My judgements and do them."

Yet he observed all that he understood the Law as demanding of a man. He gave to the poor. He abhorred the idols of the Romans, the Greeks and the Phoenicians. He wondered if perhaps there was some flaw in his character or in his relations with his family and his fellows, but could find none. Others might play fast and loose with the commandments but he would not. From the time that he first became aware, he had obeyed the laws of God.

He had searched his own soul. He respected his parents and loved them dearly. As they were getting older he used to see to it that they had every attention and every courtesy which a loving and dutiful son could give. Nor were his wife's parents neglected, for Leah called on them often, taking them gifts and doing what was needed. He did not covet, and was not jealous of others for he had all he needed and much, much more. As to sins of the flesh, he had married at eighteen when Leah was approaching sixteen. He had felt stirrings in his flesh but had kept himself strictly under control and had gone to her pure, as she had come to him.

In their house the Sabbath was a delight, as the prophet had said it should be. It was never a case of grim observance of every minute piece of legislation but of enjoyment of what God had intended to be enjoyed. He was not naïve in thinking that all were as high minded as were he and Leah. It pained him that some, who ought to have been examples, often seemed to fail. However, he did not condemn, for only God knew the state of their lives and what torments of heart or of soul they might be

לַחֲבֹשׁ לְנִשְׁבְּרֵי־לֵב זְרָא לִשְׁבוּיִם דְּרֹור וְלַאֲסוּרִים־ פְּקַח־קֹוַח׃

going through in the privacy of their minds. Job had been accused by his friends, but it was God who had vindicated him, as it was Job who had vindicated God by his refusal to allow his suffering to break him.

Musing upon the problem of righteousness led him to the words of Daniel who had spoken concerning the Messiah that he would, one day, "finish the transgression, and make an end of sins, and make reconciliation for iniquity, and bring in everlasting righteousness." He longed for that day when Messiah would visit His people and when all things would be put right. Would he have to wait many long and weary years, he wondered, before Messiah would give to the earth peace and to Israel its just place above the nations with satisfaction of every heart and of every mind? Perhaps only Messiah would have the answers to the questions which troubled him.

This was what led him to the side of the street opposite Rabbi Ephraim's gate waiting for Yeshua ben Yosef to emerge. This was his hope that, perhaps, Yeshua from Nazareth might be that Messiah. Perhaps He would be able to tell him what it was to gain eternal life, to find everlasting righteousness and to be at peace with God.

Abiel had been on a visit from Jerusalem. He admired Abiel who had excelled above all at his studies until Saul, the young student from Tarsus had arrived in the capital. Abiel had not been jealous of Saul's success; instead he had encouraged him and several of them had enjoyed disputations far into the night. Now Saul and Abiel were among the young up-and-comings in the Great Sanhedrin and he was not a little flattered that, from time to time, they should remember with pleasure their companion of student days who had remained a provincial. He and Leah enjoyed the visits when one or other of the future intellectual leaders of the nation paid

לְהַלְבִּשׁ לִנְשָׁבְּרֵי־לֵב זֶרָא לִשְׁבִּים דְּרֹור וְלַאֲסוּרִים־פְּקַח־קֹוחַ:

their respects and stayed at their house.

On these occasions they invited others who might benefit from the conversation round the meal tables. There had been quite a number at Abiel's latest visit and the subject of Yeshua from Nazareth had been discussed. The events too at Machaerus were in all their minds and the connection between John and the prophet from Nazareth had been hotly debated.

"I tell you this **is** Messiah!" argued one, hotly. He went on to cite evidence of his healings and other miracles.

Abiel had frowned. "We must expect something rather more spectacular from the true Messiah," he cautioned. " 'Messiah's feet will stand in that Day upon the Mount of Olives' and the ground will be cleft apart. He will then, 'suddenly come to his temple,' " he added. Someone had objected that this was the Lord Himself, but Abiel reasoned that Messiah was the Lord in human form.

"How can that be?" asked a sceptic.

Abiel had gone on to argue that the Angel of the Lord had to be reverenced as only God could be, by Moses, by Joshua and by the parents of Samson as well as others. It was well understood that God often visited His people and would do so again in Messiah's Day.

The discussion had then turned to John, who had said that he was not worthy to untie Yeshua's sandals and who also had pointed out Yeshua as the Lamb of God, the sin bearer. They had argued long and hard as to whether that meant Messiah or simply one of the prophets, or, what was likely, the prophet promised by Moses.

The evening had left disturbing thoughts with him. How could Yeshua be Messiah if all the other things,

לְהָבַשׁ לְנִשְׁבְּרֵי־לֵב זָּרָא לִשְׁבֹּיִם וְּרֹוּר וְלַאֲסוּרִים־ פְּקַח־קָוֹחַ:

which Abiel had asserted, were true? On the other hand His miracles were certainly of a more powerful order, and if calming the storm on the lake were true and the feeding of vast crowds with small amounts of fish and bread, then the claim was a serious one demanding of thorough investigation.

He was either that or He was an impostor. But then He had not publicly claimed to be Messiah, though once there had been an attempt to stone Him when He had uttered the seemingly blasphemous statement, "before Abraham was I am." In doing so He had claimed one of the important titles of the Most High: I Am.

He had to see Yeshua and question Him, but above all, since His wisdom seemed to be great and greater than that of the Scribes, the Pharisees and the Priests, he had to ask Him what he needed to do to have eternal life.

The previous afternoon a friend had burst in on him. "You wanted to meet that Yeshua ben Yosef," he said. "Well, He's here, staying at Rabbi Ephraim's house. He's been blessing the children."

He expressed his gratification at the news, then, with a glance at Leah and a grin on his face he said. "It's a sure means of success, bless the children. That way you get the women on your side and the men have no choice but to follow."

They laughed and Leah had shooed them out so that she could see to the meal and supervise the girl who came in to help but who was turning out to be rather less of an asset than they had hoped. He had suggested they get in someone else with rather more initiative, a girl who did not need to be shown, step by step, how to do everything so that it would have been just as quick for Leah to do it herself. But Leah had been insistent that they must employ her since her mother was a widow and

לְהַבֵּשׁ לְנִשְׁבְּרֵי־לֵב קָרָא לִשְׁבֻיִם דְּרֹור וְלַאֲסוּרִים· פְּקַח־קֽוֹחַ:

needed the money.

"And," Leah had emphasised, "she needs the money for her dowry or she will have to put up with a dreamy man such as I ended with."

"Alright my dear, I will go and dream at Asa the Smith's forge and forget that I have a strict guardian of the household to keep me in order and my feet on the ground." They had laughed, but it seemed that God was giving him a chance which might not come again.

As well as being a scene of busy activity, Asa's forge was also a good place for the men to exchange gossip. He had learned that Yeshua from Nazareth had been there since earlier in the day and would stay there overnight, when He would make an early start on another of His journeys. Where He was going no one knew and it did not really matter. All that mattered was that he got up and about long before dawn and watched from the street for the guests to leave. He could accost Yeshua as He was on His way. He had not been invited to Rabbi Ephraim's and he knew that Yeshua's disciples would be there as well, so he could not rudely intrude into an already busy household.

This was why he was lingering with only his thoughts and his anxieties in the dark before the dawn, looking up to the stars and finding no solace in their remote and inscrutable light. The tension mounted as the daylight built up and as people began to move around. It had been foolish of him to get there so early, but one never knew; it was said that Yeshua was a man like Elijah who, without warning, might rise before dawn and undertake a journey of many miles. It did not occur to him, indeed he could not have known, that Yeshua ben Yosef was a perfect gentleman and would not inconvenience his host and hostess any more than courtesy and consideration

לַחְבֹּשׁ לְנִשְׁבְּרֵי־לֵב זָרָא לִשְׁבֻיִם דְּרֹור וְלַאֲסוּרִים־ פְּקַח־קֹוחַ׃

allowed. He would not disturb them by insisting on disrupting the household arrangements for his own need for an early start. Nor could he have known the uncanny detail of the Teacher's planning so that every visit, every journey and every stop on the way, was designed beforehand to coincide with the movements of thousands of others who needed the message of the Kingdom and of Salvation. Every little detail, every word and every action was all part of the grand design.

A workman he knew, who was making a hasty breakfast on dried figs and a piece of bread, greeted him and he returned the greeting. A market trader was unloading his patient donkey and setting out his wares on a mat on the ground. The city was coming to life but, though he took in, with interest, all the varied activities and the starting of the day, he did not allow his attention to wander from the gate of Rabbi Ephraim's house over the way.

A noise of bolts being drawn and of muted conversation came from that direction. He felt the butterflies in his stomach and a sudden misgiving that he might not recognise Yeshua if he were surrounded by his friends and disciples. He shrugged the anxiety away and told himself not to be silly. He had a tongue in his head and could ask, even if it did seem a little stupid. Yeshua of Nazareth did not sound the sort of man to take offence at not being recognised. Not like some rabbis he knew; he smiled to himself, but then put the thought behind him as being unworthy.

The gate into the courtyard of Ephraim's house was pushed ajar. He heard voices, a little louder this time but could not quite distinguish what they were saying. Then the gate was closed again while the voices continued with some laughter. The overnight guests were saying their goodbyes, but with many a regret, with thanks and the

לַחֲבֹשׁ לְנִשְׁבְּרֵי־לֵב זְרֹא לִשְׁבוּיִם דְּרֹור וְלַאֲסוּרִים־ פְּקַח־קֹוחַ׃

witticisms and compliments which made such times memorable and enhanced the pleasure of the visit. The gate inched open yet again, and yet again it was swung to, but not quite closed, as if someone had their hand on it but kept hesitating as, each time of parting the conversation flared up again. The guests were leaving with reluctance, which was as it should be, and the host and hostess would see them on their way with the happiness that their home had been shared by friends who had brought to it joy and enrichment.

At last it swung open fully and, slowly, the dozen or so figures emerged. They were of all ages and types of men. There were big, brawny, muscular men, lean wiry men and men who had about them the look of the scholar or of the skilled artisan. One, indeed, had an intense, suspicious look about him and another carried himself with the jaunty, challenging air of the 'devil may care' attitude of the zealot. He wondered how such a disparate group of men could stay together and share the wandering life of their Teacher without falling out and coming to blows. It must, he thought, say something wonderful about the character of their leader and teacher if he could unite such differences of character and of outlook.

His fears of not recognising Yeshua had been groundless. Indeed if he had had merely a description it would not have availed, for Yeshua was not the tall outstanding man one thought of as a leader. Everything about him said, 'average'. He was not particularly good looking though his features were regular, and certainly one could not but be drawn to Him as soon as one looked upon Him. Those who thought of a leader and a teacher who was commanding and like a Caesar would be disappointed, he thought. On the other hand, those who looked for kindness, for gentleness, for compassion and for all the goodnesses one could ever desire, would find them, beyond their wildest imaginings, in the face of

לַחֲבֹשׁ לְנִשְׁבְּרֵי־לֵב זָרָא לִשְׁבוּיִם דְּרוֹר וְלַאֲסוּרִים־ פְּקַח־קָוֹחַ׃

this one Man. Even as he ran toward Him the thought
came to him of what the prophet Isaiah had said: "And
when we shall see Him there is no beauty that we should
desire him, he is despised and rejected of men."

He knelt before Him. He could not have said then
why he knelt. It came to him, in his inner being, that
here was Love incarnate, here was the answer to
everything he had ever desired, to everything he had ever
needed to know.

"Good Teacher," he blurted out, "what good thing
shall I do, so that I may have eternal life?"

The Teacher smiled as one does on a puzzled child.
"Why do you call Me 'good'? No one is good but One,
that is God." He paused, still looking at the man, in his
prime of life, kneeling before Him, allowing the thoughts
and their implications to sink in. Then he continued, "If
you want to enter into life, keep the commandments."

It was not the answer he had been looking for. It was
exactly what had been troubling him. What did the
Teacher mean; was there something he was missing? His
brows drew together in a frown of puzzlement. "Which?"
he exclaimed in his uncertainty and confusion.

Yeshua was patient. He was leading the young man
on so that he could find out for himself his need and,
drawing his own conclusion, so come to an understanding of his need and what he should do.

Yeshua continued: "Do not murder. Do not commit
adultery. Do not steal. Do not bear false witness. Honour
your father and your mother."

The enquirer shook his head as if to clear away the
mist of perplexity which was clouding his understanding.
"All these things have I kept from my youth. What do I
still lack?"

The answer came as a bolt from the blue. It left him
speechless. "One thing is lacking," He replied.

The young man looked up in hope but with a feeling

לְהַבֵּשׁ לְנִשְׁבְּרֵי־לֵב ׀ רָא לִשְׁבֻיִם דְּרֹור וְלַאֲסוּרִים־ פְּקַח־קֹוֹחַ:

also of dread.

"Go and sell whatever you have, give to the poor, and you will have treasure in heaven; and come and follow Me."

He could not have anticipated such an answer. His mind was in a turmoil now. Not because of confusion but because he saw it all so clearly and he could not, dare not, comply with this stark choice that was being offered him. What would Leah think? That was his first thought. How would she cope? Yet at the same time he knew that by doing that which was right he was also doing the best for her and taking her with him on the road of discipleship to that glorious blissful life eternal in the heavens.

He looked into a great chasm, a yawning gulf. There was all the emptiness of the things of this life. There lay all the pretensions and the pride of life, there lay the admiration of fellows, the success that was really failure, the glory which was in reality shame, the gain which in fact was loss. And there, beyond it all, beyond the emptiness lay the reality. Earthly loss was heavenly gain.

To be despised by men was to be loved by God. To be trodden upon by men was to be promoted by God and rewarded with riches unimaginable to the mind stuck in the rut of this life and confined by the blinkers of human conditioning and of culture.

He got up from his knees. The burden of sorrow he now felt in a heart as heavy as the gold which men craved, was heavier than the burden of unknowing he had carried before. The rabbis said that God's blessing made one rich. They said that to be poor was worse than all the plagues of Egypt.

Yet he knew that, though they encouraged almsgiving, it was in a spirit of odious boastfulness and this too he had been guilty of. He knew, for he had looked into the face of Truth and had heard from His lips. And he had rejected the Truth and he had spurned the

11 Lacking One Thing

לַחֲבֹשׁ לְנִשְׁבְּרֵי־לֵב קְרָא לִשְׁבֻיִם דְּרוֹר וְלַאֲסוּרִים־ פְּקַח־קוֹחַ׃

Love.   Only by self-sacrifice and self-denial could he
really obey the higher law of the Kingdom.   He looked
again at the face of the One who had so invited and
challenged him.   He saw there a love greater, far greater,
than his own and a sorrow deeper, far deeper than his,
which was troubling his soul, as he tore his gaze away
and stumbled to his feet and, with shaking legs hurried
as best he could, back to his own house.

Never would things be the same again.   He would be
a hollow man, a man without a soul and a spirit, a man
mechanically going about the form of living, without its
inner peace, without its reality and without its joy.   That
joy and that peace had been within his reach, yet he had
been afraid, so terribly afraid, that he could not lift his
hands and take them from the hand of One who loved
him more than his father and his mother, more than his
Leah and more than all those who would have called him
'fool' had he listened to and had he obeyed the Teacher.

As the light of that fateful day had dawned over the
town square and had shone into the passages and the
alleys as well as the streets and lanes, so had the bright
clear light of eternity dawned in his own heart.   All that
he had reckoned to be of great worth was seen in that
gentle but penetrating radiance to be but dust.   The walls
which he had built up of complacency and of confidence
had crumbled to rubble, and he was exposed to that high
calling which came from the very throne of God.

"Sell all you have?   Give to the poor?"   He responded
with horror, the shock of it all reducing him to tearful
despair and a slow, dragging journey to his home.   He
had looked on the Truth, and the Truth had looked on
him and had found him wanting.

(Based on an incident recorded by Luke, chapter 18.)

238

12

To Love Much

It was more in the nature of an invitation to an inferior than to another rabbi. It was the sort of invitation a senior might give to his junior or a very rich man to someone who was poor. It was the sort an aristocrat might give to one of the businessmen he dealt with, not quite as patronising as the invitation he might issue to one of the peasants, but expressing clearly that one man was lowering himself and conferring a privilege on the other.

Such was the invitation the teacher, Yeshua of Nazareth received. Though common courtesy made the Pharisee give the invitation, and though he was bound, again by that same courtesy, to call him 'rabbi' he felt he was possibly compromising himself somewhat in some pharisaic circles. Already it was clear that many of the brotherhood felt uneasy about the teacher from Galilee. People were even saying he was a prophet. There were even those, and Pharisees shook their heads in concern at the thought, who were saying he was the Messiah.

If Simon the Pharisee did feel he was conferring a privilege upon the teacher from Galilee he suppressed it. If there was an element of patronage in his invitation, he told himself, and others, that it was his duty to entertain visiting teachers. If there was condescension then he told himself that it was not so and that he was curious about the unusual teacher and that it was right and proper that

12 To Love Much

לַחְבֹּשׁ לְנִשְׁבְּרֵי־לֵב לִקְרֹא לִשְׁבוּיִם דְּרוֹר וְלַאֲסוּרִים־ פְּקַח־קוֹחַ:

he should investigate the man's ideas and his teachings. A Pharisee, the son of a Pharisee, he had learned from an early age always to be perfectly correct in all that he did. Indeed, he prided himself that he was perfect in etiquette, in dress, in dietary considerations, in washings, in tithes and in all the offerings required by the law.

He was curious. Such a mentality did not always sit easy with the certainties that were the laws and rules of pharisaism. He was curious about this man, Yeshua from Nazareth. He could expound the Law and the Prophets as no one else could. His teachings were easy to understand, and yet, they were profound and he felt there were depths of wisdom that the teachings of his schools and his rabbis had never yet plumbed.

The common folk heard Yeshua gladly; they rejoiced when they had been with him. There was supposed to be joy and gladness when the Law was expounded and yet, he mused, there was so little happiness in all the convoluted arguments and stern teachings of the rabbis. He thought, with some regret, that the higher echelons of the brotherhood of Pharisees had nothing to compare with the elegantly beautiful reasonings of a man, who to many, was simply a sort of hedgerow rabbi, though some of the common people were saying he was a prophet.

With a twinge of guilt, he realised that these thoughts were disloyal to the great teachers he had longed to follow and whose example he had studied to emulate. Hillel, Shammai and now Gamaliel, were the men he admired above all. And yet ... And yet! The Rabbi from Nazareth held a strange fascination, a sort of compulsion that drew people to him. He too felt he was being drawn, though he dismissed the thought and put it from him, turning his mind back to the path of duty and to obedience to the Law, the sacred Torah.

לַחְבֹּשׁ לְנִשְׁבְּרֵי-לֵב ּ קְרֹא לִשְׁבוּיִם ּ דְּרוֹר ּ וְלַאֲסוּרִים- פְּקַח-קוֹחַ ּ

Outwardly he was a senior member of the brotherhood of Pharisees. As such the touch even of the junior members of the order could be defiling and was avoided. As he walked through the streets and across the market square he would automatically pull the skirts of his garments to himself to avoiding any and all touches that could carry defilement. All the common people were thus defiled. They did not know the Law – how could they with their elementary education only? They attended the synagogue, and they listened to the lectures of the Pharisees who held universal sway in such institutions. Yet for all that they were not learned in the minutiae of the Law and so could not obey it all.

The beasts with their burdens, the children playing, anything and everything had to be avoided unless it was ritually clean. Any defiling touch made him unclean and he had been taught to avoid this at all costs. The ritual prayers and ablutions, the specific offerings for specific infringements were all a burden which he hardly knew he carried. He hardly knew it, but he longed to be free; though his mind and his understanding were darkened to think that these, these burdens, were the things which made him free. They were the things which set him apart from the common people, and which set the whole of Israel apart from the nations. With his mind he approved of them and gloried in them, though in his heart he felt the cold of dawning enlightenment. It was that cold, clear light of truth which may make a man rebel against it in fear, or which makes him lift up his eyes to heaven and cry out to God for love, for light and for life.

He sighed within himself. If only all Israel could avoid uncleanness for just one day. The rabbis taught that if they did then Messiah would come to His temple

12 To Love Much

לְחַבֵּשׁ לְנִשְׁבְּרֵי־לֵב זְרָא לִשְׁבֻיִם דְּרוֹר וְלַאֲסוּרִים־ פְּקַח־קוֹחַ׃

and restore all things. His, he was convinced, by the traditions of his family and of his culture, was a high and noble calling. That was the purpose of the Pharisee. He had to show the way, to lead, to teach that all Israel might be saved. Only thus would God send Messiah. Only thus would begin the glorious golden reign of peace, of prosperity, and of fruitfulness when Israel would be the head and not the tail of the nations. Only then would all men look to the Temple at Jerusalem as the place where God the Lord dwelt and they, Israel, would be a nation of priests and teachers, an example to the world.

Some of his brother Pharisees fiercely condemned Yeshua ben Yosef. They condemned him out of hand because he was not a Pharisee. If he were not a Pharisee, they reasoned, he could not be of God. Therefore, clearly, he was an impostor.

It all seemed so simple, so rational, and yet so trite and he sensed that something, somewhere was missing among the simplistic arguments they put forward. If he was not of God, they further reasoned, then he boded no good for the nation and, with the Romans breathing down their necks, they could not afford false Messianic hopes among the people. They dare not allow the fervour of the people to be stirred up lest the Romans send in the legions and that would be the end of Israel as a nation and an end to their God-given religion.

He could not thus easily swallow the arguments they so obligingly trotted out. He could not close his mind since his conscience kept nagging him that this was not an open and shut case and that all too flippantly they failed to investigate Yeshua properly and to hear what he had to say about himself. Disturbing thoughts kept intruding in among the pharisaic certainties with which his upbringing and his education had effectively

לְהַלְבִּשׁ לְנִשְׁבְּרֵי־לֵב זָרָא לִשְׁבֻּיִם דְּרֹור וְלַאֲסוּרִים־ פְּקַח־קֹוחַ׃

indoctrinated him. He was uneasy, and his mind unsettled. He wished he could be so sure like other Pharisees. But he could not be sure and there were times when he was wracked with doubts. These doubts he kept to himself and hid them under the calm, dignified exterior of a senior Pharisee, a Rabbi, a Teacher of the Law of Moses and of the customs of Israel

It seemed somehow inconsistent, though he fully understood the problems they faced. The Pharisees shuddered with horror whenever they thought of the Roman occupation of the sacred land, Erets Yisrael. Roman soldiers trampling everything sacred. Roman cities with theatres and all sorts of debauchery going on. A Roman governor and, worst of all, a High Priest who appeared to condone all this and who worked with them.

For all that, they recognised that the High Priest had a careful diplomatic task to perform and, grudgingly, they admitted that he managed to keep the governor off their backs and the Sanhedrin actually governing the affairs of the land.

The priests were, for the most part, members of the school of thought of the Tsadikim, the Sadducees in the Grecianised form of the name. They were the 'righteous ones' who believed in the Torah but who did not entirely believe in the existence of supernatural spirits. Nor did some of them believe in the resurrection. There were, in these ideas, to his mind glaring inconsistencies. How could they deny these things and still believe in God the Creator, Sustainer and Upholder of the universe and not believe in resurrection?

The Pharisees prided themselves that they upheld all the ancient traditions of Israel. They were descendants, the true descendants, they would have claimed, of the hassidim, the followers of the Maccabees, Jewish patriots

לַחֲבֹשׁ לְנִשְׁבְּרֵי־לֵב זְרָא לִשְׁבוּיִם דְּרֹור וְלַאֲסוּרִים־ פְּקַח־קֹוֹחַ׃

who had restored the Temple and its service after the desecration by the Seleucid king of Syria, Antiochus.

As the hated name came to his mind, Simon thought, "May he burn in the lowest hell reserved for the worst of gentile tyrants." Just as the Maccabees had rallied the faithful in Israel, so he believed that God would, one day, raise up a deliverer for Israel. God grant that it be soon, God grant deliverance to His people, may He soon visit His people.

The longing for Israel's salvation, so much part of his personality, was so much part of his very being from the earliest times he could remember. The hope for Messiah and the longings not far below the surface of all Jewish lives brought his thoughts onto yet another track. He had been brought up with the mental blinkers of pharisaism and yet the very Scriptures and the hopes and longings on every page of the Torah, taught him to hope for something more. It was a something he could not define, yet it was a something which was making him increasingly dissatisfied with the traditional views of his upbringing and his education.

Some of his brother Pharisees condemned Yeshua ben Yosef out of hand. Indeed these were in the majority, yet Simon could not find it in him to take this over-simplistic view. He could not and would not close his mind. To him it was no simple matter to be lightly dismissed, just as the Carpenter's son himself could not, in his mind, be lightly dismissed. Disturbing thoughts intruded constantly into and among the pharisaic certainties with which he had been brought up and educated. He reflected again how the common people respected him and in the hearts of many he inspired love and devotion. The man's disciples might be from the lower ranks of society, simple fishermen and the like, but

לְהַבֵּשׁ לְנִשְׁבְּרֵי־לֵב זְרָא לְשָׁבּוּיִם דְּרוֹר וְלַאֲסוּרִים־ פְּקַח־קֽוֹחַ׃

they were still Jews and they were no fools. He could not dismiss such people as his fellow Pharisees dismissed them and their ideas, their loves and their hates. They were after all, as Jews, the people of God, even if unlearned as far as the pharisaic laws were concerned. Did that make them any less, he wondered, in the eyes of God? God was, after all, so far above everyone that he doubted in his innermost mind whether God concerned Himself with such distinctions.

He tried to banish the doubts and questions from his mind but he could not. He wondered what other Pharisees would think if they could read his thoughts. He was glad they could not. He was glad that he could keep up that calm and seriously bland exterior to hide the turmoil beneath.

Maybe Yeshua was a prophet. Were not the prophets in their generations often despised and ill treated? Was not Jeremiah considered a traitor and imprisoned because he counselled surrender to the Babylonians and their king, Nebuchadnezzar? Had not Daniel been a captive in Babylon? Had not Amos been one of the herdsmen of Tekoa, a very ordinary sort of working man whom the Pharisees, had he lived in the present, would have disdained even to speak to?

More examples of the failure of Israel to listen to the prophets God sent them came to his mind and he shook his head sadly. Could it be that they were in danger of making the same mistake over this Yeshua from Nazareth? No prophet had been seen or heard in Israel since the time of Malachi; except for the Baptist, of course; they also said he was a prophet. He too had been rejected by the Pharisees as a madman or deluded and who had seemed to answer their questions with riddles.

He thought of Israel's history; how a succession of

לַחֲבֹשׁ לְנִשְׁבְּרֵי־לֵב זָרָא לִשְׁבוּיִם דְּרוֹר וְלַאֲסוּרִים־ פְּקַח־קוֹחַ׃

gentile kings had ruled over them and under some of whom they had been cruelly oppressed. True, some, such as Cyrus of Persia, Alexander the Greek and Octavian, titled Augustus, the Roman, had been favourable to the Jewish nation and had even granted them privileges.

He remembered how the festival of Purim, lots, celebrated the change of heart of the tyrannical Ahasuerus. He was known to the Greeks as Xerxes, and, by the unseen working of the God of Israel, Esther, the Queen, had prevailed on the King to undo the evil plots of the enemy Haman the Agagite to exterminate the Jews. A Jew, Mordecai, Queen Esther's older cousin, was made chief minister and the Jews "had light and gladness, and joy and honour."

These times had been all too few and now Tiberius reigned. He was a man with little time for religion and less for that of the Jews who were, to him, at best a nuisance, at worst possible enemies, alien to the culture of Rome. In Judea a Roman procurator governed who was cruel and unpredictable and, worse, related by marriage to the Emperor. The rule of the two remaining Herods, Antipas and Philip, was not much better though of the two Philip was much to be preferred. Philip's tetrarchy east of Galilee was well administered and Philip toured the province providing justice freely for all. However, his dominions included Greek cities and areas with a non-Jewish populace. It was hardly the same as Judea or the much larger province ruled by the despotic Antipas.

He cast his mind back to those rulers of old who had favoured the Jews and, national prejudice apart, it seemed to him that they were the best of them. Cyrus had caused the Temple, destroyed by the Babylonians, to

לַחְבֹּשׁ לְנִשְׁבְּרֵי־לֵב לִקְרֹא לִשְׁבוּיִם דְּרוֹר וְלַאֲסוּרִים־ פְּקַח־קֽוֹחַ׃

be rebuilt. Alexander had treated Jerusalem with respect, and had been pleasantly surprised that he was mentioned in the Jewish prophetic books. The High Priest had shown him the roll of Daniel where the four-winged Greek leopard had destroyed the mighty lumbering bear which was the empire of the Medo-Persians.

Later, after the untimely death of the great conqueror, the empire had split up among his generals; that too had been implied by the prophet. The Jews had then fallen under the power of the kings of Syria, the descendants of Seleucus. Each one of these was more corrupt than the last and under Antiochus Epiphanes, referred to by some less complimentary names by many of his own subjects as well as the Jews, they had suffered bitter persecution and the desecration of the Temple. This had provoked the revolt of the sons of Matthias, under the leadership of Judas, the Hammer. After setbacks and a gruelling campaign, the Syrians had been defeated by a vastly inferior Jewish guerrilla army. The Temple had been cleansed and its worship restored; an event celebrated annually at the festival of Hannukah.

Israel's independence did not last for long; they fell under the domination of Rome. That too was there in the prophetic book of Daniel as a multi-headed beast, rapacious and terrifyingly destructive; an apt description of the empire under its Caesar, Tiberius and his armies of officials and tax collectors. So Israel languished. It fought for its survival, not with weapons of war but with cunning, with diplomacy, and with the world-wide influence of its bankers, its business men and its merchants and the wealth of its Temple and its capital city.

This contemplation of his nation's history and of the

לְהַבֵּשׁ לְנִשְׁבְּרֵי־לֵב זְרָא לִשְׁבֻּיִם דְּרוֹר וְלַאֲסוּרִים־ פְּקַח־קוֹחַ׃

Book of Daniel led his thoughts back to the sorry state of the nation and to other promises in that same book. The exile prophet had also spoken of a time of restoration. His words were barely understood except in the most general of terms and they stirred up a longing and a hope which seemed to be so remote and so unlikely of fulfilment that they could scarcely be believed.

"Seventy weeks are determined upon thy people and upon thy holy city, to finish the transgression, and to make an end of sins, and to make reconciliation for iniquity, and to bring in everlasting righteousness and to seal up the vision and prophecy, and to anoint the Most Holy. Know therefore and understand that from the going forth of the command to restore and to build Jerusalem unto Messiah the Prince shall be seven weeks and threescore and two weeks ... and after the threescore and two weeks shall Messiah be cut off, but not for Himself. And the people of the prince that shall come shall destroy the city and the sanctuary."

Simon shook his head, confusion and sadness mixed together that there should be such hope and yet such a prophecy of dire destruction. Four hundred and ninety years decreed to the time of the end, when God would restore the world, bringing in everlasting righteousness. How could that be? There were to be four hundred and eighty-three years to Messiah's coming. Surely Messiah was to set up an everlasting kingdom; how could it be then that He was to be cut off? If he understood the passage rightly then the decree to restore and to build the city must have been that of Artaxerxes the Long, handed to Nehemiah. There was only that one decree concerning the building of the city. The previous decree by Cyrus had been to build the Temple only. What he could not understand was why Messiah would not come at the very

לְהָבֵשׁ לְנִשְׁבָּרֵי־לֵב זְרָא לִשְׁבֻיִם דְּרֹור וְלַאֲסוּרִים־ פְּקַח־קֽוֹחַ׃

end. Why was He to be "cut off"? What did it mean to be "cut off"? What were and why were there to be "troublous times"? And then, as his mind recoiled in horror at the thought, why were the city and the sanctuary to be destroyed? The great focal point of the Jewish religion and nation was the Temple and the City of Peace, Jerusalem, where it was built. Had there not been enough destruction? How could that be?

The questions came thick and fast. They poured into his mind until it could not contain them. There seemed to be no answers, unless it were to one: the very time of Messiah's coming. "From the going forth of the command to restore and to build Jerusalem unto Messiah the Prince, shall be seven weeks and threescore and two weeks."

That decree had been about four hundred and eighty years ago. Maybe four hundred and eighty-two or -three years, give or take a bit here or there. Which meant only one thing. The coming of the Messiah was imminent. How could that be? And yet it made sense. Always at Israel's lowest ebb had come deliverance from God.

Had he not raised up the righteous man, Abraham, from the East when the world was sinking into idolatry and moral degeneration? Had not Israel been slaves in Egypt, under cruel and hard bondage, and had not God raised up a deliverer, Moses, to lead them out, give them the Law and to bring them to the borders of the promised land? All through the times of the Judges had not God taken the most unusual and despised of men as saviours for His people? They had been left-handed men, terrified men, yokels and a Nazirite who broke every one of his vows with spectacular regularity. Had He not brought David to the throne at the time of great national and religious emergency and were they not now waiting

לְהָבֵשׁ לְנִשְׁבְּרֵי־לֵב זְרָא לִשְׁבֻיִּם דְּרֹור וְלַאֲסוּרֵים־ פְּקַח־קָוֹחַ ׃

for a King like both David and his son Solomon?

The prophetic year was three hundred and sixty days. What with Caesar's reformation of the calendar and the genealogies beloved by the rabbis, things were terribly confused and yet maybe, just maybe ... And yet probably, why not probably? Mathematics had never been his strong point but, he wondered, should he be actively looking for and expecting Messiah? Messiah the Prince, anytime now, or within the next two or three years?

Or was it all just words, words too difficult even for an accredited rabbi to unravel and to understand? Maybe Messiah was here already and they did not know it. Perhaps he was among them and perhaps like Moses, He was despised and rejected by His people. Was that why He was to be "cut off"?

"Despised and rejected of men; a man of sorrows and acquainted with grief." The words of Isaiah came to his mind; unbidden they insinuated themselves into his brain and burned there before he relapsed into his accustomed confusion.

He went over the more familiar teachings. Messiah was to descend out of Heaven, His feet were to stand in that day upon the Mount of Olives. He was suddenly to come to His temple. Then what was the meaning of the other prophecy of Zechariah? "Rejoice greatly, O daughter of Zion. Shout O daughter of Jerusalem. Behold thy king cometh unto thee. He is just and having salvation, lowly, and riding upon an ass, and upon a colt the foal of an ass."

He did not like the way the prophecy continued, for Israel's battle bow and chariot were to be broken, and because of that, he feared. Neither he nor any rabbi of the Pharisees, not the lawyers nor the teachers seemed able to explain satisfactorily, what it was all about. Nor did they know how to reconcile the apparent contradictions. That there must be a reconciliation he did not, for one minute, doubt; but how it could be he had no idea.

Still puzzling, his mind went back to Yeshua the carpenter's son. He had taught in all the local synagogues. He had himself heard him on more than one occasion. He had watched him and had seen the sick and the sad flocking round the prophet from Nazareth. He had seen the joy, the delight and the relief on the faces of those who had been healed and on the faces of the loved ones who had brought them. They had gone away healed, satisfied, renewed and happy. Even those who, like himself, came out of curiosity and out of civic and religious duty, were not a little moved.

But he noticed also the increasing hostility with which some of his fellow Pharisees and some of the priests regarded the Prophet Yeshua from Nazareth. Why should that be, he wondered. Why, when the man, even if that was all he was, seemed only to do good. His miracles were genuine, he had no doubt of that, so why not keep minds open and investigate his teachings further? Indeed, that was all he wanted to do; it was his duty as a leader of the community.

He had been strangely moved, and had responded with an unaccustomed warmth to the words and to the actions of the Galilean who was more than just a gifted teacher. But Simon was not a man to be swayed just by his feelings; he needed to see whether the man was consistent with all that the Scriptures taught – that was the key to understanding. As Isaiah had said: "To the Law and to the Testimony, if they speak not according to this Word, there is no light in them." That is what he would do, he would test him by the Word of the Lord.

לְחָבָשׁ לְנִשְׁבְּרֵי־לֵב ָרֵא לִשְׁבוּיִם דְּרֹור וְלַאֲסוּרֵים־ פְּקַח־קֹוחַ׃

What if God did visit His people? What if He had done so? He did not want to miss such an event. He did not want to be found wanting at such a time. What if he *were*? What if Yeshua was really a prophet? What if he were the Messiah and what if people ignored him? But how could they? How could Israel despise and reject their true Messiah?

The questions were disturbing and frightening. Frightening too was the fact that he had no answers. What had he said? "Come to me all you who labour and are heavy laden, and I will give you rest. Take my yoke upon you and learn from me; for I am gentle and lowly in heart and you will find rest for your souls. For my yoke is easy and my burden is light." Who and what was he to say such things? For them to be truth he had to be Messiah. Who else could give rest, and if he invited them to take on his yoke then he had to be equal at least to the Law itself. Or, and his mind rebelled at the thought, he had to be the giver of the Law, God Himself.

What a yoke, what a burden was the Law. It chafed many of their best minds; instead of giving rest and peace it engendered fear. Instead of something to be carried gladly, it was something which many who really understood would happily have relinquished and put down. Rest for the soul. Not just for the body but for the very innermost being. Rather than growing lighter, the burden of the Law got heavier and more terrifying each new day. They dare not put it down. They would if they could but what else did Israel have? There was nothing else which separated them from the nations. Without the Law what was it to be a Jew? Without the Law they had lost everything; and yet with the Law they gained nothing but a burden which no man could carry.

"Rest for your souls." What sort of rest was that? Not

לְהָבֵשׁ לְנִשְׁבְּרֵי־לֵב קְרֹא לִשְׁבֻוֹם דְּרֹוֹר וְלַאֲסוּרִים־פְּקַח־קֹוֹחַ׃

just rest for the body; that only lasted a night, and in the morning it was time for work again. A rest for the whole personality, for the mind and for the spirit. He tried to imagine it. A spirit at one with God, at peace with Him and at peace with itself.

How could one ever be sure? He knew he had followed every detail of the rabbinic law. And yet how could he be sure? Might it not be that in some small detail, unwittingly he had transgressed? How could he tell, how would he know if he had missed something? And if he had? In that case would God demand it of him? Would God insist on every tiny detail? He hoped not, for he was sure that he could have made mistakes; he was human; all humans were prone to error, even the best of them, even Pharisees. Though he had conned the rabbinic writings and the Holy Scriptures themselves, yet he could not be sure that he had not misunderstood something. How could he be sure?

Perhaps at the end, at the judgement – but then it would be too late. How could one put down the burden which God had laid on Israel? How could one be free? How could one have rest? Could the Law give rest? The answer had to be "No!" The Law was a terror, for it condemned one for the slightest transgression. His mind came round again in a full circle. Again he had to acknowledge that it was the Law which was the distinguishing mark of Israel. Without the Law they were but as one of the nations.

And so he had invited the prophet from Galilee to his house. And so he greeted Him with correct but with just a little courtesy. And true to His nature Yeshua ben Yosef made no attempt to correct him. He made no protest nor did He try to put the Pharisee right about who He really was and the superlatively high honours which were His

לְהָבֵשׁ לְנִשְׁבְּרֵי-לֵב זְרָא לִשְׁבּוּיִם דְּרֹור וְלַאֲסוּרִים- פְּקַח-קֹוחַ׃

by right. He had come to His own, but His own people did not receive Him. Yet one of those people had a small chink in his armour. Deep down he was hoping that the Rabbi from Nazareth might yet be able to teach him something. At worst his curiosity might be satisfied.

The questions surged and smashed against the tumbled rocks of his intellect. All was spray and confusion as the nagging guilts, the doubts and the fears sucked his emotions to and fro. Like the waves on the seashore his thoughts, restless and troubled, churned up more doubts, confusions, naggings and fears.

Outwardly he still remained calm. His manners were perfectly correct, though had he been able to understand, his concern for the niceties of social distinctions made him careless of the real meanings of courtesy and of kindness. If Yeshua had been a Pharisee of equal rank, or even senior to himself, he would have offered a kiss of greeting and would have had a servant with bowl and towel to wash his feet. He would have anointed Him too though he was, as yet, unaware of the incongruity of that thought since Yeshua, whose name meant Salvation of the Lord, was indeed the true Anointed One.

They reclined at the table with their legs stretched out behind them. Their bodies rested on a couch and they supported themselves on one elbow, using the other hand to eat with. Conversation was polite but hardly scintillating; it was correct but hardly stimulating. The Pharisee watched his guest. So far he had said nothing unusual, nor had he done anything unusual. He sat with quiet dignity and smiled gently at the other guests, almost as if he were the host and not Simon. The polite conversation began during the hand washing and while the host divided the bread to his guests. It tended to lapse when the guests began to eat. That was how it

לְהַלְבֵּשׁ לִנְשְׁבָּרֵי־לֵב זְרָא לִשְׁבּוּיִם דְּרוֹר וְלָאֲסוּרִים־פְּקַח־קוֹחַ׃

should be. If things were dull Simon did not mind. He had been concerned that his chief guest might be inclined to do or to say something outrageous, but so far he had not.

There was an attempt to turn the talk into deeper channels, but they fell silent when a woman entered. This was outrageous, for an outsider so to interrupt an important social occasion. Everyone concentrated on their food and there was a tenseness in the air. Only the Man from Nazareth seemed unconcerned. The woman made her way along the wall behind the guests.

Each man tensed as she passed him and relaxed when she moved on. She was clearly nervous, even frightened and intimidated. However, she had overcome her fear, and with determination made her way to where Yeshua reclined near his host. She stopped behind him and they all held their breath.

Simon could hardly contain the indignation and the outrage he felt at this interruption. It was all the more annoying since he would not now be able, after a polite interval, to lead the conversation in what he hoped would be an innocent manner to the subjects he wanted to hear the prophet's views on. Worse still, the woman was known to be a sinner, and by her presence she defiled his house and his person.

His self-control held and he retained his calm exterior. He would not make a scene before his guests, especially before such an unusual and special guest. The woman stopped and looked at the prophet from Nazareth. Her self-control seemed to break down, for tears welled from her eyes and she began to weep in an ecstasy of remorse and devotion.

"Come to Me," He had said. She had come to Him and the moral beauty of His presence made her own

12 To Love Much

לָחֲבֹשׁ לְנִשְׁבְּרֵי־לֵב לִקְרֹא לִשְׁבוּיִם דְּרוֹר וְלַאֲסוּרִים־ פְּקַח־קוֹחַ:

unworthiness all too real. And yet, just as He had bidden her, had bidden all of them to come to Him, so He had not turned her away. Though she just knew a little of it, she had rest for her soul. It was with trepidation that she had approached Him, and yet she knew that she could approach Him. Had He not said that He would give her rest? And had He not done so already? She wanted to be with Him and to tell Him of her devotion; she wanted to thank Him for His so great salvation and to find some way to express that devotion and that gratitude, but she had no words.

Her tears washed over His feet and wetted them and His lower legs and ankles. Fearing that she might offend, or fearing that her tears might not be worthy, she took her hair, which had become unbound and had fallen down around her face, and began to wipe His feet, to dry them with her hair. By this time she had sunk down onto her knees, still sobbing and still attempting to wipe away the tears with her hair. Yeshua made no move but turned His head to survey the Pharisee and the other guests, His expression serious and a little sad.

The woman, in the act of wiping His feet felt the alabaster bottle of perfume which she carried hanging down round her neck by a chain, nearly to her waist. She opened it and poured it over Him. Over His head, over His neck, she poured it, and it splashed onto His clothes. The room was filled with the exquisite smell. It was expensive perfume such as many Jewish women carried with them. Some, like this one, were worth more than their weight in silver. Many women spent a large proportion of their dowry on such perfume.

She had expressed herself in the only way she could, but it was a richness of expression, a glorious expression, a loving, devoted, sweetly smelling form of expression.

לְהַבֵּשׁ לְנִשְׁבְּרֵי־לֵב זְרָא לִשְׁבוּיִם דְּרוֹר וְלָאֲסוּרִים־ פְּקַח־קוֹחַ׃

She had wanted to make herself known to Him and yet she had been frightened to do so. In spite of her fears she had managed to come near to this most wonderful of men. The burden of her many sins had been lifted. The love and gratitude welled up in her heart as the tears welled up from her eyes. She kissed His feet with reverence and with tender care.

She knew not how the burden of her sin and guilt had been rolled away, but she knew that it had. He was so good, so kind, so loving and yet He was great, far above all others. His purity was incandescent, His was light greater than that of the sun and His was right, truth and peace in ways which could not be explained. This Man had lifted her out of the foul mire which had been her life and she knew not how but she loved and worshipped Him because of it. She could not have put into words what she thought, but she would follow Him to the end and she wanted Him to know that. But then, this Man, who was more than man, had called her and the wonder of it and the joy of it filled her whole being and lifted her spirit to paths of delight which were the pathways of heaven itself.

In her own eyes she had not been worthy to anoint Him nor to wash His feet. But He accepted her ministrations with a silent though wholehearted acceptance. The very silence in the room and the fact that He had not withdrawn His feet from her nor flinched at all at her touch signalled that acceptance. She crouched at His feet, still half afraid she might be roughly driven away, but at the same time knowing that she would never be driven away. She was at the place where she most wanted to be and that place was hers for eternity, at the feet of Yeshua who loved all people with that warm intensity and gentle power of His love.

לַחְבֹּשׁ לְנִשְׁבְּרֵי־לֵב גְּרָא לִשְׁבוּיִם דְּרוֹר וְלַאֲסוּרִים־ פְּקַח־קְוֹחַ׃

Meanwhile, Simon, while keeping a perfectly composed exterior, was deeply troubled. He was almost in a state of shock that this woman had so disturbed the meal and the social occasion. It seemed as if it was all happening somewhere else, in some other place. He could not believe it was happening here, in his house, so well managed and so well run. The servants were as if turned to statues. One stood with his mouth half open, a large jug of water clasped to his chest, as if it would somehow protect him. Only his eyes moved, half fearful, to the master of the house and then back to the indecorous scene where the guest reclined as if oblivious to it all, as if it were perfectly normal and right. Another nearly dropped a dish and only by a scramble managed to save the food it held from spilling all over the floor.

Still managing to keep a reasonably calm exterior, his thoughts were questioning what it was that was happening. No Pharisee would ever have anything to do with such a woman. That she had found her way into his house was horrifying, but worse still, all the ideas in his mind that this Man, Yeshua might have been a prophet, even The Prophet, the one promised by Moses, were cancelled and there was no satisfaction that he had been unmasked.

"If he were a prophet," he thought, "the man would have known the sort of woman she was." It also occurred to him that, had he been a prophet, he would have refused such treatment as being, not only defiling, but, as a sort of worship, also blasphemous. He decided that he would continue the meal as if nothing had happened, but then he would be able to tell others, with confidence, that Yeshua from Nazareth was undoubtedly not a prophet.

In a way the conclusion gave him no sense of relief.

לְהַבֵּשׁ לְנִשְׁבְּרֵי־לֵב זְרָא לִשְׁבוּיִם דְּרוֹר וְלַאֲסוּרִים־ פְּקַח־קוֹחַ׃

In a way, things were still not conclusive; the truth was that he still did not understand. And yet there was no Pharisee who would not be filled with loathing at the presence of this woman who was a sinner. There was no Pharisee who would not have recoiled with horror from her touch. So who was this man? Simon was confronted yet again by the inadequacy of all his study, of all his religious observance and of all his training in the rabbinic schools. None of it had fitted him to cope with this sort of situation and to find answers to the questions it raised. "This man, if he were a prophet, would know what sort of woman this is who is touching him, for she is a sinner."

The answers came unexpectedly from the One who had all this time remained silent. He spoke, and Simon was once more out of his depth. The water from the Temple had washed around his ankles, then round his knees and now it was water to swim in. But these waters were of the mind and of the thoughts, and it took him some time to grasp the implications of them.

Only a prophet, or One who was more than a prophet, could read the thoughts in a man's heart as clearly as that man could read the words of the book he read in the synagogue on the Sabbath. They were read as clearly as if they had been spoken aloud. They were read as clearly as if they had been written by the finger of God upon the wall of his house even as the doom of Belshazzar King of Babylon had been written by the fiery finger of God on the wall of his decadent banqueting hall. With numbing of the mind yet with shattering certainty, he was accused, he was judged and he was condemned. All was made glaringly plain and the truth was beyond all his imaginings; and the fears and the doubts returned with greater force than ever as the Galilean said:.

"Simon, I have something to say to you." Still with

259

לְהַבֹּשׁ לְנִשְׁבְּרֵי־לֵב זָרָא לִשְׁבֻיִם דְּרֹור וְלָאֲסוּרִים־ פְּקַח־קֹוחַ׃

perfectly correct manners, as to a guest, Simon replied, "Teacher, say it."

Yeshua held up His cup. It was also polite to hold the cup in one's hand for a few seconds before taking a sip. He then sipped the watered wine and, putting the cup down, he looked Simon in the eye and told a story.

It was a very brief story but no such brevity ever held such a wealth of meaning, most of which was lost in the immediate moment, on the bewildered Pharisee.

He began: "There was a certain creditor who had two debtors. One owed him five hundred denarii and the other fifty."

He paused and Simon nodded respectfully, though he had no idea where all this was going. He knew that a denarius was the day's wages for a labouring man and that though fifty was a tidy sum, five hundred was a fortune for a poor man who had only his labour to sell.

The Rabbi from Nazareth went on: "And when they had nothing with which to repay, he freely forgave them both." Again He paused and looked at Simon as if to emphasise that this story was for him. Continuing, He asked, "Tell me therefore, which of them will love him more?"

The answer was an obvious certainty to the calculating mind of the Pharisees. It did not occur to them that love was impossible to measure out as if weighing it with the merchant's scales. Simon did not stop to think. Even had he done so it is doubtful whether he would have been able to give any different answer. "I suppose," he replied, "the one whom he forgave more."

Simon had behaved with correctness though with a lack of that love which characterised the concern of God as shown in the Torah for the poor, the fatherless and the widow, and that joy when sinners repented. If Simon had

לְהַבֵּשׁ לִנְשָׁבָּרֵי־לֵב זָרָא לִשָׁבֻיִם דְּרוֹר וְלַאֲסוּרִים פְּקַח־קוֹחַ׃

shown a lack of that courtesy which was as far above that mere correctness as the heavens are above the earth, then the reply he then received was a marvel of gentle restraint and of sensitive consideration for the feelings of a host from a guest. It was a rebuke, but a rebuke offered so wisely that no one could have recognised it as such except for the man himself who was addressed.

It reached down into the depths of his being and it brought him an enlightenment which few people dare look upon. It shone into the depths and Simon saw himself in the light of God as he truly was. He saw the pride, the arrogance and the dogmatism of his certainties which were but short cuts to knowledge and to understanding.

He saw the chains of rabbinic teaching with which he had burdened and shackled himself over all the years he had studied without learning. He saw how he had been blind to the human need for love, for compassion and for real courtesy and kindness, qualities which his pride had robbed him of, and in robbing him, had left him the poorer. He saw how the tradition he followed had cut him off from his fellow human beings and how its arid outward show had dried up all the springs of compassion which ought to have watered all his dealings with his fellows. He was cut off from them and he was, without knowing it, cut off from God. It was as if he had come out into the brightness of the sun after languishing for long in some dark and dismal dungeon where the convolutions of rabbinic teaching had kept him bound and away from light, from life, from health and from true happiness. He saw also that it might have been that the roles were actually reversed and that it was he who was the great debtor, for he had thought himself righteous when he was not. He had thought his religious

לְחֲבֹשׁ לְנִשְׁבְּרֵי־לֵב זָרָא לִשְׁבוּיִם דְּרוֹר וְלַאֲסוּרִים־ פְּקַח־קֽוֹחֵ׃

observance and his prayers made him acceptable in the sight of God when they really pushed him further away and the burden of the Law only served to condemn him.

It suddenly became simple to understand that the woman who could show such love was really the better person than he who had grown cold and correct yet emotionally starved while all the time longing for love, and to be at one with God. All this flooded into his mind and so much that had been hidden from him was revealed. Yet there was more to come. The Teacher continued, gently but firmly, to push the lesson home.

He said, "You have rightly judged." He turned to the woman and spoke to Simon indicating her. "Do you see this woman? I entered your house; you gave me no water for my feet, but she has washed my feet with her tears, and wiped them with the hair of her head.

"You gave me no kiss, but this woman since the time I came in has not ceased to kiss my feet. You did not anoint my head with oil, but this woman has anointed my feet with fragrant oil."

Simon began to understand, but there was more. Taking the Pharisees' measure He added: "Her sins, which are many, are forgiven, for she loved much. But to whom little is forgiven, the same loves little." Turning more fully to the woman He said: "Your sins are forgiven."

The other guests, local worthies deemed fit companions to eat at the table of a local ruler of the synagogue, were somewhat shocked. They tried to understand. How could this man say that sins were forgiven? That was surely for God to say.

"Who does he think he is?" they thought to themselves. "Who is this that forgives sins?" There was indignation there; Yeshua from Nazareth was making Himself God. They could not, perhaps they would not,

לְהַכֵּשׁ לְנִשְׁבְּרֵי־לֵב זְרָא לִשְׁבוּיִם דְּרוֹר וְלַאֲסוּרִים־ פְּקַח־קוֹחַ:

or, perhaps, they were not yet ready to take in the implications of the words and to recognise the simple truth that only God can forgive sins, so therefore, this man, Yeshua son of the carpenter, was also God.

So mighty and majestic a truth was it that God should become flesh, that unaided human reason could not take it in. But then, only where there is a simple willingness, only where there is an awareness of sin and of unworthiness, can the Spirit of God break through the encrustations of human tradition to show reality as it actually is. That is to show real truth in the person of Him who is the Truth, the Way and the Life.

Her sin had already been forgiven. Her tears were not for a burden of sin which she no longer carried, but for the joy that it had been removed. She had heard and responded to His loving and all-embracing invitation: "Come to Me all you who labour and are heavy laden, and I will give you rest. Take My yoke upon you and learn from Me, for I am gentle and lowly in heart, and you will find rest for your souls. For My yoke is easy and My burden is light."

She had done what He said to do. She had come to Him and she had cast her burden of sin and the awful yoke of the Law down at His feet. She had taken His yoke instead and had gladly put it on and she longed to be with Him, knew she would ever be with Him, and she longed and determined to learn from Him. She now had rest; the yoke of the Kingdom of God lay lightly on her shoulders, and her soul rejoiced in God her Saviour.

Having braved the contempt of the Pharisee and his guests, knowing too that He whom she loved above all others, would also be "despised and rejected of men", she lifted her head a little. As she did so the Teacher addressed her directly: "Your faith has saved you. Go into

12 To Love Much

לְחַבֵּשׁ לְנִשְׁבְּרֵי־לֵב לִקְרֹא לִשְׁבוּיִם דְּרוֹר וְלַאֲסוּרִים פְּקַח־קוֹחַ׃

peace."

She got up, and stood happily heedless of the disapproval which was still reflected in the faces of many there. With fresh confidence she knew that the love she felt would grow and would encompass others.

"Into peace." With head held high, but with wonder in her heart and confidence in her step she left the house. In that confidence she saw others and their needs. She saw their failings and the futility of their petty triumphs. She longed to bring them to Him who had given her peace and who had filled her with this confidence and with a love for others who needed Him too.

The party continued, but for Simon the Pharisee it was as if he were in a dream. At the end he bade his guests Godspeed and then, with eyes downcast and a deepening sense of shame, he faced the guest who had changed his life and his thoughts for ever.

There was a fresh realisation, a disturbing realisation dawning on his soul. With difficulty he raised his eyes to the Man who had seen deep into his being and who had shown him the dark places there. As he faced that steady gaze the lamps seemed suddenly to burn with a brighter flame. He saw by that light, in the depths of those eyes, deep into a soul and spirit which burned with Love and Truth. He understood that the parable of the two debtors was the conclusion of his own pharisaical thinking. He saw himself as a greater debtor. He saw it clearly and, with some surprise and some embarrassment, realised that this Man who was more than man, was smiling at him. Gently and kindly but with warm laughter too He was smiling, and he realised that he too was loved who deserved no love. Understanding bore deeper understanding. Such love could not be earned; it was freely given.

לַחֲבֹשׁ לְנִשְׁבְּרֵי־לֵב ;רָא לִשְׁבוּיִם דְּרוֹר וְלַאֲסוּרִים· פְּקַח־קוֹחַ:

Not all the observances, not all the prayers, nor the Sabbaths, nor the sacrifices and the offerings on the altar could earn that love. It was there all the time and the Law, while it condemned, showed that they were all dependent upon that love for salvation.

What a fool he had been. The woman he had condemned as unclean was forgiven and was clean in the sight of God, whatever foolish Pharisees might think. He too, who had been so blind and so stupid, he realised could also be forgiven by that same freely forgiving grace. Yeshua was not laughing *at* him, rather he was laughing *with* him and inviting him to laugh at himself. He was not mocking him, would never mock him, but was smiling as a friend smiled, as a father or an older relation, a kinsman who was also a redeemer smiled.

He was grateful. Hitherto he had believed that God was somehow grateful to him for keeping some of the Law. How foolish he had been to think that God could ever see him in that light when it had all been arrogance and pride. On the one hand he was mortified that his hypocrisy and pride had been shown to him for what it really was. On the other he was overjoyed that he too could begin to feel the cleansing as those shadowy depths of his soul were swept free of the contamination and the loathsome follies that dwelt there.

He smiled back, shyly at first, then with confidence. The words of God by Jeremiah came into his mind; "I will forgive iniquity, and their sin will I remember no more." His smile grew broader and it was answered with a smile of welcome and of acceptance.

(Based on the incident described in Luke's Gospel, chapter 7.)

Epilogue

Empathy enables one to imagine oneself inside the thoughts and feelings of the character one wishes to portray or to understand. When we read that the 'Rich Young Ruler', "went away sorrowful, for he had great possessions," we have to try to become that young man and to feel his regret, his sense of desolation and his fear, as the Lord Jesus laid bare his motives and his inner misconceptions derived from his culture and his own insecurities. We also find ourselves challenged as we feel with that young man and realise, if we dare, that the challenge also comes to us to lose our life so that we might save it.

The lady with the haemorrhage problem, for example, had clearly experienced great hurt, awful disappointment and a measure of disillusionment. I have tried to show that. In so doing I have done no more and no less than what any preacher on a Sunday morning or a Sunday evening tries to do. However I have added the pure fiction of a budding romantic involvement with a kindly and gentle man of her own social class and upbringing. But then, is that so fictional? Have not most of us felt the thrill and the glowing euphoria of developing love and have we not also felt the tearful loss of a loved one? These are common human experiences and, though manufactured in my mind, they are not that far from the truth I believe.

For many of the details of Jewish life in the first century I have relied on Dr Alfred Edersheim, himself a learned Jew, who converted to Christianity and became a minister in the Church of England. I recommend all his works. I have used those devoted to the era which saw

לְהֲבֵשׁ לְנִשְׁבָּרֵי־לֵב קְרָא לִשְׁבוּיִם דְּרוֹר וְלַאֲסוּרִים־פְּקַח־קוֹחַ:

the Lord and His disciples visiting the cities, towns and villages of Palestine. *Life and Times of Jesus the Messiah* is a must for anyone seriously studying the period. Also helpful are: *The Temple – Its Ministry and Service*, and *Sketches of Jewish Social Life*, by the same author. Josephus also, the contemporary Jewish historian, though sometimes heavy going because he mentions places, people and events we are ignorant of, is also essential.

To a lesser degree I need to mention two other volumes which somehow came into my possession and which I have used. These are: *The Social Life of the Jew*, by Rev. E. Keith, and *A Student's Guide to the Talmud* by Chajes. The former is very readable.

I found Portsmouth central library reference section extremely helpful when it came to books on Herod the Great and his building projects. They had materials giving me the archaeologists' findings and reconstructions of the various fortresses with which he surrounded himself.

There is a vast library of books on the Romans and their empire so I will not mention them all. I wanted to find out about trade and craftsmanship customs but found that there were gaps. Traditionally historians have been interested in 'the big names' and the doings of Caesars and of their rivals for power, or their underlings. What the ordinary Joe Bloggs in the suburbia in Rome or in provincial Syria got up to was only incidental if he happened to come across one of the major players. Generally speaking they were in different leagues and played by different rules.

The Roman writers tell us a lot about the careers of the generals who came from a different social class from the centurions and the ordinary soldiers. Centurions were also officers and, unlike the generals they were professional soldiers, recruited from the middle and lower middle classes or promoted from the ranks of the

לְהָבֵשׁ לְנִשְׁבְּרֵי־לֵב זְרָא לִשְׁבֻיִם דְּרֹור וְלַאֲסוּרִים־ פְּקַח־קָוֹחַ׃

footsloggers. Promotion in the Roman army was a sort of inclined plane sideways.

We know a lot about the ordinary legionaries; there are training manuals and reports innumerable which tell us details of their lives and work. We know about the centurions; there are two of them in the New Testament who are noted for their great faith and a centurion was in charge of the execution where the Lord Jesus occupied the central cross. Two more centurions are mentioned sharing the command of about five hundred men between them when they were charged by the commander (a chiliarch) to escort the prisoner, Paul, from Jerusalem to Caesarea.

The matter of NCOs is, as far as I can see, something of a mystery. Maybe someone somewhere is busy deciphering an inscription which will tell us more about them. We know their names, 'cornicularis', 'signifer', 'optio', and the 'aquilifer' who had the honour of carrying the eagle standard of the legion. These might have been senior sergeants or warrant officers. I have heard it said that there was a decurion, a sort of corporal; but 'decurion' was also a civic office and the writer may have been confused. I have called the man in charge 'sergeant'; that is what I think he probably was and his Roman title was one of the above, probably 'optio'. Herod's army and the temple 'watch' were almost certainly modelled on Roman lines. What we can be sure about is that NCOs and centurions did inflict beatings on their men. They could not, however, put a man to death; that was the privilege of the general, or 'legate'. My sergeant is like sergeants everywhere and, if I may say so, like the gunnery and drill Petty Officers I suffered under as a boy in the Royal Navy. I later learned that most of them were quite human; some even became friends of mine, though I had my doubts about some. I believe that

לַחֲבֹשׁ לְנִשְׁבְּרֵי־לֵב לִקְרֹא לִשְׁבוּיִם דְּרוֹר וְלַאֲסוּרִים פְּקַח־קוֹחַ׃

an army is an army and soldiers are soldiers whether in first century Palestine or modern-day Aldershot. *The Roman Soldier* by G.R.Watson is a scholarly work. On the NCOs Leonard Cottrell in his *The Great Invasion* gives a very readable summary of Roman ranks and titles with what little is known of their duties.

For the rest, the Gospels themselves are the main sources. They say so much in so few words that we often miss their depth and their wisdom.